Know Your Personality

A Self-Guide for Sharpening Your Competitive Edge to Achieve Success in Life

R. M. Onkar
(Lt. Col. Retd.)
B.E.(Hons), M.E.,F.I.T.E.
Ex. Jt. Managing Director
Punjab Communications Limited, Mohali, (Punjab)

Published by

F-2/16, Ansari Road, Daryaganj, New Delhi-110002
011-23240026, 011-23240027 • *Fax* 011-23240028
Email info@vspublishers.com • *Website* www.vspublishers.com

Regional Office Hyderabad
5-1-707/1, Brij Bhawan (Beside Central Bank of India Lane)
Bank Street, Koti, Hyderabad - 500 095
040-24737290
E-mail vspublishershyd@gmail.com

Branch Office : Mumbai
Jaywant Industrial Estate, 2nd Floor-222, Tardeo Road
Opposite Sobo Central, Mumbai - 400 034
022-23510736
E-mail: vspublishersmum@gmail.com

Follow us on

All books available at **www.vspublishers.com**

© Copyright : V&S PUBLISHERS
ISBN 978-93-505718-8-0
Edition 2016

The Copyright of this book, as well as all matter contained herein (including illustrations) rests with the Publisher. No person shall copy the name of the book, its title design, matter and illustrations in any form and in any language, totally or partially or in any form. Anybody doing so shall face legal action and will be responsible for damages.

Printed at Param Offseters Okhla New Delhi-110020

PREAMBLE

Your **'Self'** is apparently synonymous with your 'Destiny'. In turn, your 'Self' is holistically represented by your **'Personality'**. Thus, there is an indirect interconnectedness of your *Personality* with your *Destiny*. In this way, when you blame your 'Destiny' for your failures or loss of fortunes, you should, in fact, blame your 'Self'. Unfortunately, you don't realise this indirect linkage. It is therefore imperative in life that you should know this linkage of your Personality with your Destiny through your Self.

Generally, there is a tendency of looking at Human Destiny from philosophical and spiritual point of view. As such, it is treated as the myth called NIYATI. It is therefore considered beyond human control and understanding. Hence, it is strongly believed that you can't do anything for your failures or misfortunes. Consequently, you helplessly accept them with despair and remorse.

In this respect, I wish to remind you through the medium of this comprehensive and thoughtful book that the divine power which is associated with your *Destiny* is already gifted to you by the God at the time of your birth in the form of your *Personality*. It is then entirely left to you to discover and develop it under the influence of the existing circumstantial conditions and forces through your personal efforts called the **KARMAS**.

In fact, when you visit a temple or worship or seek blessings of the Saints, the indirect message is conveyed to you to look inwards at your 'Self' and discover your *positive and negative qualities, shortcomings, strengths* and *weaknesses*. You should then properly harness your strengths and take corrective action to overcome your mistakes, so far committed knowingly or unknowingly. What this message means that you should know your personality and discover your 'Self'. Unfortunately, this basic message is lost due to human greed and ego and you adopt easy means of seeking blessings for achieving wealth or fortune or success without doing efforts of looking at your Self for taking effective actions.

I have identified this general human tendency. So, I have tried to bring out in this book the **indirect relationship of your Personality with your Destiny by undertaking an in-depth search of your Self.** I have examined your Personality and its various dimensional aspects that enable you to discover your Self and eventually, become an **Architect of your Destiny.** Hence, the Preamble to this book giving the gist and core message is given in a summarised form as follows:

Your 'Self' Represents Your 'Personality'
Which Is Exclusively Identified
with
The Divine Gift of Your Hidden Treasure of X-Power Factor
in the Form of Several Important Personal Positive Qualities
Hence, Remaining Ignorant about Your Personality
is Ignoring Destiny
and
Missing the Bus of Your Career Growth and Prosperity.
So, Realise Your Personal Moral Responsibility
for Discovering and Assessing It.
So that You Avail Material and Spiritual Benefits
and
Avoid the Escapist Blame Game
for Your Failures, Losses and Misfortunes in Life.

FOREWORD

I feel indebted to Shri R. M. Onkar (Lt. Col. Retd.) for bringing out this book, titled, *'Know Your Personality and Discover Your Self'* primarily due to the fact that he has very distinctively and effectively brought out this co-relation in a scientific manner. The entire pursuit undertaken by him has resulted in evolving a creative manifestation, wherein, *he has evolved an appropriate and logical modality for deciphering as well as quantifying multi-faceted dimensions and aspects that include strengths and weaknesses of the individual in his self-conceived personality.* On an objective evaluation of this realisation, one would be in a position to invoke which would go in for a meaningful development and enrichment of one's pursuits in his life.

In the preamble itself, the author very candidly describes one's personality to be a divine gift extended on him which amounts to an occult treasure of meaningful qualities of which if one is ignorant then he is equally ignorant about his own destiny and thereby misses the carriage for a meaningful prosperity and success.

As such, it is imperative that *one needs to realise one's personal and moral responsibility for not only discovering one's personality, but also fathoming it, so that he is in a position to invoke material and spiritual benefits in the domain of satisfying success.* In view of this very realisation, one also gets immunity from the escapist blame-game of passing on the buck of his failures, losses and misfortunes onto situations, circumstances on any other things, but for himself.

The author has very deftly handled the various concepts of 'personality' and has gone to establish *that it is the 'mind' which is the 'ring master' of one's personality.* One is therefore, required to acquire a mindset, which is blended with a *'positive attitude' and a resultant 'positive thinking', which would end up in a 'positive action'*, which is devoid of fear, worry, anticipated failure, anger and criticisms. Each one of us is blessed with 'intellect' as well as 'talent'. It is imperative that both of them need to be chiselled and articulated through appropriate acquiring of skills, which include memory, learning skills, interpersonal skills, communication skills and actualisation of the leadership qualities innate in the personality itself.

It is imperative that by invoking appropriate and diligent inter-personal behavioural skills, one is in a position to win not only friends but also is able to influence people. This mandates 'empowerment' of the personality for which the author has brought into focus distinct approaches which facilitate this very process. It is pertinent that *the personality gets depicted through 'performance' and is reflected in an 'Acquirable Success'*.

The most curious aspect that he has *brought into focus pertains to the realisation that 'destiny' is hidden in one's own 'personality'. It is necessary that one is able to co-relate the interconnectedness of the 'personal attributes' with the 'destiny' and linkages of 'positive attributes' to acquiring successes and 'negative attributes' resulting in gross failures.* He has also very diligently brought into focus the **'role, relevance, scope and influence'** of *'cosmic laws' and 'its forces' on human personality.*

His erudite dispositions on the laws of *'Mentalism, Correspondence, Vibration, Polarity, Rhythm, Cause and Effectas well as, Gender'* are very vivid and free flowing. He has brought into focus the unison of the human life and its personality with the 'cosmos' and its forces, wherein the continuous cosmic influences affect one's personality since the day of one's birth and there-from on the subsequent activities all throughout one's life. *As this cosmic action is invisible and is 'imperceptible', hence, its impact on the personality is not realised physically, but, it gets manifested in several occurrences of 'fortunate' and 'unfortunate' events in life.* It is true that one gets a solace by attributing this to one's 'destiny', however, *the author has gone an extra mile to emphatically bring into focus the co-relation of the 'cosmos and its forces' with the 'destiny' of the individual. Therefore, an inevitable conclusion that one's personality is an inseparable part from one's destiny is a fact and together, they turn out to be the 'two sides of the same coin'.*

The author has *very scientifically approached this difficult co-relation in a deft and subtle manner, whereby things have become easy and discernable for which he merits all accolades and appreciation. I ardently believe that this CREATIVE WORK of the author will turn out to be of significant use to all it readers in interpretation of their 'personality' and it's neat and clear interpolation with their 'destiny'.*

Dr. Vedprakash Misra (Pro-Chancellor, Deemed University)

PREFACE

I strongly feel that the *process of personality development* has *two parts*. The first part covers the objective of knowing completely about your personality and the second part of undertaking subsequently the program of its development. These two distinct phases of activities if properly and systematically coordinated and executed will certainly result into an *effective, productive* and *meaningful* development of your personality. In view of this factual position, there is a tendency to undertake a direct program of personality development and surprisingly, *all commercial advising and consulting agencies proceed directly for advising personality development without giving an iota of importance for deeply knowing and understanding about your personality except giving a very superficial introductory information at the beginning.* The result is obvious. The entire program of personality development remains impersonal, unproductive and advisory like a religious sermon with total washout of its result.

It is therefore emphasised that unless you have an in-depth holistic picture of your personality and especially *take cognizance of your inner personality along with its innate soft skills and controlling factors like the brain, mind, memory and sense organs of your body, you will remain blank about yourself along with the strong and weak areas of your personality.* Consequently, the entire, sincere and expensive exercise of your personality development will become infructuous and frustrating with *wastage of your time, money and efforts.*

Having conviction in light of my above observation, I am pleased to offer you this comprehensive treatise on your personality and project its various domains covering your both outer and inner personality. As a result, *you are appraised about your nature, character, behaviour, talents, intelligence, communication skills, performance and public relations. In fact, these are your career related aspects and oriented towards achievement of materialist gains, career prospects and advancements.*

In the books on psychology, *human personality* is the centric theme for its study and projection. Since it is a complex treatment and lacks objectivity and practicability, I have given in this book a simplified representation of your personality in the form of *Five Star Pentagon Type Model highlighting five distinct domains of your personality i.e., mental, intellectual, communicative, physical and spiritual. This closed model is expressive, comprehensive and pragmatic for holistic projection of your personality in an objective manner, thereby covering its multi-dimensional star aspects unlike any other model presented by the management gurus and different psychologists.*

It is pointed out that all the domains of your personality are of *star category* and evantually, equally important in the sense that if you lack in one aspect, your personality becomes unbalanced and inharmonious. Consequently, your living and survival become inconsistent, unstable and unproductive. Even *spiritual aspect* which appears to be least bothered and often neglected is significant in the sense that if you don't have character, you lack in moral strength, spirit and ethical values. As a result, you receive a terrific setback in your image, reputation, prestige and dignity and consequently, your personality becomes unimpressive, repulsive and hateful in the public eye. The end result is that you lose sympathy and respect of the people and finally, you lead a lonely, frustrated, neglected and forlorn retired life with nobody around to take care and look after you. Besides, you leave behind the legacy of bad memories pertaining to your vicious, immoral nature and character. This is my factual observation about some high ranking professional persons from public services.

While examining the first domain of your personality, it is seen that *your mind controls all your career related activities and life events. Thus, it becomes the ring master of your personality although it remains in the background unseen, but indirectly exercises strong control on all your karma and on-job performance in an imperceptible manner.* Thus, you need to be *conscious of the vital role of your mind and its various mental aspects in shaping and conditioning your personality.*

As far as the functional aspect of your personality is concerned, it plays a very important role in your public interviews and subsequently in your career-oriented performances and career growth. So, you need to be aware about this aspect and see *how far your inner personality and its soft skills become instrumental in finally determining success or failure in your life.*

Finally, as the title of the book refers to *Destiny, associated with your personality*, it implies that those who deeply know their personality, they discover their destiny therein. In other words, *your destiny is integrally related to your personality and remains hidden therein.* Since you get your personality as the *Divine Gift* at the time of your birth, your destiny is obviously associated with your personality since birth. Hence, it is *entirely left to you to discover, understand, develop and use it for your personal benefits. Eventually, it becomes your personal responsibility to look after, develop and protect it from service, incidental hazards and from deterioration.* So long as *you are aware and sincerely realise this aspect, you will finally end up your career happily, peacefully and prosperously with the satisfaction of having done your best efforts with full awareness and consciousness.*

As far as the contents of this book are concerned, they are covered in *twenty-one chapters* with FOREWORD and EPILOGUE, posing finally a question CAN YOU CHANGE YOUR PERSONALITY *which becomes the forerunner for the next phase of* PERSONALITY DEVEOPMENT. These chapters profusely cover the following distinct parts as under:-

- (a) **Five domains of your personality, each having sub-titles of various subjects referring to the role of mind, different characteristics of mental state, intellect, intelligence, learning skills, memory, motivation, communication** skills, physical fitness, appearance and spiritual aspects, dealing with human character and empowerment of your personality. .

(b) The role of personality in public interviews and performance on different jobs based on the hard and soft skills of your inner personality.

(c) Different methods for discovering personality for measurement and self-projection and writing comprehensive report on your personality.

(d) Popular issues of gender difference in male and female personalities and service incidental hazards, creating stress, tensions and deteriorating your personality.

(e) Hidden aspect of Destiny in your personality.

(f) Cosmic influence and its governing laws on human personality

These are the diversified subjects which provide the holistic picture of your personality in an objective manner. Your personality development program will certainly become *effective, meaningful* and *result-oriented* only when you take cognizance of these multi-dimensional aspects of your personality as a whole at the beginning.

With these words, giving you outline and purpose of offering this book in its comprehensive version, you will **look up to your personality as your personal baggage and try to discover it by adopting the technique of Introspection and Self-Assessment.** This **Self-Addressed Exercise of Self-Interrogation** will effectively provide you a detailed information about your strong and weak areas, nature, character, talents and abilities in an objective manner. **Remember that knowing yourself is the most significant sacred duty of fundamental nature, left by the God to you since the time of your birth. It is entirely left to you to perform it honestly, sincerely and diligently and enjoy the fruits of your Karma. Your efforts to approach an Astrologer or Palmist or Tantric will not help you in any way and it becomes an escapist way of evading your personal duties and responsibilitiese. If you ignore your duty and responsibility towards your personality, you ignore your destiny.** Consequently, you will remain an ordinary, discontented, frustrated, lonely and unhappy person, blaming unnecessarily your **Destiny and God** for your acts of *commission* and *omission*.

Gratitude

I am grateful to Shri Sahil Gupta, Director, Shri Subhash Tyagi and his Editorial team of V&S Publishers for the publication of my book. I hope that their gesture by publishing this book will enable the students of all streams and the younger lot to definitely get the benefit by referring to this book for their efforts to successfully go through various types of interviews and also for giving effective and beneficial performance in their service careers.

CONTENTS

Preamble 3
Foreword 5
Preface 7

Chapter 1	Personality- Concepts and Projection..	13
Chapter 2	Human Mind – The Ring Master of your Personality	28
Chapter 3	Mental Domain of your Personality	35
Chapter 4	Salient Mental Parameters of Your Personality	39
Chapter 5	Adverse Parameters of Mental Domain.......................................	54
Chapter 6	Intellect and Talent	63
Chapter 7	Intelligence And Intelligence Quotient (I.Q.)	67
Chapter 8	Memory, Learning Will and Creative Power	75
Chapter 9	Communication Skill	86
Chapter 10	Leadership Aspects of your Personality	99
Chapter 11	Forming Relations with People	109
Chapter 12	Health, Appearance and Body Features of your Personality....	122
Chapter 13	Character of your Personality...	129
Chapter 14	Empowering Your Personality	136
Chapter 15	Discovering Your Personality for Measurement and Self-Projection..	142
Chapter 16	Role of your Personality in Public Interview	158
Chapter 17	Projection of Personality in your Performance and Success	168
Chapter 18	Hazards for Deteriorating your Personality................................	178
Chapter 19	Gender Difference in Personalities	186
Chapter 20	Destiny Hidden in your Personality...	194
Chapter 21	Influence of Cosmic Laws on Human Personality	202

Epilogues – Can you Change your Personality... 210
Annexure 1 to Chapter 15 – Performa for Writing Report on your own Personality 213

CHAPTER - 1

PERSONALITY – CONCEPTS AND PROJECTION

Abstract

In the present highly advancing and competitive age, your personality has assumed demonstrative and functional nature in your service career. It offers you a *unique identity* and *individuality*. Being your personal baggage, it is your responsibility for its proper development and application. Various Models are projected by different psychologists demonstrates the   . Your *mind controls your inner personality* which mostly determines your *soft skills*. There are different

growth ladder of your service career.

Background

This is a highly advancing and challenging age which has created stiff and severe selection of proper manpower and its judicious employment in an economic manner. The persons so selected have to meet certain job qualitative requirements and standards and possess organisational and managerial skills which should help the employers to sustain and survive against the market driven forces and competition.

As you pass out and get a degree of your desired branch, your struggle to get proper career and subsequent employment starts. You come across a lot of different careers and new to the dynamics of job market and unaware of its demands, challenges and different modalities. *You have only the degree in your hand and you are required to face different career and employment prospects.* Now, the question is - How will you face? On what basis, will you face? 21st *Century* and its challenges about the *newly emerging job market and employment expectations*. You are just of *communications* and *computer sciences* which have revolutionised systems processes, procedures and operations with tremendous changes in the concepts of *operations*, *organisations, managements and recruitments of manpower.* It has resulted in new concepts, such as *global economy, global marketing, global village, global mercantile family, global trading* and *formation of World Trade Organisation* (WTO). Hence, conventional and traditional concepts of marketing, trading, employment, selling and servicing are no longer valid and have given rise to new concepts, such as *skill developments, outsourcing, total package, networking, stock market remuneration options*, etc.

Market Environment

Hence, as you pass out and enter the career/job market, you have to face *interviews, service selection boards, placement agencies* and undergo through different work practices, work culture and apprenticeship. So, you start feeling the heat of the market system arising from the following factors:-

1. Employer's specific Demands and Different Job Qualitative Requirements
2. Diversified market needs and competitions
3. Different working environments and required adaptation techniques
4. Risks and Challenges arising from new developments and technologies.
5. Technological developments and advancements and its impact on the society.
6. Learning new professional and communication skills, manpower recruitment, training and management
7. Global impact and influence on local market conditions due to free flow of technology, foreign investment funds and trade expertise.
8. Political and social demands, structure and policies

In this respect, the following questions arise as under:-

(g) How far are you prepared?
(h) On what basis will you face the competition in the job market?
(i) What treasure of yours will you look up to face the situation?
(j) How will you project and market your personality for seeking different careers and jobs?

The answers to all these questions lie in your *inherent personality* which you have been *endowed at the time of your birth and how far you have developed and strengthened it* so that it has sufficiently become strong, robust and mature for facing *rough and tough aspects of your career,* its demands and challenges. In this respect, the assistance, guidance and exposure which you get from your school and college authorities for apprising you about your personality is very meagre and inadequate. Even if you are properly exposed to it, it is sufficient for you to mentally prepare and *put you on the self-realisation and guidance path so that you can independently proceed for its proper development and application.*

Awareness

Adoption of a particular career and its pursuit is essential in order to meet the *basic needs of the human beings* and lead a life of *reasonable comforts, quality, style and standards.* If you do not follow a specific career, the only job left for you is to do *manual labour work* throughout and *lead a life of a clerk, worker or a labourer* with no hope for comforts and rise for decent life. In this respect, you should know and have awareness about your following inherent or inborn features as under:-

1. Life expectations and aspirations which are related to your ambitions
2. Aptitudes to do specific types of work and performances
3. Interests and hobbies for deriving your mental pleasures
4. Strong likes and dislikes in the form of your strengths and weaknesses
5. Urge to exploit available opportunities and resources for deriving and enjoying maximum material benefits
6. Long-term desires for leading a peaceful, happy and prosperous life

Now, that your purpose is clear and you are aware of *your potential abilities,* you have to track and pursue a *specific career.* **Your personality becomes a significant factor because it affects your selection, employment, performance, image, promotions, advancements and happiness. It also affects your growth, environmental adaptability, adjustments and self-image.** Thus, the quality and standard of your personality become not only your concern but also of your family, society and organisation wherein you live and work. It also becomes an important driving element for leading you to success in different careers and jobs. However, it remains a background player and pulls from the background the strings of control over your performance under different situations and working conditions.

Since, you embody in yourself with many operating forces of different nature and character, the consequential impact, although slow and unseen is definitely effective, significant and decisive for the final outcome. Thus, you are able to observe the impact of your personality from many indicators which will be described in later chapters. At this stage, it is essential to *know and realise the multi-dimensional aspects of your personality along with its basic definition.*

What is Personality

The word *personality* is quite fascinating, as it projects and demonstrates you for public viewing and interaction. It also means your personal baggage and possession which you fully own and exercise your full control on its working and behaviour. In common parlance, **personality is the projection of yourself and your qualities that make you attractive or unattractive, impressive or unimpressive to the people outside in your contact.** In other words, it is the **demonstration of your physical appearance, dress, general bearing, communication skills, intellect or something which strikes to the eye about an individual.**

The word, 'personality' comes from the Latin word, 'Persona' which originally means mask that was worn by Roman actors to hide their faces and perform roles of others. Progressively over the period, it got interpreted as the *'Projected Behaviour and Appearance'.*

Psychological Definition of Personality

Personality can be defined in terms of directly observable behaviour of an individual or in other words, traits which are inferred from one's behaviour. It can also be defined in terms of the ways in which individuals interact with other individuals or according to the roles, an individual adopts for himself for his functioning in the society. Leaving aside other technicalities, the most widely accepted definition of personality as given by Gordon Allport is as under:-

"The personality is the dynamic organisation within the individual of those psycho-physical systems that determine his unique identity and adjustments to his environment."

Of course, there are different ways of looking at your personality. According to Freud, he looks at the personality in the form of *self-ego, self-image or self-conscious and sub-conscious mental process.* Behavioural theorists primarily look at observable responses while others emphasise the *behavioural process.* Trait theorists attempt to categorise the people according to general modes of thinking or acting while humanistic psychologists dwell upon the *development or self-awareness and self-actualisation.* All theories of personality try to describe the *constant pattern of individual differences and explain why a person thinks, feels and behaves differently in a given situation or environment and finally forces people to change their opinions, thoughts and feelings.*

Simplified Personality Concept

The word, 'Personality' of a human being is a fascinating visible factor when its complete profile and picture are presented before you. It basically becomes a qualitative factor of a person as you decide your likes or dislike or form a favourable or unfavorable opinion or become impressed or unimpressed about him at the first look. So, let us take a look at its scientific analysis which reveals that

1. **The outer aspect of personality consists of physical features and characteristics which pertain to his physical, appearance, body organs and their conditions, expressions, movements and performance.**
2. **The inner aspect of personality consists of qualitative and behavioural features and characteristics which pertain to his mental, emotional, psychic, intellect and behavioural factors.**

Personality is the most important demonstrative aspect of a human being. It indicates his nature, character, behaviour, habits, relationship and performance in personal as well as public life. It is the personality which determines the *apparent suitability, acceptability,* and *accountability* of a person in his career as well as during service period. Obviously, this aspect is often highly emphasised and eventually, his becomes the most important criteria for selection during public interviews and later placement in services in any organisation and industry.

The reason for emphasising the personality aspect is that *it demonstrates its functional role in bringing out certain prominent personal qualities which are related to behaviour, character, conduct, habits, bearing, health and expression.* Incidentally, these qualities can't be tested in written examinations, wherein emphasis is on written expressions about technical and general knowledge and I.Q. level. As such, this becomes the criteria for assessing the candidate's intellectual abilities and expressions along with his performance in a single as well as group activities and verbal interviews. It is obvious that your personality plays the dominant role in demonstrating your intellect, abilities, power of expression, behaviour and physical fitness. It is natural that your efforts should be focussed on the development of your personality. Now, *the question is where and how you should direct your efforts and full attention for its development.* So, let us try to understand the *true meaning and theory of personality.*

Theory of Personality — Basis

Personality is based on the 'Self' which is the *nuclear concept in this theory*. It is developed from interaction of the individual with his environment. It strives for achieving *balance, stability* and *consistency*. Let us see the basic factors on which this theory is based. These factors are closely related to human being as under:-

He, i.e., a Human Being exists in a constantly changing world of his own experience in which he remains at the centre.

1. He is the best source of information about himself.
2. People react differently to the same stimuli because of different perceptions.
3. He reacts as a whole to the phenomenal field. As such, it is always a total organised system and any change affects the whole system.
4. He has the basic tendency to actualise, maintain and enhance his powers and potentials.
5. Behaviour is basically directed to a specific objective and it is an expression of his perceptions.
6. Feelings and emotions are always present in the goal-directed behaviour and facilitate its expression. They are significantly required for maintaining and enhancing his entire organism.
7. The modes of behaviour adopted by him are consistent with the concept of the 'Self'. Hence, desired changes in behaviour can be brought out by altering the concept about the Self.
8. Behaviour is also caused by organic experience and needs.
9. Psychologically, adjustments are possible in which he accepts all his experiences and integrate them into his self- structure.
10. When a human being is able to *accept experience without any distortion*, he is able to lead a *healthy and integrated life*.

From the above, it is broadly observed that there are basically three distinct aspects of your personality as under:-

(a) *Physical cum Biological*
(b) *Psychological cum Psychic*
(c) *Sociological cum behavioural*

Salient Features of Different Theories of Personality

Modern research and classical theories offer a balanced and coherent viewpoint of personality from the synthesis of psychological research which covers many issues, such as your *nature, psycho-biology, learning theories, trait theories* and *social psychology*. As a result, *eight basic aspects* are projected by different psychologists for getting a real insight into the personality of a person as under:-

1. **Psycho-analytic:-** It deals with the psychic aspect of human nature thereby giving attention to the brain, mind, sexual drive, nature, socialisation.
2. **Neo-Analytic/Ego:-** Here, emphasis is given to the Self as it struggles to cope with emotions and drives that cause *Self-Image* and *Self-esteem*. These factors are responsible for giving identity which is an urge from inner side.
3. **Biological:-** It focusses on tendencies and limits imposed on potential for growth and change by biological inheritance that relates to *geneinstinct* and brain structure for controlling functions of the body organs.
4. **Behaviourist:-** It relates to conditioning and reinforcing of individual behaviours, relations, learning skills and experience. .
5. **Cognitive:-** It captures the active nature of *human thoughts, perceptions, observations* and *decision making* tasks. It ignores the emotional aspect of one's personality.
6. **Traits:-** It involves understanding and assessment of personal attributes and abilities forming a part of one's personality.
7. **Humanistic:-** It pertains to spiritual nature and emphasises struggle for self fulfilment, dignity and enlightenment.
8. **Interactionist**:- It pertains to understanding about interactions between different roles and identities under different situations.

Well, it is too difficult to understand and comprehend such *multi-dimensional aspects of personality* in such a form which is based on the *classical theories* and *research of personality with emphasis* mainly on *psychological, neo-analytical* and *cognitive aspects*. With this approach, the *subject of personality development* truly and definitely becomes *complex and intricate*. It will not positively serve your purpose as the studies will not lead us to practical gains and achievements. So, let us examine the alternative aspects of personality which are pragmatic and easily understandable for implementation.

Simplified Approach for Representing its Physical and Psychic Aspects

While taking a simple and practical approach, the *personality of an individual is seen and observed from two angles.* One angle is the *outer side which is visible and perceptible.* The other is the *inner side* which is *invisible and imperceptible.* As such, personality gets a two-dimensional view, If you add *time factor* as you grow from childhood and pass through different stages, thereby affecting the outer phase of your personality. It gets a three-dimensional view for deep consideration. Incidentally, you are endowed at the time of birth a specific personality which is grown and developed over the period as you grow and pass through different stages of your life, such as *childhood, adolescence, adult* and *old age.* Two factors have exerted tremendous influence and determined your personality, one is the **genetic or hereditary factor and other is the cosmic and geo-magnetic forces, as existing at the time of birth and place.** As a matter of the fact, *a child gets its unique identity and "the so called the God's Gift of special appearance, talents and qualities" which eventually constitutes his heavenly luck.*

Since no two persons are alike in all respects, they have obviously different personalities, thereby indicating that they possess different outer and inner attributes. The outer attributes are observed in the visible and perceptible forms, such as *physical body features, bearing, behaviour, habits, movements, manners* and *performance.* The inner attributes are manifested in the form of your *nature, character, talents, abilities* and *potential.* Both the outer and inner attributes of your personality are very important and are significantly recognised for determining the difference in human beings. Since **they are based on cosmic and genetic factors, they cause differences in personal appearance, tendencies and responses to variations in environment, such as education, upbringing, training, etc.** Hence, let us consider the *significant indicators* of your personality.

Personality Traits
Broadly, these are of two types as under:-

    (a) The outer traits of personality pertaining to its visible and perceptible aspects.

    (b) The inner traits of personality pertaining to its invisible and imperceptible aspects.

Physical Aspects - Outer Traits of Personality
These are physically seen and they demonstrate different features of your personality. They form its integral part and create an impression about your *overall appearance at the first sight.* Although it does not give a complete picture of your personality, it does help to form an impression at the first glance from prominent visible features. Thus, the visible features as given below certainly play a significant role for the assessment of your personality:-

    (a) Body features and their size, shape and sharpness, such as the nose, eyes, lips, ears, forehead, height, hairstyle, appearance, bearing, hands, legs, palm, body structure, etc.

    (b) Dress, style, make up, colour and texture.

    (c) Behaviour and conduct, while dealing with relatives, friends, subordinates and colleagues.

(d) Mannerisms, pertaining to the style of walking, gesticulation, seating and standing posture, etc.
(e) Expression-verbal as well as written, its style, toning, articulation and depth.
(f) Intellectual abilities pertaining to questions by the members in the interview apart from your intellectual performance in the written tests or examinations, etc.
(g) Temperament, emotional outbreak and reaction, especially to provocative, irrelevant and absurd questions and situations under difficult conditions in group activities leading to give valuable expressions to your emotive feelings and mental state.
(h) Performance, pertaining to your job activities and the results produced by you with respect to economy in manpower and resources.
(i) Physical fitness, endurance, physical outlook and tenacity.
(j) Body language pertaining to your body movements, indicating functional and operational parameters, each conveying its own meaning and impression.

It is however pointed out that action and reaction of the above stated body features and physical acts are mainly controlled by your inner traits or qualities.

Qualitative Aspects – Inner Traits of Personality

The qualitative aspects of your personality are actually projected in *six distinct domains* as under:-

(a) **Mental**
(b) **Emotional**
(c) **Psychic**
(d) **Intellectual**
(e) **Communicative - Relations**
(f) **Spiritual**

Now, the inner personality is manifested in the form of *inner traits* which are normally referred to as *personal qualities or attributes*. They actually belong to *different domains* of *mental, emotional, psychic* and *intellectual* aspects which are eventually responsible for causing influence on functional and developmental activities of your personality. Each aspect covers a set of positive and negative human behavioural qualities. Numerous personal qualities of both positive and negative types are mentioned below as a part of each domain:-

(g) **Mental** – Related to the mind, such as *ambition, will power, tenacity, firmness, integrity, loyalty, determination, responsiveness, willingness, awareness*, etc.

(h) **Emotional** – Related to emotions, feelings and passions, such as *sensitivity, sincerity, anger, temperament, politeness, adamancy, morality, selfishness, greed, arrogance, perseverance, consistence, consciousness,* etc.

(i) **Psychic** – Related to psychic attitudes, such as *maturity, stability, outlook, initiative, passiveness, sulky, mindset, critical, casualness, restlessness, attitude,* *extrovert / introvert, loneliness, possessiveness, demanding,* etc.

(j) **Intellectual** – Related to the thinking power of the mind, such as *intellect, logic, expression, creativity, memory, reasoning, ingenuity,* etc.

(k) **Communicative** – Related to your *skill of communication being done with different types of persons and agencies* for establishing relations, interactions, dialogues, networking and expressions of your work, proposals and thoughts to the concerned authorities and public.

(l) **Spiritual** -- Related to *character, values, principles, morality, ethics* and *etiquettes* which cover the *spiritual aspects of one's personality.*

These inner qualities/attributes are prominently manifested in you under the following personal characteristics:-

(a) Nature and character
(b) Behaviour and conduct
(c) Aptitude and interest areas
(d) Attitude and mindset
(e) Intelligence and motivation
(f) Relations and contacts
(g) Habits and hobbies
(h) Professional skills
(i) Organising and administrative skills
(j) Expression and communication skills
(k) Performance
(l) Leadership
(m) Learning and updating skills
(n) Self- image and self-esteem
(o) Morality with respect to values, etiquettes and ethos

Different Versions of Models for Representation of Human Personality

So far, the psychologists have considered *various models for representation of human personality* purely from the psychological point of view by dividing it into *eight basic aspects* as projected above. One management Guru considers personality from *three aspects* such as **Attitude, Knowledge and Skills (ASK)**, while another management Guru projects the personality in a fours dimensional model of *four Ds, such as Desire, Direction, Determination and Dedication.* Other model of personality is projected on the basis of *four letters of Ls, covering the basic life aspects of Living, Loving, Learning and Legacy.* Each aspect of your personality in this model covers a wide range of activities and functions which are directly or indirectly related to your *career and quality of your life.* **Living** is an activity of your personality which is related to your *work and performance* for *survival and progress* by maintaining health of both the *body and mind.* **Loving** activity deals with your relations, behaviour, conduct, manners, expressions and communication skills. *Learning* stands for your capacity to learn new skills, knowledge, wisdom and enrichment required for your career advancement. The last aspect *legacy* is your need which works in the spiritual domain of values, principles, morality and ethics which enhance your self-image, reputation, dignity, grace, nobility and continue to exist in the society even after your retirement and death. Thus, they are basically found four distinct need-based corner stones of your personality.

The modern conceptual model for your personality is thought and projected from the *Employer's angle*. In fact, your employer writes your *Annual Confidential Report* which *covers basically seven distinct aspects of your personality* which are given below:-

    (a) Behaviour, conduct and values
    (b) Personal characteristics
    (c) Intellectual abilities
    (d) Performance and stability
    (e) Work motivation
    (f) Interpersonal skills
    (g) Administrative skills

The above model is mainly based on the *soft skills of your personality.* They are distinctly related to your *aptitude, abilities, personal attributes, character traits* and *attitude*. In fact, *this model is quite pragmatic and gives a comprehensive and realistic kaleidoscope of your personality because emphasis is here given on the functional demonstrative aspects of your personality and exploitation of skills for personal, public and social applications.* Unfortunately, this model does not cater to the physical and spiritual domains of your personality.

Five Star Model for Representation of Human Personality

With due considerations to all these models used for representation of human personality, I feel that these models do not project its holistic picture. So, I would like to consider a simplified but comprehensive model by covering both the inner and outer aspects and project it in the form of a *Pentagon model,* thereby giving representation in the form of five stars where each nodal point represents the *star aspect of the human personality* as stated below. It will be seen from this *eye catching model given below that these* five distinguishable but separate domains are slightly modified to become broad based and generalised for comprehensively highlighting their important roles in shaping and conditioning your personality.

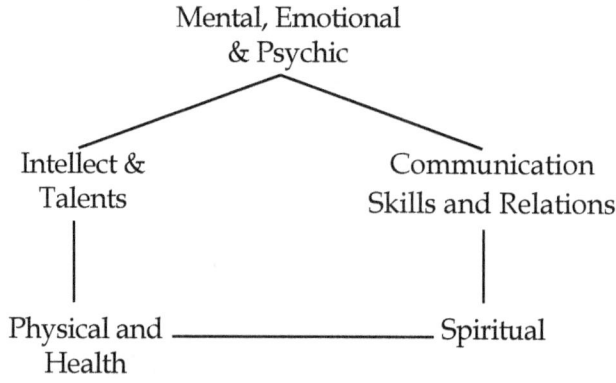

It is evident that this *five star representation becomes the paradigm of your personality and summarises its main functional aspects in a realistic and pragmatic manner with a long-term perspective.* Let us now take a critical look at them and ascertain if they can be significantly and singularly identified for development.

(a) Mental, Emotional and Psychic nature basically related to your mind

(b) Intellect and Talent for learning professional and management skills and improving knowledge and wisdom

(c) Communication skills for expressions and forming relations

(d) Physical and Health related to your body features and appearance

(e) Spirituality representing character, values, principles, morality, ethics and etiquettes

These distinct domains of personality lead to highlight the following behavioural and functional aspects of a person:-

(a) *Mental, emotional and psychic factors* which are basically related to your mind, thereby leading to formation of your nature, mindset, attitude, habits and manners covering a wide spectrum of your *personal characteristics of both positive and negative types.* Consequently, they are responsible for your *effective performance and stability.*

(b) *Intellect and Talent* indicate your intellectual and thinking abilities in order to understand, respond, grasp, assimilate and express. It sets in your thought process and decision making mechanism. It also enables you to learn different jobs, professional and management skills and techniques and enhances your knowledge, expertise and wisdom for availing opportunities for fairly high career advancement. So, it stands for your *intellectual abilities and work motivation.*

(c) *Communication skills and behaviour* enables you to express in writing or verbally project your thoughts, ideas, work proposals with effective presentation before your boss, colleagues and senior officials. It also enables you to form relations and address your team, group or committee members in meeting or discussion and lead them in a project or mission. So, it stands for your *interpersonal, organizing and administrative skills.*

(d) *Spiritual domain* like character, values, principles, morality and ethics enhance your spiritual power that offers happiness, bliss, peace and contentment. Since it deals with the moral and spiritual aspect of your personality, you adhere to the path of high dignity, morality and grace and stay on to enjoy the reputation of being a noble, ethical, dignified and respected person who stays away from vices, bad habits and conflicts. As a result, you become a source for preventing corrupt practices in your organisation. Eventually, they stand for your *behaviour, conduct* and *values.*

(e) *Physical and health related to your body features and appearance that* lead to the formation of your appearance, attractive or unattractive, impressive or unimpressive. Your health fitness offers mental soundness, coolness, robustness, stamina, tenacity and endurance. It also controls your habits and temperament.

Such is the inherent representation of your personality in this model that gets a holistic view of a multi-dimensional nature and consequently becomes the whole projection of your complete Self with a unique identity and individuality. Incidentally, you will find the detailed information about various domains of your personality in the succeeding chapters. In this respect, I may say that this model is the much improved realistic representation over the *psychometric model of human personality known as the OCEAN* of which each letter stands for :-

- (a) O – Openness to experience and appreciate art, emotions, adventure, curiosity
- (b) C – Consciousness showing tendency to show self-respect, discipline, act dutifully, planned work, etc.
- (c) E --- Extraversion, showing enthusiasm, emotion, cooperative and helpful to people.
- (d) A – Agreeableness- a tendency to be friendly, compassionate, cooperative.
- (e) N – Neuroticism indicating sensitive, nervous tendency for negative attributes, such as anger, anxiety and depression.

It will be seen that the five star model of your personality as given above is highly realistic, pragmatic and it is in tune with the demands of the day. Besides, it represents the needs of your employer, present work culture and your own aspirations. *Consequently, it has become fairly expressive, identifiable and distinctive about the overall structure of your personality and more so visible about its functional and qualitative aspects.*

Centric Factor of a Your Personality

It is generally observed that some persons look *more impressive* and *influential* than others because of the *aura* around them and *radiance* reflected from their face. Their bearing, movements, style of walking and conduct appear stylish, dignified and lofty. They demonstrate liveliness in their bearing, behaviour and actions. They catch your special attention and get prominently marked in a group on the basis of their distinct individuality which is in fact manifested from their personality. Now, the questions obviously arising in your mind are as under:-

- (a) Why do you get so impressed and influenced by such a class of persons?
- (b) Why do they look so distinct and prominent in a group so that they quickly catch your attention?
- (c) Why do some persons behave, act and conduct themselves in the stylish and dignified manner?
- (d) How did they get such impressive bearing and personality and where from?

It is well known that each person carries the *spirit of liveliness called 'CHETNA' which is caused by the inner mental, emotional and psychic forces.* They activate the human mind and brain and convey their presence to various organs of the body through various personal attributes of both positive and negative types. The resulting proactive spirit is present in all human beings but its degree and level or in other words its strength and quality which is distinctly determined by different personal attributes and their associated levels will vary over wide range in human beings. Since the human mind is the depository of both positive and negative attributes, this proactive self emitting energy level *'Chetna'* is linked with your mind and brain and their combined response, activation and consequent decision. In fact, decision taken by you to act is eventually determined by the personal attributes as possessed by you.

As a result, you act properly, positively gently and justly that begets confidence in you. Consequently, you get self image and a sense of satisfaction which is generally perceived from your face and expression. Thus, indication of a person having impressive personality is given by his mind which works fast, responds and grasps the situation and act fast in a decisive manner. On the other hand, the mind of a person who is passive and unimpressive in personality works slowly, responds and grasps little and does not act in a decisive manner. Thus, the energy forces which are generated within a person from his personal attributes eventually determine the activity level of his mind and brain combination which in turn gets manifested in his personality.

So, it is ultimately your mind and your associated attributes of both positive and negative types which set in the control mechanism for your personality. So, simple advice is ' *You control your mind and personal attributes, you will consequently determine the quality and value of your personality* '.

Different Stages of Personality Growth

Personality of a person is not stable and varies from his childhood to adult and later to senior citizen stage. Of course, variations in your personality from childhood to adult stage are quite significant and prominently visible. It is natural because your body grows physically and the growth in its physic brings out remarkable changes in your appearance, body features, movements, habits, manners and styles. Changes also take place in the behaviour patterns and reactions due to psychological, physiological and sociological aspects of personality. *Because of these transitional factors, personality becomes a dynamic organisation of yourselves that consequently determine your unique reactions and adjustments with your environment.* There are different outlooks and theories that are associated with the personality thereby emphasizing its different aspects during particular stages.

Some may consider the development of self-image or ego or self-awareness while others give emphasis to its behavioural process. All these aspects point out the *dynamic factor of personality with individual differences in their patterns, emotional response and reaction.*

Although there are different stages of growth, we are specifically concerned to your late adolescent stage extending from 14 to 25 years and later up to adult stage. At this stage, the youth are expected to attain physical, mental and emotional maturity. The physical growth is almost complete and you fully start observing, thinking and reacting. As a result, they start assuming vocational and civic responsibilities. As your mental, emotional and psychic factors which have fully undergone social interaction, engineering and adjustment dominate with their associated attributes of both positive and negative types and consequently determine your personality and its many functional and behavioural aspects. In fact, major changes in your nature, character, behaviour, conduct and performance take place during this stage due to these factors which usher in totality and maturity thereby leaving little scope for change during the later part of your adult stage. Ultimately, all of them affect your performance and determine its grade and excellence from career advancement point of view. So, this becomes the critical stage when the personal qualities of the adolescent children should be discovered, identified, assessed and objectively developed.

Projection of Your Personality

You know that *your personality uniquely establishes your identity and individuality*. It marks your unique presence and it becomes your specific personal commodity for marketing in a highly competitive market. Now, it has *really become an art of packaging yourself and skill fully projecting in the employment market for seeking career jobs*. So, the question is -How will you project your personality or what are the indicators of your personality?

One way is your physical presentation before the members of an interview board with full preparation. Another way is to project through the medium of preparing comprehensive Resume called Personal Bio-Data or CV in which you write about yourself in a skilful and forceful manner so that others get a complete picture about your personality. This aspect will be seen later in a separate chapter

Indicators of Your Personality

Your personality is mainly projected through the following indicating factors :

1. Ancestral or heredity features and family background and upbringing
2. Physical and body features
3. Appearance and conduct
4. Dress/clothing symbolising gender, identification, individuality, maturity and desire for fashion and novelty. It offers smartness or drabness to the personality
5. Intellectual ability and emotional response, such as your feelings, reactions, expressions, etc.
6. Material or non-material status and outlook
7. Knowledge, wisdom and experience
8. Social behaviour, mannerisms and relations
9. Communication skills
10. Social adoption and adjustments
11. Moral values, principles and ethics
12. Etiquettes, manners and ethos

Additional factors of equal importance are given as under :-
   (a) Economic and educational environment and facilities
   (b) Academic performance and achievements

(c) Psychic response such as outlook, mindset, vision, attitude, etc.

(d) Vision, aspiration and approach

The above indicators make your personality quite representative of your complete Self. In fact, they determine the holistic organisation and constitution of your personality. Thus, projection of personality has today become a specialised art and it requires special techniques for presentation. It should be ensured that your projection is realistic and convincing and it does not inflate or blow out your personality in any way. In this respect, you have to be honest, sincere and truthful to yourself in discovering and projecting true picture of your personality. You will see the method for projection in the next few chapters.

Concluding Remarks

Well, you have seen the definition of personality and its important inner and outer aspects as being two distinct sides of a coin. Five starred paradigm is the comprehensively worked out representative model of human personality which is logical, rational and practical without having conceptual wrappings of psychological thinking and research which is found too complex and confusing for execution and follow up. You have observed close correlation of your personality with your nature, character, behaviour, conduct, habits and performance through your personal attributes. You also know that you are the master of your personality and you hold the keys for its control and positive developments.

Your personality is your unique identity and establishes your individuality. It is your personal treasure which has immense hidden potential and strength. Unfortunately, you do not know, nor you are generally bothered to know. But, you should remember that it is *your personality alone that will take you up the growth ladder of your career.* It is the only means you trade, exchange with others and gain your position and status in your service career, society and public life. In fact, a leader is no doubt born but born with a unique personality that brings bundles of dominating positive qualities as heavenly gifts that determines the glorious positive direction of his destiny.

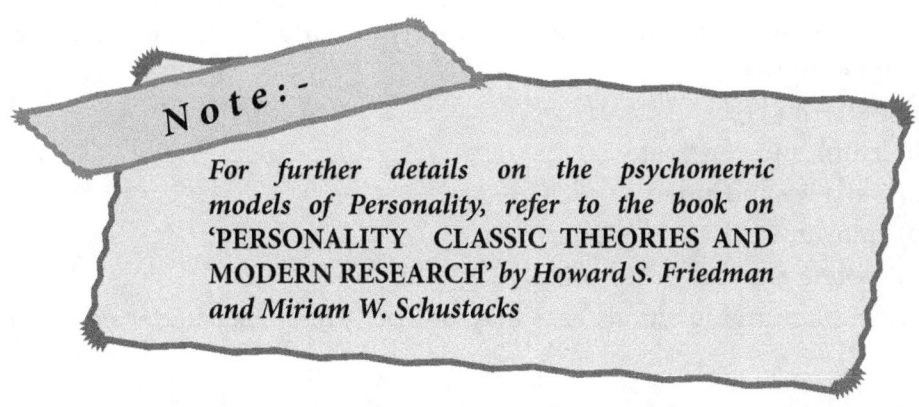

Note:-

For further details on the psychometric models of Personality, refer to the book on **'PERSONALITY CLASSIC THEORIES AND MODERN RESEARCH'** *by Howard S. Friedman and Miriam W. Schustacks*

CHAPTER - 2

HUMAN MIND – THE RING MASTER OF YOUR PERSONALITY

▪Abstract▪

Human mind stays as an invisible controlling agency in the background and exercises a very subtle and effective control on your personality as the Ringmaster and remains the supreme boss of your performing show. Nobody can ignore its hold and control or else, a person is out of the arena and vanishes. Human mind steers your personality and drives it over the predetermined course of your objective. Unfortunately, human mind remains ignored, overlooked and often neglected despite its strongly perceptible talked subject in the spirituality, it remains the least noticed and cared in practice.

Controlling Factor

the inner personality of an individual and as such they are mostly controlled by his mind. Unfortunately, you are not aware that all your activities, performance, routines of the days and months are in fact controlled by your mind. This exercise of control is indirect and invisible but you do experience this aspect at every stage whenever you say that *" I feel like this way or I think this way "*
and indirect control of the mind on your activities. Thus, the controller of your activities remains in the background but your **personality is driven to act according to its dictates. Let us now see how the mind conducts you in your daily activities, you normally act and function as under :-**

    (a) Sense and feel
    (b) Think and anticipate
    (c) Perceive and judge
    (d) Look inwards or outwards
    (e) Decide one way or the other

These are your routine functions and they are performed not under control of your person, it becomes his specific identity which incidentally remains embedded in his personality and is reflected in the form of his specific nature, character, habits, behaviour, and performance.

Ultimately, the human mind holds the stick to control all your personalized activities but your personality becomes the front end demonstrative face of your action. *How is this control exercised?* Obviously, the human mind is the faculty by virtue of which you remain conscious and aware about existence of yourself. *Hence, consciousness, awareness, thinking power and actualization of the Self are the basic characteristics of the mind which distinguishes a person from another person through manifestation of his personality.* Hence, the link of the mind with your personality is so obvious that *your body takes an order from your mind and not from brain.* It means that you do not act independently but through your mind and that too after fully processing the input data with full thought before taking the decision to act in a particular way.

Since your mind thinks, reasons, analyses, discriminates, feels good or bad, senses pleasure or pain, imagines, worries, etc, it plays the pivotal role in shaping and conditioning your personality to act in a particular way. Thus, it is within control of your mind to offer you good or bad, healthy or sick personality. This aspect will be seen in the succeeding paragraphs and emphasizes its supreme role in governing and controlling your personality. Before that, let us examine the characteristics of your mind

Characteristics of the Mind

These are stated in the specific forms as under :-
- (a) It is not a physical entity. So, it is not seen or weighed or quantified by any measure.
- (b) It is a faculty for sensing and feeling. As such, it can't be analyzed chemically in any laboratory.
- (c) Mind grows and its capacity is enhanced by experience and maturity instead of aging and decaying.
- (d) Mind is a different entity from brain as it is capable of sensing, thinking, reasoning, feeling, perceiving, judging etc.
- (e) Mind is self-luminous and self-energized unlike physical objects which require source of energy for activation. Mind does not need outside energy to function. It functions of its own.
- (f) Body stays active and live as long as mind functions.
- (g) *Mind and body are very closely inter-linked. Any change in mental state affects the health of the body. Hence, mind and body act and react together but the influence of the mind over body is pronounced and overriding.*
- (h) The power of the mind can be enhanced by adopting certain means and Yogic exercises
- (i) *Mind experiences the stress and fatigue which can be reduced by deep breathing and Yogic exercises.*

Levels of the Mind

There are three levels of human mind. They together give the mind a single entity. These levels are given below :-

(a) **Conscious Mind** – It is that part of the mind which on receipt of input signals from the sense organs through brain reasons, thinks, analyses, discriminates and then decides for a specific action. Before that, it calls for information from the sub-conscious mind and its treasure house. Once the conscious mind completes processing, it takes decision and conveys to brain for action.

(b) **Sub-conscious Mind** --- It is an another level of mind and is accessed by the conscious mind for relevant data from its treasure-house where all that you have seen, heard, thought, talked, done, are stored in the form of personalized impressions, emotions, images and personal attributes in different folders. The sub-conscious mind plays the significant role in enabling the conscious mind to take an appropriate decision which corresponds to the levels of personal attributes as stored in its different folders. The urges, impulses and emotions arising from the sub-conscious mind keeps the conscious mind ticking its clock for taking proper decisions In fact, sub-conscious mind becomes the storehouse for keeping and maintaining *SANSKARS which demonstrate different types of impressions, predispositions, tendencies, biases, phobias and apprehensions of individualistic nature.*

(c) **Unconscious Mind** – It is a mind which functions independent of the brain when the link or connection with the conscious mind is broken and it functions in a free style mode. Here, sub-conscious mind dominates over the conscious mind and keep feeding it all irrelevant data. The mind generally goes in an unconscious state when drunk, or brain damaged in an accident or hypnotized.

It is thus seen that the human mind is a powerful invisible entity and indirectly exercise control on his entire range of action, activities and performance. That is why the mind is called the *Ring Master of the human personality.* It is a repository of thoughts, emotions, impressions and feelings. Negative and evil thoughts make the mind weak. Hence, such a person is said to have weak personality because he always succumbs to temptation and bad habits. So, *you have two types of persons, one having strong personality which is identified by possessing a strong mind and another having weak personality with a weak mind.*

Let us see the characteristics of a strong mind and weak mind as under:-

A Strong Mind

(a) **It always remains cool, calm and composed under difficult and challenging conditions**. It exercises control on anger and does not get provoked.

(b) It never succumbs to temptation, greed, envy, vices and develops immense courage to say ' NO ' to immoral demands and actions.

(c) It always remains free from prejudice, suspicion and jealousy.

(d) It has clarity in thinking and action that enables him to take right decision and come to right judgment.

(e) It does not harbor against anyone evil emotions and feelings such as desire, anger, greed, fear, hatred. So, he is always guided by right thinking and intentions.

(f) It develops positive thinking, positive attitude, concentration, fearlessness and self-confidence.

A Weak Mind

A weak mind gets irritated and loses temper over trivial matters and reacts violently.

(a) It easily succumbs to temptation, immoral demands and vices.

(b) It fails to take right decision due to confusion, suspicion and prejudice and delivers partial and biased judgments.

(c) It easily compromises and surrenders to evil forces and temptations from corrupt persons.

(d) It can't face challenges in life and tries to escape from them by adopting easy and cheap methods.

(e) It does not appreciate good qualities, work and offers uncharitable comments and criticism.

(f) It remains restless, grumbling, lazy, frustrating and in a negative thinking mood.

With this background information, characteristics and quality of the mind and its pivotal role in personal life by shaping our personality, let us now examine closed relationship of personality with human mind.

Personality through Your Mind

Your mind mainly stands for your mindset, thought process, vision and attitude. Your mind plays a very important role in shaping these factors. Your mindset is basically formed by the combination of your positive and negative attributes and its nature whether positive or negative is determined by the dominating profile of positive or negative attributes. If the dominating part is negative, your mindset becomes negative and if it is positive, then your mindset is positive. *This mindset becomes one of the important factors in determining quality of your personality.* How does it happen? How does mindset affect the personality?

Your mind is exercised through the personal traits. When these traits or personal attributes are considered and closely observed, they represent a mirror reflection of your mind. Its function and activity get truly and faithfully manifested into these personal traits. They influence working of the mind in a positive or a negative way. Consequently, your nature and characteristics are greatly affected by the mindset because of its positive or negative nature. It is the process of affirmation in your mind that builds the strength and force and gives direction to your work, values, principles and ethics that eventually become indicators of a good personality.

Mind and Its Control

Your mind exercises a strong influence and power on your nature, habits, behaviour, conduct and performance. Your personal characteristics are highly affected by your mindset and many of them get reflected into your personality. The biggest contribution from your mindset results in formation of relations, liaison and networking with others. This in turn affects your attitude, visibility, patronage cum anchor support, communication skills and finally relations with your friends, relatives, subordinates, seniors and especially with your boss. These aspects will be dealt in later chapters.

Let us take a further look at the mind. All human qualities / attributes pertaining to mental, emotional, feelings, psychic and intellectual aspects originate from your mind. As such, your mind with its personal attributes and their characteristics makes tremendous impact on your nature, performance and personality. Many of them contribute to form the positive mindset and offer the power of positive thinking and attitude. *The positive mindset is undoubtedly a key player of your personality and has positive impact on your work, activities and performance.* This aspect is further elaborated in order to get clear understanding about the role of your positive mindset in various fields so as to :- :

1. Avoid the feeling of inferiority complex which creates self doubt on account of our parentage, cast, creed, gender and social environment.
2. Generate self confidence to always think that "I can do it or I will do it ".
3. Carry always the spirit and power to win and succeed.
4. Have implicit faith in the God and believe that He is always there to help and protect me.
5. Banish negative thoughts about your personal power, strength and courage and replace them by positive thoughts.
6. Stop unnecessary imagination about probability of obstacles and adverse happenings. Instead, anticipate and plan for avoiding them.
7. Seek an advice from a competent, knowledgeable and experienced Advisor or Counselor to overcome any complex feelings and doubts. Also try to seek self-knowledge in order to keep ourselves updated in organizing and managing skills.
8. Assess fairly the areas of your strengths and weaknesses. Enhance your strengths and try to substantially reduce your weaknesses step by step
9. Take a risk and face a challenge, arising from difficult and adverse situation. Always say that "the God's is with me in all my endeavors.

Mental Attitude

Besides the above aspects which directly affect your mindset, it is the state of your mind which too matters considerably as it is related to form and change your mental attitude. It is *based on a thought process which generates within you different thoughts, moods and temperaments.* If those are pleasant, peaceful and quiet, they generate power, strength and good spirit in your functioning, activities and performance. As a result, your living, behaviour and habits get much improved and your personality is consequently enriched.

What do we mean by a peaceful and quiet mind? It means that the mind has practically banished negative thoughts and ideas, pertaining to fears, worries, hatred, greed, anger, grief, anxiety, despair and guilty consciousness. The moment you get rid of the negative thoughts, you feel immediate relief and your mind is occupied by creative, positive, productive, healthy and inspiring thoughts. In fact, they start entering the mind one by one and you start feeling at ease, composed and relaxed and your spirit and morale are rejuvenated. Whenever you come across unpleasant and uncomfortable situations, your attitude and approach of looking at them are positive because your mind is occupied by positive thoughts which drive you to act and react in the positive direction. This is perceived as a direct advantage of a peaceful mind which enables you to listen to the deep sound of bliss and harmony, as if coming from the divine power of the God. As a result, you gain deep spiritual power, experience and moral strength and you are able to concentrate more on your work, performance, relations, behaviour and body movements for their improvement and enrichment.

Driving Factors

Thus, it is seen that *your positive mindset, attitude, positive thinking and peaceful state of mind are truly big driving factors and greatly affect the quality, grade, grace, standard and style of your personality and its performance.* It is predominantly your performance and its result which is watched, observed, assessed and finally judged by your senior officials. Now, meaningful, healthy, productive and excellent performance is positively expected from a healthy and peaceful mind. *So, healthy mind eventually becomes an indicator of your good fortune, prosperity and happiness.* In case, you have negative mindset and attitude, you should try to change to positive side by adopting suitable and corrective measures which should be pragmatic, self reliant, spiritual, moral, ethical, noble and down the earth. *In this entire self centric process, you should not be egotistical, casual and easy going but cultivate seriousness, intensive interest and commitment for improvement.*

In order to give a fairly good idea about the role of your mind in shaping the personality, a few set of questions which are directly addressed to you are given below for your consideration :-

1. Do I realise my mindset? Is it positive or negative type?
2. Am I optimistic or pessimistic in my outlook?
3. Am I hopeful or hopeless?
4. Am I thoughtful, conscious, mindful and rational?
5. Are my thinking, outlook and approach positive or negative, forward or backward considering my present conditions?
6. Do I start my mission with a firm hope of winning success or anticipate failure and then hesitate or keep brooding on its pros and cons?
7. While planning and executing, do I see and think loudly, pointedly, openly and widely or keep considering about restraints, controls, checks and balances?
8. Do I jump to a conclusion or think step by step and then conclude?
9. Am I forward looking or back ward look?

10. Have I progressive approach or regressive approach?
11. Do I apply logic, reasoning, rationality and sensibility in my thinking?
12. Do I envisage and think about my objective with a definite, clear and firm purpose in mind?
13. Do I have a tendency to act fast without a thought or on the spur of a moment without fully understanding about an issue and its complex problems?
14. Am I happy, smiling, graceful and dignified while performing and executing my duties?
15. Do I display courage, strength, firmness and clarity after I decide to act and perform?
16. How do I respond to risks and challenges? Do I maintain cool, composed, and thoughtful and then focus my maximum attention on tackling the risk while facing the challenge?
17. How do I behave with my relations, friends, colleagues and subordinates? Is my behaviour amicable, polite, gentle or stubborn, aggressive and arrogant?
18. Do I offer my critical remarks in a graceful and dignified manner?

These are typical action-oriented, thoughtful questions which are listed here in order to assess the condition of our mind and its thoughtprocess. From the nature of answers, if they are found affirmative, you can fairly conclude that you have got positive mindset and it becomes a positive indicator of your bright destiny

Concluding Remarks

Human mind is the key player of your positive or negative, good or bad personality. The strength and quality of your personality is known by the type of mind you possess. Whether it is strong, weak, robust, composed, visionary determines the quality of your personality and eventually becomes its indicator. Hence, you must remain aware and conscious about the role your mind plays in your life activities. You should ensure that it plays positive role by adopting positive thinking and positive attitude. You should therefore improve its quality and strength by adopting good habits, reading wholesome literature and doing regular Yoga and meditation. *A disciplined mind with positive mindset will always keep you away from vices, bad habits and bad companies.* Besides, it will instill in you vigor, drive, values and enthusiasm for doing positive work. *Remember that your mind is the basic identity of your personality*

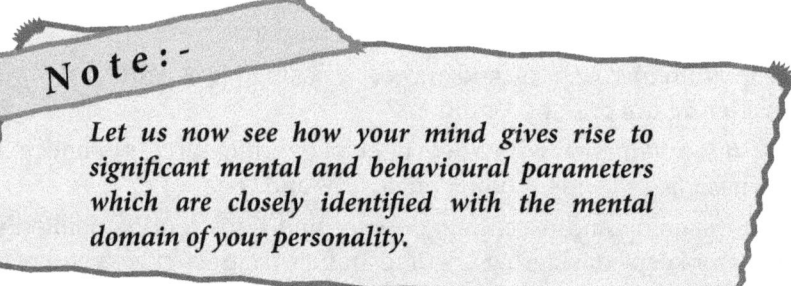

Note:-

Let us now see how your mind gives rise to significant mental and behavioural parameters which are closely identified with the mental domain of your personality.

CHAPTER - 3

MENTAL DOMAIN OF YOUR PERSONALITY

> **Abstract**
>
> state, mental health and mental strength. Mental health is projected through mental, emotional and psychic attributes which are personal characteristics of an individual. There are various indicators of your mental health. Incidentally, your mental state
>
> mind. Hence, your mental health becomes the key factor for winning success or causing failure in your service career.

First Domain of Your Personality

This is the most important domain of your personality and it is a direct offshoot of your mind. So, it is manifested in the form of your feelings, emotions, passions, impulses, instincts and behaviour. Consequently, they directly affect your nature, character, habits, relations and performance. Obviously, it dominates functional, behavioural and attitudinal aspects of your personality. In fact, your personality will have the positive or negative dimension and

Mental State

Mental state deals with the health of your mind and its healthy projection. In fact, your nature, behaviour and performance depend upon your mental state which involves your feelings, emotions, thoughts and passions. These factors are generated from your mind and its mindset detects their functioning either positive or negative way. Mind and brain are two combined faculties of a human body and their combined operation results in a decision which is conveyed by the brain to the body organs to sense and act accordingly. Since this is an imperceptible process which takes place deep inside your inner self, its evidence is felt through your certain

Mental Health

Mental well-being depends upon the mental health. Robust state of mind is neither affected by misfortunes nor by the cheerful and pleasant events.

So, the mental health is broadly considered in terms of the following aspects of an individual:-.
- (a) Attitude towards oneself
- (b) Growth, development and self-actualization
- (c) Integration and autonomy
- (d) Perception of reality
- (e) Environmental adaptability and accommodativeness

The *attitude of an individual towards himself pertains to self-acceptance, self-confidence, self-reliance, self-dependence and initiative. You are able to express your ideas and feelings with full awareness, confidence and consciousness.* You are able to observe yourself realistically and objectively and accept without bias and distortion ideas and perceptions about your self-identity, self-image and self-esteem. You always try to *realise your potential and abilities through self-actualization.* A mentally healthy person has a positive self-concept and is motivated to strive for self-actualisation. When you are an *integrated person, there is a balance of psychic forces in you. You have a unifying outlook on life and have reasonable capacity to resist stress.* As a result, you exhibit a sense of autonomy in relation to the environment and in your decision making process. You also exhibit a healthy and objective perception of reality and social responsibility.

Projection of Mental Health

Once the correlation of your mind-body with your attributes is perceived, the mental state can be projected in the form of your personal attributes. They have close bearing with your mental function and projection. So, it is enough to focus on the personal attributes of a person if it is required to observe his mental state. For this purpose, let us consider the following attributes :-

1. Mental
- (a) Ambition and will power.
- (b) Firmness, tenacity and determination
- (c) Devotion, dedication and dependability.
- (d) Integrity and loyalty.
- (e) Awareness and responsiveness.
- (f) Adaptability and accommodation
- (g) Responsibility and commitment
- (h) Foresight and vision

2. Emotional State
- (a) Sensitivity and tolerance.
- (b) Sincerity and humbleness.
- (c) Anger, sulkiness, adamancy and temperament.
- (d) Ego and self-image.
- (e) Politeness, morality and softness.

(f) Temptation, greed, envy, selfishness and possessiveness.
(g) Calmness, consistence and persistence.

3. Psychic State
(a) Maturity, stability and consistency
(b) Outlook and consciousness
(c) Casualness, carelessness and passiveness
(d) Loneliness and indifference
(e) Cheerfulness and liveliness
(f) Initiative and keenness
(g) Temperamental balance and restlessness
(h) Extrovert and introvert

In fact, the mental state is inclusive of emotional and psychic state and all of them constitute the mental health. So, it demonstrates an integrated effect of all these three factors and their respective attributes have positive or negative bearing on them. As a result, you get the following indications.

Indicators of a Healthy Mental State
(a) Positive attitude and positive thinking
(b) Calm, composed and positive outlook
(c) Balanced and controlled temperament
(d) Relaxed, pleasant and cheerful facial expression with glare of self-satisfaction and self-confidence
(e) Self-reliance and bright self-image
(f) Dignified behaviour, conduct and body movements
(g) Flexibility and maturity in understanding and responsiveness
(h) Cordiality, amiability, openness and human face in relations
(i) Loyalty, dependability and integrity
(j) Love, laughter and sense of happiness

In fact, you experience yourself that you have got the healthy mental state in light of the above stated feelers, indicators and markers. You feel your mind at rest and you are able to focus it on your performance and responsibilities. As a result, your output is increased considerably, your working efficiency goes up and you become quite proficient and creative in your performance. You are thus able get direct benefits of a healthy mental state. Now, you should remember that your mental state is controlled by *five universal laws* as under:-

(a) *The law of cause and effect,* pertaining to generate thoughts that lead to particular activities.
(b) *The law of control* that enables you to assume responsibilities only when you are able to control.

(c) *The law of belief.* It means that each of your belief is a choice that creates change in your life.
(d) *The law of concentration.* It leads to the growth of your knowledge, wisdom, skills and experience.
(e) *The law of attraction.* It means that whatever you have in your consciousness or dream or intensive feelings, you will attract it in life like love attracts love, friend attracts friend.

It may be noted that your personal attributes are conditioned under the influence of these laws. So, your mental state gets eventually conditioned accordingly.

Mental Strength

It is seen that *strong mind generates mental strength. It comes from strong will power, determination, firmness and focused objective.* In fact, when you have set your objective for achievement with clear vision, you build up your mental strength from your tremendous hidden power which is stored within you as your hidden treasure. This power is further *enhanced by reading good, wholesome and knowledgeable literature which provides healthy food to your mind, its positive thinking and attitude*. The selection of such reading material and the company of good knowledgeable persons will certainly enhance your mental strength. In this respect, contribution by practicing Yoga and meditation will be substantial for overcoming your depression, tension, stress and restlessness. It makes mind fresh by banishing negative thoughts and emotions by concentrating your attention and energy on your desired objectives.

Concluding Remarks

To conclude, it is emphasised that your mental health is the key factor for winning success in life. *The way you think in your mental domain determines the way you act and function in your physical domain.* Finally, this factor together with your physical factor produces either constructive or destructive end results. *It is your mind and its mental positive state that makes your body and eventually your personality rich and dignified.* While it is possible to measure the level of physical fitness through medical tests, it is difficult to measure level of your mental health. Ultimately, *you have to exercise control on your attitude, feelings, emotions, thinking, physical fitness, diet, etc. according to the dictates and constraints of the working condition and environment.*

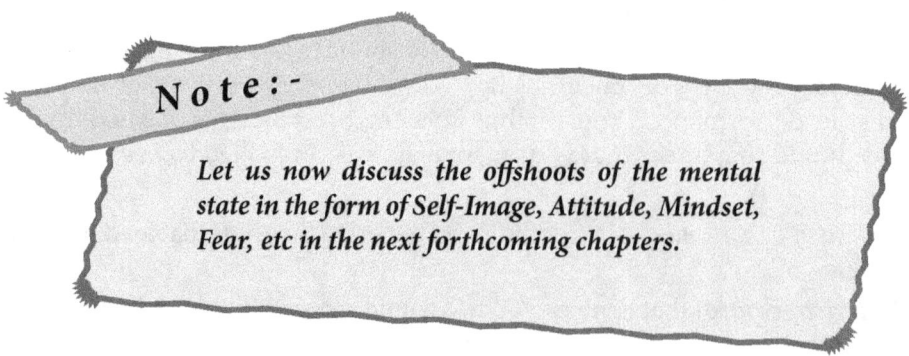

Note:-

Let us now discuss the offshoots of the mental state in the form of Self-Image, Attitude, Mindset, Fear, etc in the next forthcoming chapters.

CHAPTER - 4

SALIENT MENTAL PARAMETERS OF YOUR PERSONALITY

Abstract

Mental parameters, such as *Self-image, Attitude and Positive thinking* are the offshoots of your mind and its mindset. There are many psychological forces which are responsible for generating them from your mental state. While self-image pertains to your opinion and impression about yourself, attitude refers to your mental state about feeling, thinking, judging and reacting to a situation. Your attitude depends on your beliefs that determine way of your action. Accordingly, you may have positive or negative attitude. Positive thinking is the healthy process of your positive attitude and positive mindset. Each of them is comprehensively described in this chapter.

Scope

study of the psychological forces reveals that the people act, behave and perform because of these forces, acting on their mind that make them uniquely individualistic and establish their individuality in the society. Since the inner part of yourself dominates on your personality, the psychological forces eventually control your mind and its functioning *How are these forces generated?*

The psychologists have often put forth many factors; a few of them are listed below:-

(a) Ego factor of a person which provides a sense of identity called ' Self '.

(b) Biological factor which offers genetically physical, physiological and temperamental nature.

(c) Environmental factor conditions and shapes the mind of a person who believes and responds in certain ways under varying cultures and traditions.

(d) Conceptual factor pertains to a perception, observation, understanding and decision making process of a person.

(e)
like music, singing, drama, painting, etc.

(f) Ongoing interactive factor that sets interaction between a person and his particular surrounding and environment for living and inter personal communication.

(g) Spiritual factor that sets religious thoughts for understanding human existence, soul, wisdom and divinity for getting mental peace and happiness.

A human mind is definitely affected by these psychological factors as stated above. As a result, *the thought process of the mind which is the main characteristic feature of a human being gives rise to the following aspects of your personality :-*

(a) Self-Image
(b) Attitude
(c) Mindset
(d) Positive or Negative thinking
(e) Anger, Sorrow, Loneliness
(f) Success or Failure
(g) Fear, Worry, Anxiety and Criticisms

Let us take a critical look at each of them and understand them in the succeeding paragraphs.

SELF-IMAGE

Personality *vs* Self-Image

The words like 'I', 'Self' or 'me' are commonly used by individuals while talking about their achievements or conducting a mission or leading a task force or commission or committee for work study or evaluation. In these words, you see a glare and glimpse about the reference to your Self as the centric figure as you want to project your image of a *prominent striving person, achiever, doer and main conductor. All these roles are structured around you so as to give personalized impression to others about your unique personality and its image.* Although, it appears to be egoistic yet, it *projects your personality glorified, dignified and self centric. It gives an aura and charm of self activity, self achievement and self esteem to your personality.* It is perceived as your creation thereby encouraging you to use such words like ' I did ', ' I want ', ' I will '. You are thus hijacking your personality in the direction of yourself. Perhaps, it is judicious association of your personality with your Self-Image that may keep you away from the evils of excessive self esteem, self pride, self ego and arrogance.

Meaning

It simply means your opinion and impression about yourself which is either conveyed to others or generated by your physical presence, behaviour and communication skills. In other words, others see your behaviour, expression and performance that project visible features of your 'Self'. Consequently, they create your image in public eye and enable others to form opinion and impression about you.

It is pointed out that self-image is a part of the self concept factor and is mainly based on your belief system. Your mind and thinking which drives you to form idea, concept or impression about yourself allows you to accept new ideas and advice if there are consistent with the ideas or concept already present within you or held by you. Thus, *your Self Image becomes your mental face and your inner mirror in which you see your own reflection. As a result, your Self-Image becomes a key to your personality for understanding your behaviour and performance and eventually sets boundaries and limitations on your capacity for accomplishment.* If you are rigid and pretentious in your Self Image, then there is hardly any scope for its improvement or enhancement because you will not accept new ideas, learning, advice and suggestions.

Self-Image directs your mental thought process in a particular direction and your body responds to it accordingly in your behaviour and performance. You should therefore think in a positive direction and turn down undesirable negative thoughts. In other words, *Self-Image reveals dominance of either positive or negative attributes and your behaviour, personality and performance get affected accordingly* through your corresponding body movements and language as well as facial expression and general postures. *A person who keeps himself isolated and aloof from friends, society and community and behaves rigidly or expresses bitterly, has generally low and poor self image.*

Process of Self-Image

Human mind is divided in two parts. One is the conscious mind and other is the sub-conscious mind. Now, the process of transformation of self image into your behaviour, habits, manners and typical working style takes place entirely at the sub-conscious level. As a result of various factors as stated above, the psychological forces have conditioned your mind to think, perceive, believe and see the outside objects and activities on your mental screen in a particular way and activate your nervous system to respond and direct you through brain to behave and perform in a manner consistent to your image. Thus, *your behaviour and performance become physical manifestation of your Self image which is not clearly perceptible to you.* But, you come to know about it when you carefully listen to what others talk about you, monitor the way others react to you and compare your current performance with previous performance.

Your *Self-Image Factor (SIF)* is the dominant parameter that affects everything you do in life. It is looked upon as *the driving factor of your personality that empowers your Self to act and behave in a particular way thereby determining the chances of success in your performance.* That is how you have to accept full responsibility for the consequence of the type of the self image which you possess and project on appropriate occasions.

Salient Features

Finally, to recapitulate, the salient features of your Self-image are summarised as under:-
- (a) It pertains to your ideas, concepts, opinions and impressions you hold about you.
- (b) It becomes an indicator of your behaviour and performance which consequently affects your relations with outside persons as well as agencies.

(c) It projects your confidence, self-respect and values in performance and business dealings
(d) It reflects your mental face in the form of your inner mirror to yourself.
(e) It sets boundaries/limitations on your accomplishment.
(f) It imbibes you with new spirit, energy, enthusiasm and moral strength that may finally turn your failure in success.
(g) *It makes your personality winning through positive and assertive technique.*

Discovering your Self-Image
Now, how are you going to discover your Self-Image?

Since it is based on your thinking about yourself and what others feel and think about you, the *best way for you is to look up to .yourself and ask a question whether I am like this or do I think about myself in this manner.* You should address to yourself a set of questions related to your behaviour, habits, body movements, manners, conduct, relations, working styles, hobbies and performance and find out whether your self-image is something like as under :-

1. Angry, aggressive, adamant
2. Temperamental, passionate, sensitive
3. Egoistic, talkative, self-eulogizing
4. Inspiring, encouraging, motivating
5. Self-centred, centric, inward-looking
6. Casual, indifferent, carefree
7. Moody, unstable, restless
8. Cheerful, joyous, pleasing
9. Frank, straightforward, open
10. Generous, supportive, helpful
11. Impressive, dignified, graceful
12. Honest, sincere, dependable
13. Selfless, truthful, virtuous
14. Strict, disciplined, moralistic
15. Rational, logical, thoughtful, systematic
16. Forward-looking, visionary, reformist
17. Religious, spiritual, ritualistic
18. Critical, nasty, sadist
19. Dare-devil, bold, fearless, risk-taking, adventurist

You are thus able to ascertain your *self-image* by addressing to yourself a *set of queries in a sequential manner,* as given above and list out the *corresponding answers,* as applicable to you. **Whether you have a positive or negative self-image is determined by the number** *of affirmative or negative answers.* However, you should be careful and discreet while drawing conclusion. In fact, you are able to collect proper personal data that you should properly and carefully analyze and then draw the correct inference about your self-image. *You should not be hasty, illogical and irrational but you should properly carry out introspection and self-assessment.in order to get your realistic and pragmatic self-image.*

This is the way your reputation about your self-image is created or spread or projected. *Persons whosoever come in contact with you have prior information about your self-image and are therefore careful while dealing with you.* Sometimes, *your self-image becomes your double edged weapon in the sense that it prevents you from doing bad jobs as well as it protects you from the vicious and corruptive environment. In the process, you are likely to displease your boss or other senior persons who may spoil your annual reports and jeopardize chances of your promotions.* You are however required to be *discreet in order to ensure that your self-image does not affect your normal performance, activities, relationships and promotional prospects.*

Control Mechanism of Self-Image

It is generally observed that some persons look more impressive and influential than others because of the aura around them and radiance reflected from their face. Their bearing, movements, style of walking and conduct appear stylish, dignified and lofty. They demonstrate liveliness in their bearing, behaviour and action. They catch your special attention and get prominently marked in a group on the basis of their distinct individuality and self-image which is in fact manifested from their personality.

It is observed that the inner mental, emotional and psychic forces activate various organs of the body through different personal attributes of both positive and negative types. As a result, they cause reactions and impressions on your body features more predominantly on your face that has proactive and self-actualizing feature. Whenever these forces act properly, positively and justly, it begets feelings of confidence, grace and dignity in you. Consequently, *you get self-image and a sense of satisfaction which is generally perceived from your face, bearing and expression.* Thus, a person having impressive personality gives the indication of positive self image On the other hand, a person who has passive and unimpressive personality exhibits dull, morose and depressive self image. It is ultimately your mind and your associated attributes of both positive and negative types which set in the control mechanism for creating your self-image of either positive or negative type. .

Negative Self-Image

Negative Self-Image is reflected as the poor self-image and demonstrates dominance of the negative attributes of your personality. Its influence is directly visible on your face, behaviour and conduct. These negative attributes cause a significant setback in your attitude, performance and progress. Let us see the influence of these negative attributes on personal characteristics of your self-image as under :-

- (a) Lack of self-confidence and reliance
- (b) Restless, temperamental and inconsistent nature and behaviour
- (c) Indifferent and casual attitude and outlook
- (d) Lack of ambition, vision, objective and definite direction to personal career
- (e) Lack of focus, concentration on personal profession and diversion of attention and efforts on wayward and wishful issues of material gains
- (f) Lack of learning, professional knowledge and information on current affairs
- (g) Ego and over-confidence in personal abilities
- (h) Lack of desire to follow morality and ethics in profession and personal life
- (i) Self-centeredness and a narrow-minded approach

Consequently, these negative functional aspects of your personality adversely affect your basic nature, character, behaviour and conduct and indirectly lead to form and project your self-image as shaky, intemperate, egoist, self-centric, evasive and unresponsive.

Image Management

In this competitive world, projection of an impressive image is recognized as a creative art. You are often given proper professional lessons for adopting its technique. It is also treated as the *Image Management Technique with the emphasis on optimally utilizing the resources of clothing, grooming practices, body language, etiquettes and vocal communications for projecting the desired image in every situation in life.* Considering the wide scope and market demand, *image consultants and image consulting business institutes are coming up in metro cities along with advertisements in print and electronic media.*

ATTITUDE

Meaning

It is basically the way you feel, think, judge and react to a situation whenever you come across. So, it is defined as your habitual manner of acting, feeling .and thinking that shows your disposition, opinion and beliefs about life. Here, the key words are *habitual, thinking, belief and acting* that significantly affect your nature. It is the most outwardly visible characteristic of what you think about you on your mental screen. Presentation of your personality is simply the outward expression of your inner attributes, emotions, feelings and passions. Consequently, they are reflected in your behaviour and the manner you behave is considered your attitude in action. *Your attitude is the visible expression on your face about all the beliefs you hold and thought process you engage for thinking.*

Key Factor

Thus, the key to your mental attitude is your beliefs and your beliefs in turn determine the way you think, behave and act. For example, some people select to adopt firm belief in honesty, integrity, loyalty, gentleness, humbleness and regards for their fellow human beings. Others do not believe in their own interest, wealth, property, fortunes and do not bother whether it hurts others. Some believe in following certain values, principles and ethics for enriching their personal life while others believe in spiritual pursuits. Here, it should be noted that you adopt a particular belief only after thinking of those who are associated with you and the environment in which you live in. In fact, your living conditions, traditions, culture and the people you are associated with have significant influence on your belief formation process. Perhaps, your attitude so formed happens to be the end result of your thinking and reaction and finally reflected in your typical behaviour and facial expression. Of course, external events, all types of people and circumstances, both good and bad are found everywhere in the world and they are defined as the activating agents and you have no control on them. But certainly, you can control the way you think and react to such event by adopting a positive or negative attitude. In other words, *it depends upon what type of mental thought process you have developed on the basis of your beliefs and reaction to external events.* Here, it is *your mind and its inner traits which play the main ball game in the background.* And you must realise that they ultimately hold the key in forming your mental attitude.

Positive Attitude

Positive attitude comes from your positive attributes and its response level is determined by their respective strengths as possessed by you.

The main positive attributes which are responsible for creating positive attitude in you are stated as under:

(a) Maturity, flexibility, openness and forward outlook
(b) Tolerance, endurance and forbearance
(c) Politeness, gentleness, patience and calmness
(d) Responsiveness, awareness, respectfulness and softness
(e) Creativity, perceptiveness and adaptability
(f) Alertness, self-discipline and diligence

It is seen that these positive attributes basically form part of your nature, character and behaviour. In fact, they are so important that they eventually determine the quality of your life i.e. good or bad, happy or unhappy, peaceful or otherwise. Incidentally, *your wisdom is in turn determined by your positive attitude which contributes to a large extent for enhancing your knowledge and career prospects.* It also paves the way for gaining enlightenment in your life.

Benefits of Positive Attitude

What are the benefits of possessing a positive attitude? So, let us look at a person who has positive attitude and you carefully observe him. You will invariably find that

(a) He enjoys good health.
(b) He remains peaceful, patient, joyous and cheerful.
(c) He maintains a calm, quiet and composed posture with spirit and liveliness in his behaviour and performance.

(d) His mind is also robust and healthy, and as such, he possesses a positive mindset and always demonstrates positive approach to wards life.

(e) He focusses his energy and attention on achievement of his objectives and does not vile away his time and efforts in meaningless activities.

(f) He has clarity in his thinking and farsightedness in his vision.

(g) He avoids emotive issues and unpleasant response.

(h) He does not waste his time in brooding over the past events.

Developing Positive Attitude

There is no doubt that you must possess the positive attributes as stated above for giving you positive mental attitude. They will come into action and become effective when you act and take proper steps for initialising and energising them as under:-

(a) Develop a positive self-image

(b) Develop confidence and trust in your potential and abilities

(c) Avoid criticism, foul language and negative remarks

(d) Banish the thoughts of the past events. Refer them only to learn from mistakes and errors committed and take their positive cognizance

(e) Create a positive environment. It means that you should not associate yourself with loser or pessimist persons and stay away from lazy persons

(f) Remain always keen and enthusiastic to learn and update your knowledge and skills

(g) Be optimistic and never think of failure or losses. Imagine about success with proper backing of well though action plan

(h) Remain in touch and on the listening watch. Monitor the situation with alertness and cautionary approach

(i) Maintain cordiality, amenability, politeness and patience in approach and performance

(j) Seek the advice and guidance from your superiors and other competent and knowledgeable persons whenever in doubt

POSITIVE THINKING

Mental Process

Positive thinking is again the handiwork of your mental process and it remains embedded in your positive attitude. In a way, it is the reflection of your positive attributes and their influence on your mental attitude and thought process. Since you have the positive attitude, you will always think in the positive manner. As a result, you will experience the following benefits :-

(a) Your approach and outlook will be positive.

(b) Your reaction to external factors and environment will be positive.

(c) You will appreciate the work of your subordinates without giving any critical and sarcastic remarks.

(d) Your advice, guidance and direction to your staff will be positive, inspiring and encouraging.

(e) You will encourage and cheer up your staff for giving their best output.

(f) Your approach to administrative issues will be human, generous and upright.

(g) You will be able to maintain a proper balance between work and home commitments.

(h) You will suffer less mental stain and stress and feel fresh, relief and relaxed.

(i) Your face is lit with smile, radiance and cheerfulness thereby revealing the spirit of inner joy and satisfaction.

These are the ***direct benefits of having positive thinking.*** It makes substantial difference to the quality and style of your life. You stay away from vices and bad company. You are able to utilize your time and energy in a productive and purposeful manner. As a result, you are able to enhance your work and interactive effectiveness and efficiency and improve your image, reputation and position in your organisation.

Ways to Develop Positive Thinking

Since your positive thinking is linked with your positive attitude, your mind has to be addressed and conditioned for thinking positive. As you know, thinking, thoughts, thought process are the creations and functions of your mind. So, it is just not possible to banish and isolate thoughts from your mind. In that case, it is possible to discipline the mind to think in a positive way and adopt positive approach to all the inward issues and tackle them in the positive manner. In this respect, you have to resolve that you will always direct your mind to :_

1. Adopt positive mental attitude and pragmatic approach.
2. Believe in yourself that you are capable and worthy for making high achievements.
3. Eliminate criticism and impatience from your life.
4. Accept full responsibility for all your actions especially bad one and pay compensation if you cause any damage to them.
5. Value your health physically and don't do anything that may cause harm to your health.
6. Believe in having good effective interpersonal relationship and offer your total respect and attention.
7. Believe in spiritual power and strength for empowering your personality.
8. Adopt values, principles and ethos in your works and duties.
9. Become mentally and emotionally strong to bear adverse events of your life.
10. Seek advice and guidance for remaining on the right track and face risks and challenges.

11. Manage your time effectively and maintain priority work-wise.
12. Stay away from vices, bad company and in-house politics.
13. Don't think too much of the past events and engage in thinking for the present and having vision for the future.
14. Pursue self development program for enrichment of your career.

Now when you task your mind for doing above things and keep it engaged on them, your mind has to think positively in order to achieve positive results thereof. Remember that you have to control and govern your mind for positive thinking and engage it for positive thinking by loading it with the above tasks which are of course positive, pragmatic and rational in nature. Alternatively, you may train and motivate your mind to think by adopting following measures

(a) Keep reminding yourself about achieving your long term objectives and goals.
(b) Meditate and focus your attention on your duties, responsibilities and commitments.
(c) Follow certain values, principles and ethos in your performance.
(d) Engage your mind in creating and productive thinking.
(e) Offer respect and regards to your seniors and elderly persons and heed their advice.
(f) Attend religious functions, offer prayers whenever you visit a worshipping place and pray for giving you wisdom, positive thinking, knowledge and moral strength.
(g) Read biographies of great leaders and think of their struggle and success.
(h) Always appreciate the work done by others and don't criticize even if you don't like it.
(i) Be polite and gentle in welcoming the visitors.
(j) Maintain cheerfulness and smile on your face. Remain relaxed and don't be stiff.
(k) Learn to receive the bad news with a seed of goodness in the future. Take the failure with an element of luck in the future.

It is needless to state that *your positive attitude and positive thinking are both complementary to each other in creating positive effects in your performance and social behaviour.* At the same time, they determine the trend of your mind and mindset. In fact, they offer extra power to your personality which eventually becomes forceful, impressive and highly influential. They create liveliness, optimism, cheerfulness and interest in your activities and performance. They drive your personality and activate within you the power to move forward towards your destination without fear of risks and challenges on the way. They create in you remarkable energy, eagerness and enthusiasm so that your presence is distinctly felt among others. In a way, *this combination becomes another life force that drives you to set higher goals for achievement with capacity to overcome hardships and adversities. You remain focused on your objective with remarkable concentration and high spirit*

Confidence and Optimism

Positive attitude and positive thinking generate in you extra power and potential and thus they enhance your power, spirit and moral. As a result, *you experience dynamism and momentum in your personality and feel remarkable change in your outlook, health, social behaviour and relation.* Your self-image and self-confidence undergo a remarkable change. The overall effect is that *your personality becomes forceful, active, distinct and dominating with confidence and optimism to face any unfortunate situation in life like :-*

- (a) Failure or loss of property, vehicle or set back in business or promotion.
- (b) Injury or loss of your family member, friend or relation in an accident.
- (c) Crises arising from misunderstanding, miss-management and financial melt-down.

Your response and reaction to such a bad situation will be " *So what and how do you know it is a bad luck?* " This is indeed a pragmatic and courageous approach which you can have if you possess positive mental attitude and positive thinking. *This only combination is capable to remove darkness of fear, apprehension, suspicion, disappointment, depression and bring the light of courage, moral strength, optimism, high spirit and progressive outlook at the critical times in your life.*

"It is said that winning a battle is not a chance or luck. Its success lies in the positive attitude and positive thinking of their
COMMANDERS

MINDSET

Functional Aspect of Mind

Another word which is commonly associated with your personality is the mindset and it basically reflects the psychic aspect of your personality along its self-image and mental attitude. In fact, mindset is projected in strange and uncommon behaviour of a person at certain times with slight provocation and sometime without it too. Since it deals with the human mind, it involves his certain personal attributes and faculties which cause him to think, behave and act in that way. The mindset of a person could be :-

- (a) Positive or negative
- (b) Optimistic or pessimistic
- (c) Encouraging or discouraging
- (d) Progressive or regressive

As a result, this aspect of your personality assumes importance because it has much to do with your nature and behaviour. As you deeply look into this aspect, it is observed that mindset is the direct result of the way, your mind is functioning and its immediate impact is felt on your mindset. Once the mind comes in picture, it brings all complexities of its nervous system and brain-mind combined operation. Leaving aside them, let us consider the role of certain prominent positive and negative attributes of your inner self which eventually form part of your mind and become its representative. Now, whenever your positive attributes dominates over negative attributes or you dominantly possess positive attributes, your mind is influenced with the positive thought process. As a result, your mind thinks, decides and acts in a positive manner which is reflected in your mindset for positive projection and action. Similarly, whenever the negative attributes dominate over the positive attributes, your mind thinks, decides and acts in the negative manner which conveys then the negative impression and picture of your personality. Negative attributes such as being highly adamant, emotional, possessive, suspicious, impulsive, sensitive and temperamental are responsible to cause negative mindset which results in uncommon, abnormal and temperamental behaviour. It should be noted that your mindset becomes negative when certain behavioural negative attributes as stated above are present in your inner self in excessive proportions beyond tolerable limits.

Positive Mindset

On the other hand, the positive attributes such as being self-driven, motivated, ambitious, extrovert, visionary, dedicated, strongly willed, responsive, confident, communicative, adaptable, etc make your mindset positive. As a result, your approach, thinking and behaviour become positive. Here, the dominant effect of your positive attributes is to set your thought process to think in the positive manner and this is how your mindset is affected in the positive manner. *With the positive mindset, you take things even worst in the right, sporting and pragmatic manner and you look for good thing even in the worst, unfavorable conditions and situations with the remarks ' It may have good luck tomorrow, who knows "* . They have the approach to turn today's failure in tomorrow's success without creeping and blaming others. They will never keep brooding over the past events and they would not like to discuss except to learn from the mistakes. It is all possible because you have the positive mindset that offers you a broad vision, forward and optimistic outlook and positive thinking. You become a calm, composed and stable person with smile and cheer on your face. You project a contended, cool and self-reliant posture with your mind always remaining in the positive thinking mode. Your face remains free from stress, strain and tension. As a result, your mind is fresh and thinks in a rational, logical and pragmatic manner that is highly conducive to friendship, comradeship and team spirit for achieving success in a collective mission

Negative Mindset

Negative mindset has to do much with your attitude which is mostly negative in this respect. Your attitude becomes negative because of the dominant influence of certain prominent negative attributes. They are part of your inner self and adversely affect your performance and relations.

Let us try to identify these negative attributes affecting your mindset as under:-

(a) Anger - Getting quickly in a fit of anger thereby losing control and judgment
(b) Carelessness, casualness and indifference
(c) Egoistic and self-assuming
(d) Adamancy and stubbornness
(e) Rigidity, obstinacy and rudeness
(f) Possessiveness
(g) Self-centeredness and short-sightedness
(h) Craziness and sulkiness
(i) Loneliness and aloofness

Indicators of Negative Mindset

These negative attributes make your vision, perception and outlook short-sighted, polluted and perverted. You become narrow-minded and lose your rational, logical and judicious way of thinking thereby making your mindset negative. Consequently, your mental attitude becomes negative and you start thinking in a negative manner. Your approach and reaction to any event howsoever good may remain negative as indicated below :-

(a) You will discourage a person by your negative comments.
(b) You will harshly criticise his actions and pass unpleasant remarks.
(c) Your remarks will be sarcastic, distasteful and annoying.
(d) You will behave in a possessive manner and your style of working will be obnoxious and hateful.
(e) Your face will look sulky and rigid.
(f) Your voice and expression will be sharp, impolite and husky.
(g) Your movements will be jerky and noisy.
(h) Your body language will be incoherent and unpleasant.

Negative Thinking

Consequently, a person who shows the above stated symptoms has the negative thinking which is reflected in his nature and behaviour as under:-

(a) He speaks in an incoherent manner.
(b) He behaves in a restless and irrational manner.
(c) He shirks his responsibilities and has a casual approach to his job.
(d) His remarks will be negative and contradicts to the normal and accepted way of life.
(e) He lacks confidence, interest and urge for a new work.
(f) He expresses opposite views and shows tendency to oppose in a meeting or group discussion
(g) His doubts and questions is directed to why I should do it and will remain unending.

(h) He does not generally like the success of others and feels elated over their failures.

Obviously, a negative mindset seriously affects your personality and makes it unpleasant, unattractive and repulsive. All the grace and charm of your personality are lost and you eventually become a lonely, isolated, disliked and unsocial person. You are hardly able mix with others or others find difficult to form amicable friendship with you.

Causes

There are many theories of psychological nature for causing negative mindset and why a person should behave in such an irrational manner. Of course, one of the causes which point out the finger at your negative attributes and adversely affects your mindset appears to be simple for easily understanding. Besides, there appears to be perpetual fear, apprehension, suspicion and insecurity which a person subconsciously feels in his mind. It is also observed that a person having negative mindset suffers from peculiar inferiority complex which he tries to hide by demonstrating behavioural boastful actions as stated above which are basically psychic in nature. Here, he makes a miserable effort to prove about his superiority but actually, since he possesses negative attributes, *he tries to exploit them in order to establish his name and identity in a negative manner.* It is obvious that fear of losing identity and other complex factors keep constantly playing on his mind. Let us examine this aspect of fear in the next chapter.

Improvements in Mindset

It is pointed out that you can improve mindset quite effectively provided you realise that you possess a negative mindset and it is causing a lot of harm, setback and damage to you in your performance, relations and social contacts. Besides, you have to further realise that if you continue with your negative mindset, you will be left alone, isolated and neglected without any help, sympathy and compassion. *You have to realise that your friends will look at you as a rigid, possessive, sulky, unfriendly and unsocial person and so, they will keep away from you or avoid your association.* So, it is you who has to bear all these adverse remarks and consequences, arising from your negative mindset. Naturally, you should foresee the advantages of having positive mindset. This realisation and awareness enable you to take a firm decision for switching over from negative mindset to positive mindset.

Now, the question is how to do it. The following steps are suggested knowing fully that it is not so easy to:-

(a) Become fully aware of the drawbacks of having negative mindset and its adverse consequences on your performance and relations.

(b) Become voluntarily willing, keen and anxious to changeover.

(c) Do introspection and self-assessment.

(d) Search and find out your prominent negative attributes such as, *anger, sulkiness, adamancy, possessiveness, impulsiveness, indifference, suspicion, introvert, nervousness*, rudeness, stubbornness, maliciousness, craziness, etc.

(e) Ascertain whether you are able to control them or let loose them to have their free way.

(f) Firm up your mind and be determined to control and bring them below tolerable limits

(g) Take corrective and remedial measures for minimising their effects.

(h) Mix frankly and openly with your friends and relative and try to get feedback from them about the significant change in your nature and behaviour.

(i) Seek the advice from the elderly persons for improving your behaviour.

(j) Pray God to grant you good sense and a positive mindset.

You are thus initiating the process of monitoring and controlling your negative attributes. Once you control and bring them below the threshold levels, you start progressively switching over to a positive mindset and begin experiencing its benefits.

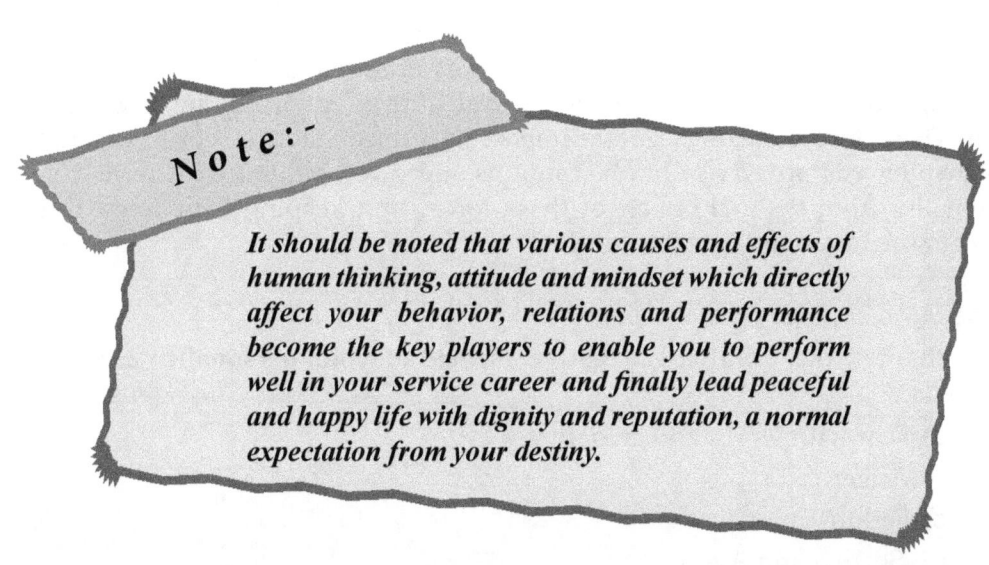

Note:-

It should be noted that various causes and effects of human thinking, attitude and mindset which directly affect your behavior, relations and performance become the key players to enable you to perform well in your service career and finally lead peaceful and happy life with dignity and reputation, a normal expectation from your destiny.

CHAPTER - 5

ADVERSE PARAMETERS OF MENTAL DOMAIN

Abstract

Adverse parameters of your mental domain such as Fear, failure, anxiety, anger and sorrow are basically psychological forces of negative type. As such, they are looked upon as the enemy of your personality since they project your negative picture to the public. These forces arise from your negative attitude and mindset. Consequently, they play negative role in your service career by creating setbacks in the process of your career advancement. You should remain aware about their adverse consequences and impact on your career and therefore do all efforts for controlling and overcoming them. These forces create negative impact and impression of your personality. In this chapter, you are advised to be cautious and given guidance for protecting your personality from the evil effects of these forces and keeping their impact on your career to the minimum possible level.

Scope

In this chapter, the following negative aspects of your personality are extensively discussed:-

    (a) Fear with worry and anxiety

    (b) Anger

    (c) Failure

    (d) Sorrow and Agony

These are basically *negative psychological aspects of your personality*. As these features belong to the mental and emotional domain of your personality, they adversely affect your nature, character, behaviour, conduct and performance. Consequently, they becomes responsible for establishing a negative identity of your personality. Hence, discussion in this chapter about the above stated factors should be treated as an extension of the previous chapter.

FEAR

What is Fear?

Fear is the demonstrative behavioural aspect of your personality and is an important offshoot of your negative mental attitude. Fear is a psychological feeling of insecurity, losing property, meeting failure in one's mission, inability to bear losses, punishment, torture, famine and so on. So, it is basically a mental factor because your mind senses the fear and creates the sense of panic in you about its unforeseen unfavourable and unpleasant consequences. In fact, it is arising from your strong desire to achieve wealth, fortune and prosperity.

Your ambitious nature and strong feelings to succeed and win the race exert pressure on your mind. The thought of failure or loss whenever it occurs creates panic and fear in your mind. Thus, fear is seen from two angles, one related to your desire and ambition and another related to your thought or apprehension or perception to fail or lose or miss. Hence, both factors of psychological nature co-exist in the word fear which becomes one of the important weak points of a person. It gets further associated with your negative attributes like, selfishness, greed, envy, hatred, possessiveness and self-centeredness. In other words, these special negative attributes give rise to the fear of losing material fortunes.

Apart from becoming part of your personality, fear also exists in organisations, institutions and industries for their survival or efficient management. Top executives are worried about the future of their companies and that worry is sufficient to cause fear in their minds. Thus, *fear leads to create unsafe feelings of insecurity.*

How to Overcome Fear

Once, you look at the fear as the creation from your negative attributes as stated in the previous chapter, you find a way out to control and overcome it according to the guidelines as given below :-:

(a) Do not set very high goals and objectives.

(b) Do not be too ambitious for their achievement

(c) Be reasonable and rational in your self interest and greed.

(d) Scale down your procurement targets to suit your abilities, position and status.

(e) Believe in doing right things at right times.

(f) Always focus on your job, duties, responsibilities and obligations.

(g) Stay away from vices, gossips and petty politics.

(h) Observe certain values, ethics and uphold the principles of morality and uprightness in your performance.

(i) Be gentle, polite, and calm and maintain composed state of mind despite provocation.

(j) Plan your activities carefully and properly and take care of all possibilities. That makes you feel bold, secure and confident.

(k) Remember God and offer prayers by doing meditation. This enhances your spiritual power for fighting fear.
(l) Practise Yoga and Meditation. This improves your mental fitness and keeps away from *mental stress, strain, disorders and depressions.*
(m) Improve your knowledge and professional skills so as to enable you to enhance your abilities, potential for facing difficult and unforeseen circumstances.

The list of guidelines which include practical steps and measures offers you a viable and valuable advice of highly effective nature. No doubt, you have to work hard, practise and train yourself for rigorously adopting these measures. Consequently, your self-confidence and self-image improve and that leads to overcome and win your fear. *Remember that your self-confidence and positive self-image hold the key to fight and remove the fear from your mind.*

Worry and Anxiety

Offshoots of fear is worry and anxiety. They are closely associated with your feelings, emotions and attitude. As such, they are *psychic in nature* and arise from the *psychological forces of your mind*. In fact, worry and anxiety appear to be synonymous in nature but they differ in their basic cause factor. Both should be considered together because one can't exist without other and both adversely affect your mental health.

Worry is related with some *definite event, incident* or *factual phenomena* whether *past, present or future* which has occurred or likely to occur for which fear definitely exists. On the other hand, anxiety can exist in the state of your mind that arise feelings of *fear, apprehension* and *insecurity* about the situation that may or may not exist. So, it cause becomes imaginary and arises from your feelings of attachment, close relationship and association. Like a mother, she is always anxious about her child not because he is ill or in trouble but she nurses an imaginary fear about its well-being, security and safety that keep her mind occupied and tense. As a result, she becomes uncomfortable and restless and behaves in an irrational manner. Because of her anxiety, she starts thinking and imagining about all sorts of causes, discover grievances and blame others. Anxiety eventually leads her to a disturbed state of mind and saps her energy and cheerfulness from her face.

Worry causes *depression, restlessness, irritation* and *forgetfulness*. You start thinking much about yourself in an apprehensive manner that takes off much of the shine and luster of your personality and reduces your efficiency and enthusiasm. Your attention is diverted to yourself and becomes less focused on your job and performance. Under such situation, your tendency is to take some ant-depressive medicine for overcoming your anxiety and worry. The only rational course under such situation is to remain cool, calm and composed and analyse the cause of your worry and take reasonable steps for overcoming them. You should sit quietly and do meditation for relaxing your mind and focusing on your performance. There is no point in keeping your worries and anxiety to yourself and keep musing over it without undertaking any corrective actions. *Remember that if you remain in worrying and anxious state, you develop sick and unhealthy personality in no time. You will consequently make your personal life miserable and unhappy.* So, keep away worry and anxiety and banish them from your thinking and attitude. It is better to remain active and occupied on the job with positive thinking, approach and attitude. Ask yourself a question *'SO WHAT, HEAVEN HAS NOT FALLEN'* and shade off the negative thoughts that cause you worry and anxiety. By adopting this pragmatic approach, you will keep your personality healthy and cheerful and save its downfall.

ANGER

Temperamental Nature

It is basically a strong negative attribute of your personality. It constantly needs monitoring and control. It should be kept under limit since it is the manifestation of the temperamental state of your mind. Its sudden outburst gives vent to your strong feelings which are expressed in hot, loud, rough and unpleasant manner

Anger is the worst enemy of your personality. It is a unique singular visible parameter of adverse nature that causes severe setback in progress of your career. It certainly jeopardizes your promotional prospects and at the same time, it creates ill-wishers around you. Nobody likes an angry person. *They do not dare to stay around him as his personality becomes fearsome, frightening and threatening.* His colleges like to stay away from him and avoid his company because they do not know when he will get angry. .

Now, anger occurs whenever the things happen against your strong likes and dislikes. So, in a way, anger becomes indication of your displeasure and expressed in high pitched hot tone with strong feelings displayed on your face. *Anger is an indication of your negative attribute along with the presence of hyper sensitivity, sensibility, less tolerance level, self centeredness, selfishness, indifference, egoistic and strong self-image.*

Anger is expressed in different levels. Some may become very angry, others moderately and some may become angry but only express on face. Similarly, some becomes angry very often, some occasionally and some only when a thing occurs beyond their tolerable limits. Now, the persons who often get very angry are dangerous and tend to create raucous and querulous situation that leads to cause damage bodily and materially. Such persons are socially disliked and many would like to stay away from them or avoid their company. They really face the major setback in their career. These are the persons who should control their temper and win over anger otherwise they soon get isolated and alienated.

Advice for Controlling Anger

The following measures are advised for controlling your anger:-

    (a) Be conscious and remain aware that you get highly angry and that poses dander to others as well as to you.

    (b) Write down in bold letters in front of you that *'Control your Feelings and Temper'* and be patient to fully understand the situation and working conditions.

(c) Think of unpleasant consequences and damage likely to occur to your name, image and position.
(d) Improve your tolerance level.
(e) Learn to pause, think and then react.
(f) Let the other person fully understand the cause of your annoyance. For this purpose, pin point the mistake, loss and time delay so caused
(g) Whenever you get angry, just utter a word *'Oh Sheet'* that vents out your feelings and outburst.
(h) Don't utter harsh and abusive words. Only express anger on your face and certain body motions.
(i) Keep the dignity and position of other person in mind while expressing your anger.

Persons who get occasionally and moderately angry need little advice as they have apparently control on their temper. Your staff members also know that you become angry only when there is a substantial reason. Sometime, this type of anger moderately controlled produce desired effect on the staff so that you are not taken for granted for tolerating their lapses. *A person who gets seldom angry is the one who is temperamentally sober, quiet and cool and is diplomatic, tactful and well trained in management techniques.*

RESPONSE FACTOR

As far as you are concerned while dealing with a person who gets angry, you should show patience, coolness and gentleness. You should not react but listen and if you are at fault then you should accept your fault without trying to give justification. You should tender your apology at the onset that will cool down his temper and become less angry. In fact, this is the best philosophy which you should follow if you are at fault. You immediate admission of fault and submission of apology will evade an unpleasant situation. In case you are not at fault and even then your boss is angry, then you should think of other reasons and be patient to observe and listen to it so long as the anger and abusive words are not directed at you. In fact, your boss may look forward for your advice after he gets cooled down. All you need to be careful, cautious and watchful with full control on your feelings and expression.

FAILURE

Meaning and Analysis

What do you mean by failure? It is simply non-achievement of your objective as desired and planned by you. Your efforts which you have sincerely and diligently made as felt by you have not materialised in fruitful, purposeful and intended result. Here, the end result is not as per your expectations. So, you interpret or conceive it as a failure and that eventually brings despair and disappointment to you. Here, the most important point to note is your mental and emotional state of mind for looking at the achievement of the end result. Someone may see it as failure because you are emotionally looking at it with expectation of preconceived idea of achievement. When it does not occur, you accept it as failure. There is another class of persons who are optimistic and they give more importance to their sincere, honest intensive efforts and proper planning. Then, they do not much bother about the end result which they do strongly feel that they will get positive result at the end but don't get disheartened if the end result is found otherwise. . .

Whenever failure occurs, you should try to properly analyze and interpret it and make all out efforts to ascertain its causes. The best person to evaluate the causes is you because you have planned and executed the task / assignment. Unfortunately, the general tendency is to pass total blame on the external agencies and much less to yourself with the remark that the situation was beyond your control. Now, *when you point out your finger for accusing at the external agencies, it is observed that your three fingers point at yourself thereby meaning that your personal share in the blame game is nearly seventy five percent.* It is obvious that you are not consciously aware of your contribution to failure because it occurs due to your certain negative attributes which indirectly play the role in your committing significant mistakes without your awareness and consciousness.

Causes of Failure

You should be dispassionate and unbiased while analyzing the reasons for your failure. You should keep your ego and confidence a bit aside and become humble, polite and self-introspection. You should pause and take a look inward of your Self for seriously thinking about the factors that have caused failure despite your sincere efforts. You should admit that these factors are personal and they should have arisen from my negative personal characteristics such as:-

   (a) Indifferent and casual attitude
   (b) Lack of planning and organising efforts
   (c) Lack of focussed and concentrated efforts on job
   (d) Inadequate professional skills and indifference to updating
   (e) Mismanagement of time, resources and efforts
   (f) Lack of drive and motivation
   (g) Lack of coordinated efforts and support
   (h) Reluctance to seek advice from the professional competent persons
   (i) Lack of involvement, commitment, patience and perseverance
   (j) Unwillingness to admit and accept mistakes for correction
   (k) Unresponsiveness to accept advice, suggestion, guidance from friends, relatives and knowledgeable persons
   (l) Lack of drive and momentum in pushing forward

Overcoming Your Failure

So, the best way to overcome the failure is to take the following steps and systematically proceed.

(a) Carry out detailed study and appreciation of the task and make honest, sincere and dedicated efforts for execution.

(b) Plan and work out systematic approach before commencement of the work.

(c) Remain really dedicated and fully involved in your mission.

(d) Remain committed and determined throughout execution of the task.

(e) Seek proper guidance and advice from your seniors and elderly person whenever faced with problems and difficulties and even before you commence the task.

(f) Appraise your seniors from time to time about your progress, problems, difficulties and shortcomings whenever you come across.

(g) Plan for your financial resources for supporting your mission.

(h) Create an amicable and congenial environment for carrying out your task.

(i) Do not get disturbed mentally or emotionally from your domestic or family side problems during your mission period.

(j) Maintain physical fitness and avoid any health problem such as injury or pain or agony during your mission.

(k) Do not get disturbed by external noise or criticism or uncharitable remarks.

(l) Remain fully focused on your mission and do not deviate from your planned path.

(m) Do not carry any fear, tension or apprehension or worry or pressure on your mind.

Optimistic Approach

This is also the way for carrying out introspection and evaluation of failure in your mission by asking introspective questions on the above lines. External forces and agencies should be considered and fully cared during the planning stage along with suitable alternatives. In this respect, it should be remembered that failure is not the end of life. In fact, it paves the way to success in your subsequent missions. *What is required is to take failure gracefully and coolly and maintain composed state of mind without getting disturbed emotionally and losing morale and courage.* You should pay special attention to the mistakes and slippages you have unknowingly committed from your dominating negative attributes and be aware of their adverse effect on your mission. For this purpose, it is necessary for you to realise about your significant negative factors and omissions which you have done out of over-confidence. Hence, you should remain aware of them and try to take suitable remedial measures for neutralizing their adverse effects. *Remember that you can look at your failure with the optimistic viewpoint of implied good luck in the near future. You should not keep musing over the failure without realising your mistakes for causing the failure. You should also avoid temptation of running to an Astrologer for seeking remedy on occurrence of repeated failures which will continue to occur if you keep committing the same mistakes or keep shifting to different tasks. Also remember that your first failure sows the seed of success in your future tasks and missions.*

SORROW AND AGONY

Causes for Sorrow and Agony

Here, sorrow and agony cause grief and sadness. Both cause sufferings in your life. You become upset and demoralized. You remain in a gloomy mood with a loss of cheer from your face. That makes your personality sick and repulsive. Sorrow and agony are manifestation of your mental state in time of distress and despair. .As such, *they become indicator of your sensitive, emotional and temperamental nature. It also indicates your tolerant and forbearing capacity and moral strength.*

Sorrow and agony mainly arise from many factors such as failure, loss, death of the nearest and dearest person from your family or friend circle. You also become sad and feel agonized on account of non fulfillment of your missions and aspirations. Another reason for you to remain sad is from having a disturbed unhappy married life or not having a child from fairly long married life or having mentally retarded child, ailing wife or child or your own fallen health. So, there are many reasons for you to become sad and unhappy and these reasons are mostly personal.

How to Overcome Sorrow and Agony

As such, the measures as suggested below are also personal for you to follow :-

(a) Believe in the God and dispensation of His justice.

(b) Avoid loneliness and mix up with your friends.

(c) Have good, selfless friends and develop friendship on moral, ethical and selfless basis.

(d) Practice Yoga, meditation and pranayam for relieving your pain.

(e) Be vocal and discreetly speak out your feelings, thoughts without causing harm to others.

(f) Believe in your Destiny which is the divine agency for giving you relief.

(g) Strengthen your certain positive attributes such as self confidence, self-image, self-esteem, tolerance, endurance, courage, dedication, etc.

(h) Listen to religious sermons, advice and counseling from elderly persons.

(i) Read wholesome books on theology, philosophy and spiritual subjects and increase your knowledge and wisdom. In this respect, advise you to read the book on *Unfolding Secrets of Human Destiny by the Author*.

(j) Be open minded, free and frank with your family members especially wife and very close friend.

You will be able to mitigate and overcome your sadness and agony to a greater extent by observing the above stated steps. You have to remain mentally strong and robust. You should adopt the attitude of '*So What*' as stated before. You should never disturb your mental balance and you should take the things in right stride and spirit. Since all sorrow and agony causing agencies are outside and out of your control, you should enhance your fighting strength, courage and spirit. In fact, *you should concentrate on the things which are under your own control and the least bother about what is not under your control.* You should always remember this *mantra* when you want to win over your sorrow and agony.

Note:-

Refer to the book on Unfolding Secrets of Human Destiny by R.M. Onkar, published by AUTHORSPRESS, New Delhi for getting solace and relief from Agony and Grief occurring from happening of Unfortunate events in life.

CHAPTER - 6

INTELLECT AND TALENT

> ### Abstract
> Intellect and talent are two important features of your personality that distinguishes you uniquely from the other species of animals. As a result, you are able to learn, in your service career. Intellect enables you learn skills for different jobs and careers and professional manner. Talent needs support of your certain positive attributes difference *It is possible to discover your talent by adopting self-addressed questionnaire.*

Distinctive Feature

Intellect and talent of a person is the distinctive feature of the human species and It is because of this feature that a person is able to think, learn, create, respond, grasp and express new things and diverse subjects. He is able to discover and invent new engineering skills and technologies for

talent for developing his personality and managing his career in such a way that he avails higher promotions and appointments in rank and status according to the level and grade of intellect and talent, possessed by him.

So, in short, intellect and talent is a very important domain of your personality that enables you to achieve materialistic and spiritual development and advancement all round in your life. They effectively decide the level of your rise and fall or success and failure or progress and regress in any career oriented professional mission of your life.

some are rich, well up, well to do, some middle or moderate type, some below middle class and the rest in poor worker's class. Similarly, some are learned, highly educated, some have cleared high level competitive examinations, some are moderately educated with

Intellect

Intellect is the special ability of a person to learn a skill of different work, job, trade, administration and management. It enables a person to understand, express and reason out the assigned subject. It is mainly the faculty of his brain and assisted by his memory that enables him to remember names, places, words, events, techniques and methods. By virtue of his intellect, he can read, study and answer your questions quickly. He understands and grasps different skills, procedures of different jobs and systems and expresses them properly. He displays his ability to reason out both positive and negative aspects of any system with logic and constancy in his arguments. He is backed by a good memory for giving references to previously related events, data or works. It makes a lot of difference to the successful performance of a manager if his intellect works and responds properly with the timely back-up from his memory.

While elaborating on the subject of intellect, *its most important useful aspect is the expression and projection of the information and knowledge gained by him. Unless you are able to express in writing or verbal form or both as visible and demonstrative outlet, your intellect has no meaning as it serves no purpose or meaning for the specific interest of your employer, society and your Self.*

Your intellect plays very important role in learning new skills and updating your professional knowledge. You are able to improve the level, capacity and quality of your intellect by periodically undergoing organized training and attending workshops. In this respect, you should always remember that *your intellect plays very important role in enhancing your productivity and employability in diverse fields.* You gain different types of experience and exposure to different work cultures and environments thereby strongly *empowering your personality in the form of enhanced self-confidence, self-reliance and self-actualisation.*

Talent

It is another important faculty of the combined power of your brain and mind and it is demonstrated in the form of your special ability to learn, grasp and reproduce a particular professional or artistic act in a systematic, highly skillful and meticulous manner with excellence and unique style. This ability is invariably in-born, natural and gifted to a child and is progressively reflected in his performance and behaviour.

It is seen that talent is not a stand-alone ability but there is a substantial contribution from some of your positive qualities in designing and conditioning talent for its skillful output. *Positive attributes, such as determination, hard strenuous work, focus, ambition, pursuit and perseverance are responsible for maturing, nourishing and flourishing your talent to an excellent state under any situation.*

Talent is slightly synonymous to intellect as it appears to be a *special intellectual ability of excellence for performance of a specific act or activity.* While an intellect is your ability to learn any trade or job, *the scope of talent is restricted to expression of a particular task or act which you carry as the natural gift from your childhood and you nourish and make sincere efforts to develop and mature it in a highly professional manner for commercial demonstration like a performing singer, actor, artist etc.*

Normally, talent remains hidden in a child till he or she gets an opportunity to demonstrate it through school performance in academics, singing or acting on the public platform. A child also is not aware about its talent till it gets a chance to perform and it is brought to the notice of the public. At present, you are watching the talent of the little champs in singing, dancing, mimicry, etc in the reality shows on Television screen. You would have not known the talent of these children if they had not got the chance for demonstrating their talent in a public show. Similarly, for the service persons, talent of some of them comes out when they face risks and challenging situations and how they use their talent in handling the difficult situation and coming out successfully. Now, it is evident that there are *three aspects of talent, one refers to get a chance, second is to utilize talent in the most skillful and meticulous way and third one is to get wide recognition, applause and appreciation.* But, before that, you have to work hard in consistent manner for nurturing and maturing your talent for the specific purpose. .

As stated earlier, your talent has to be supported by your certain positive attributes. Some persons, having talent but if they lack certain relevant positive attributes such as determination, ambition, hard work, focus, pursuit, persistency and persuasiveness will waste their talent, remain inactive and casual and eventually lead a life of common category. *They will not do any remarkable work and project their talent because they have no ambition and determination. In fact, these positive attributes act as the driving force to motivate such persons to utilise their talent in the productive and pragmatic manner.* On the other hand there is also a tendency for you to use your talent for unhealthy and antisocial activities if you possess negative attributes and if they dominate your mental state and mindset. Hence, *your talent becomes a double edged weapon and its proper use is governed by the right type of attributes, you possess.*

Discovering Your Talents

Finally, when you wish to discover your talent, you should observe your abilities to perform in a specific activity of importance covering any field of organisation, management, academics, social activities, public services, defense services, paramilitary forces etc simply by asking yourself a simple question as under :-

Do you have the special ability to:-

    (a) Listen and communicate

    (b) Plan, execute and monitor

    (c) Organise and manage events

    (d) Optimise use of money and manpower

    (e) Form teams and work together with team spirit.

    (f) Set goals and motivate others for achievement

    (g) Express verbally in a public speech in a forceful manner

It is seen that there are number of ways for utilising your talents. You should be keen to discover it and use it for public interest in a dedicated and sincere manner. You should look ahead for grabbing opportunities where you can fully use your talents in a fruitful and supporting manner. *Remember that if you don't use your talent, you are throwing away and discarding the natural divine gift which you got at the time of your birth for your career advancement.*

At the end, while highlighting the difference between these two factors, talent is demonstrated in the form of articulate ability for performing a specific skillful task and its right utilisation by harnessing the positive attributes. On the other hand, intellect does not need such driving force. Its only force is your urge to gain employment for a job and sufficiently earn for livelihood. Naturally, you have to learn skills for different jobs and keep progressively improving your job performance for decent living. For this purpose, you keep improving your intellect by undergoing intensive training and learning.

Your talent needs no such training as it is inherently present within you. In fact, what you definitely need to gain experience and exposure so that you can use it under different job and market environments. You have to work hard and learn different techniques for exploiting your talent in such a way that you substantially contribute to your organisation and it is adequately accepted for recognition. It is obvious that your talent has the basic role in improving the strength and quality of your organisation while your intellect keeps running it for giving you an employment and promotion

It is seen that intellect and talent are both part of your brain and mental power. Both are supported by the memory which determines the quality and grade of your intellect and talent. Both need continuous learning skill for improvement and becoming excellent. They differ in their creative power and need memory back-up and learning skill., Let us proceed to see the roles of these aspects in the next chapter.

> **Note:-**
> *One can never think of developing one's personality without Intellect which is basically the ability of the human mind to come to correct conclusions and Talent is of course, something which is natural or inborn.*

CHAPTER - 7

INTELLIGENCE AND INTELLIGENCE QUOTIENT(I.Q.)

Abstract

Intelligence has got a broad based domain of your personality. Its meaning and purpose are expansive and comprehensive so as to cover a broad spectrum of your personal characteristics of positive type. A combination of intellect and intelligence constitutes the key to your bright career prospects and material prosperity. There is a self-addressed method for discovering your intelligence level besides the modern concept of measuring **intelligence** called **Intelligence Quotient (I.Q.)**. There are certain people who carry the false sense about their intelligence and sensing themselves highly intelligent because of the misunderstood concept of intellect.

Basic Concept

It is basically a broad based intellectual domain of your personality. It does not merely pertain to intellect or talent but covers a whole lot of personal attributes of both positive and negative types. In fact, they substantially contribute to build up your intelligence in a holistic manner and inherently offer a lot of synergy to your intellect and talent. Eventually, level and quality of your intelligence indirectly becomes positive indicator of your personal characteristics. *Consequently, your mind is involved along with the brain in a combined operation for manifesting your intelligence unlike intellect and talent which happen to be exclusive result of your brain and memory power*

Meaning

Intelligence basically means your ability to understand, reason out and apply. Besides, you access, acquire, analyse, distinguish any data and discriminate information to a

wide, it implies that if a person is intelligent, he has the abilities to

- (a) Adopt and adjust to the system and its environment
- (b) Learn new professional skills and techniques
- (c) Update his/her knowledge and wisdom
- (d) Think, plan and execute

(e) Identify lacunas in the existing system and apply his/her skills and knowledge for updating the existing system
(f) Work with dedication for accomplishing objectives of the organisation
(g) Communicate with people and develop amicable, friendly and fruitful relations of mutual benefits with them

Thus, intelligence has a totally different but practical angle and viewpoint. It is therefore defined in a practical manner as under:-

Intelligence is an integrated total capacity of an individual to act purposefully, think rationally, express effectively, adapt to an environment without demur, deal and interact amicably, but firmly with the people. Thus, intelligence is the aggregate result of various positive attributes of an individual.

Identity of Intelligence

Intelligence is not identified by your mere capacity of scoring high marks in the examinations or by memorising and reproducing verses or extracts. You may not do well in one discipline, but may do well in other discipline of your intimate interest and liking. It is evident that your mental faculties do not tie you to one discipline but enable you to look beyond and reach out for other streams of equally importance. It means that you may not do well in engineering or medical stream but it does not mean that you will not do well or you do not have abilities to do well in other disciplines. Here, you have to discover your intelligence to ascertain your abilities, aptitude, interests and liking for a particular job or profession which suits your intellect and temperament.

Intelligence does indicate element of your intellect with fairly good memory as an asset but it can never become the representative of intellect or talent. In view of the *above definition of intelligence, it indirectly demonstrates your inner attributes such as initiative, awareness, determination, dedication, willpower, adaptability, consistency, diligence, persuasiveness apart from your expressive power of responsiveness, assimilation, comprehension and presentation.*

Thus, a person having these inner attributes has to be called an intelligent person because he has a *forethought, vision and motivation to look around and beyond as well and think forward and act with quick and positive response to proper advice and instructions from competent sources.* In other words, a person may be intellectual or talented but can't effectively interact with people, environment and express his views and opinion in public interactive sessions forcefully, confidently and convincingly, he is obviously found to lack intelligence. Such persons, despite holding high academic qualifications and having high academic performance will remain obscure, unseen and unheard from public and Government view. They remain confined to their limited working field and are eventually deprived of public recognition, awards, super status and national/international fame despite their high level of intellect and talents.

Discovering Intelligence through Introspective Questionnaire

Now, you are keen to know and discover your intelligence and how does it differ from the brain faculty of intellect. Here is given the direct method in which you are questioning yourself and you seek honest answers after proper deliberation. There is no hurry and you take your time since this is *your Self-Addressed Exercise of an introspective nature.*
A set of questions are framed for discovering your intelligence as under:-

1. Do you have urge to become someone significant in your life and someone to recognise you?
2. Do you feel the urge to do something which is different from the routine and has some new features?
3. Do you feel keen to study, analyse and find answers to something which whenever you find baffling, confusing and strange?
4. Do you hate ignorance on your part about any issue of personal and public interest?
5. Have you got the strong will and drive to push yourself in the right direction for achievement of your goal?
6. Do you wish to keep yourself updated and are you keen to know more and add to your knowledge?
7. Do you want to discuss your issues with some competent and knowledgeable persons by asking searching and informative questions and seek clarification and advice?
8. Are you keen and enthusiastic to read, write and express of what you know and share with your friends and colleagues?
9. Do you often find and select issues for your self-study and thinking or look up to someone to specifically tell you?
10. Is your attitude a specific job or profession oriented? Do you concentrate attention on your own profession and try to get maximum benefits, comfort and self-image from it?
11. Are you open, friendly and amicable while dealing and interacting with your friends and relatives?
12. Do you have argumentative or consolatory approach while discussing issues or giving instructions to your colleagues, subordinates or seniors?
13. Do you have vision, foresight and forethought for future events or scenarios or situations pertaining to your profession or project or mission in hand?
14. What is your grasping power and assimilative level when you study a specific report or article or thesis? Can you express confidently your opinion and clarify your views on what you read and understood?
15. Can you carry out review of any article, mission or operation or news item meticulously and comprehensively in a simple manner for understanding of others?

16. Can you give specific instructions or do briefing to your subordinates, teammates. or colleagues for performing a certain task or mission?
17. Are you frank, candid and honest for admitting your mistakes or errors or weaknesses? Would you like to express regret privately or openly or try to justify even after realizing your mistakes?
18. Do you adapt easily to new environment, people, working place and culture or do you take time for adjustment?
19. Do you willingly accept responsibilities and undertake works with positive and pragmatic approach?
20. Are you punctual in attending your office and meeting? Do you submit or complete the assigned work within stipulate time or do you need reminder?
21. Do you participate in brain storming sessions organized by your management or organisational head? Do you offer your proposal/suggestion for improvement of the system?
22. Do you accept challenging job/responsibility/assignment/tasks on the basis of your gut feelings or deliberate thinking of pros &con?
23. Do you have the competitive spirit for advancing your career growth? Do you work sincerely, honestly and truthfully for your career advancement?
24. Do you often try to seek advice, guidance for gaining enrichment in your performance? Do you feel inspired, driven and motivated on getting proper advice and guidance?
25. What is the scope of your satisfaction? Is it limited to satisfy your personal needs and growth or can it go beyond limits of your personal gratification?

This is a set of typical questions which cover a wide range of your activities pertaining to your nature, character, behaviour, performance, communication and learning skills and personal management. You are probing into the mental faculties of a person or you would like to discover yourself about your intelligence level and its quality from the answers which you will give to these introspective questions. These questions are no doubt simple and self-addressed but each reaches out to focus on a particular attribute or a group of attributes and reflects a specified act which is visible and performance oriented but it leads to form a firm opinion about a person, his abilities and skill.

Now, let us try to see another way of measuring your intellectual level.

Intelligence Quotient (I.Q.)

Your intelligence is measured by a factor called I.Q. In the modern practice, this measure is used to assess your intelligence level. Since it pertains to your mental abilities and functions, it leads to *your mental process for understanding, judgment, responsiveness, comprehension, assimilation and reasoning of any issue or problem, assigned to you for execution. It is a factor which speaks of many other positive attributes of an individual besides his intellect and memory.*

I.Q. has become the most important index for determining the intellectual level which is required in different proportions for pursuing different careers, professions and also seeking promotions and career advancement. *It is however advised that I.Q. of a candidate should be assessed in his field of interest and liking.* Judgment alone in the academic field is likely to mislead us. Now, there are standard tests and methods which are worked out on the basis of psychological concepts and objective observation of your performance.

Classifying Intelligence

From the answers you get by questioning yourself in the above stated manner which will be in the form of yes or no and counting their respective numbers, you can now classify your intelligence on the basis of positive or negative nature of responses you get from your answers. You should tabulate the result of positive and negative responses after doing proper analysis of answers. If the set of positive responses exceeds 50 percent of the total, you may have high I.Q. and if less than 50 percent, then it may be classified as low or average intelligence. Now, you can't expect remarkable or outstanding or excellent performance from the persons of average intelligence nor they would be able to contribute much to their personal prosperity and career advancement.

While doing this exercise, you should note that you can have such a realistic assessment of your intelligence provided you have answered those loaded meaningful questions sincerely, honestly and truthfully with deep thinking, knowledge, awareness and forethought. It is after all your personal assessment and you are not answerable to anyone outside agency. So, *you should be quite fair and objective in observing your personal characteristics such as nature, character, behaviour, conduct, performance and objectives.*

Intellect and Intelligence

These two aspects of your personality in the intellectual domain appear to be same but distinctly differ in the sense that intellect stands for your brain and memory power while intelligence indicates combined power of your brain and mind and adequately supported by your memory. In this combination, your mind plays the dominating role in your decision making process. Once the mind enters the scenario, it brings many of its positive attributes for determining the grade and quality of your intelligence. In fact, what actually happens in the process is that your positive attributes become responsible in effectively harnessing your intellect while you are executing your career oriented activities and profession. There is an indirect relationship between your intelligence and positive attributes in such a way that high level of your intelligence becomes indicator of your certain important positive attributes which, of course, substantially contribute to your better and enriched performance.

Inter-relationship Matrix of Intellect and Intelligence

With a view to examine an impact and influence of intellect and intelligence and their intra-relationship, let us treat each of them as single entity and work out the matrix of their different combinations on the basis of their individual level, as high or average. You are then in a position to look into each combination, possessed by four classes of different persons and their performance and career oriented achievements in their long professional life in any organisation, industry and institution. Since qualitative aspects of intellect and intelligence are already discussed under their respective group heading, each combination is now assessed for causing overall impact and influence on their service / business career and you tabulate the result achieved thereof. This overall result is projected as under :-

Sr.	Level of Intellect	Level of Intelligence	Overall Achievement in Career Growth
1	High	High	Top position/rank/status like Chairman, Managing Director, CEO
2	Average	High	Higher positions/rank/status like Div/Dept Head, General Manager
3	High	Average	Senior/Middle level rank/Position Like Manager, Sr. Executive
4	Average	Average	Low level position/rank like Sec Head, Supervisor

Note :- **There may be further divisions in levels such as Very High, High Average, Low, etc., and accordingly, there would be numerous combinations and their impacts on ranks and positions.**

Since I have gone through different career growth in the Army as well as Industry, I have clearly and closely observed the impact and influence of these two factors on the careers of several officers and executives. So, I have given this impact in the above tabular form on the basis of my observation and experience. *Intellect and intelligence and their levels have made a lot of difference to the careers of many people in service and business. Since intelligence implies presence of important positive attributes, they will certainly make a remarkable difference to performance and its assessment for your career prospects*

False Sense of Intelligence

Some persons are found to carry a high sense about their intelligence. It is apparent that they will definitely feel high sense of their intelligence because of the following reasons :-

    (a) Having passed the school and college level examinations with high grade

    (b) Having obtained the degree from the professional college like an Engineering or Medical College

(c) Having obtained additional professional qualifications from other institutions
(d) Having got the Govt. service of reasonable grade
(e) Having passed departmental promotion examinations for achieving higher grades and class
(f) Having proficiency in a particular subject, art, literature or faculty

It is obvious that such a person will definitely be considered intelligent by others too. What happens in practice is that the professional performance of such persons is not found to match with their material and career prosperity. They are no doubt ambitious, hardworking and persuasive but they are found to lack in certain positive attributes such as keeping focus on their main profession, concentration on the tasks in hand, sense of time management, involvement in non-priority work, humility, openness, flexibility, brevity and clarity.

Besides, they don't follow certain moral and ethical rules while dealing with friends and relations in commercial matters. They have demanding and arrogant nature without doing any benevolent and supporting gesture. They have high self-ego, over-confidence and rigidity in their views and will not seek advice or guidance from experienced and competent persons. This is apparently the result because they consider themselves to be highly intelligent. So, they feel with their high self-ego that they have fairly good self-image and reputation in public.

Unfortunately, they don't realise that they are no doubt highly intellectual guys but certainly not intelligent and they even lack in average intelligence In fact, a person of average intelligence is found to lead a much comfortable, stable, settled and contended life with the least liabilities especially on retirement beside having a fairly good public image.

Here, such incidents are mentioned after observing persons with different levels of intellect and intelligence and their performance with achievements in their life in terms prosperity, rank, reputation and public image. It is evident that intellect alone does not contribute to your materialistic prosperity. On the other hand, it may land you in trouble. Hence, a combination of intellect with even an average intelligence makes a lot of difference to your prosperity and quality of life.

Concluding Remarks

To conclude, intellect and intelligence are two unique distinct features of your personality and both are basically responsible for your materialistic growth. Intellect is essential for acquiring different professional skills and proficiency. You gain knowledge and experience through your intellect but you definitely need intelligence to effectively use it for your career growth and advancement. Now, intelligence implies indirect combination of intellect and positive attributes. It clearly means that positive attributes enable you to effectively utilise your intellect for specific purpose and their combined role in a particular manner constitutes your intelligence for public manifestation and perception. In other words, if you lack in possessing certain positive attributes, you will not be able to use your intellect effectively. In fact, it may be wasted and you remain without availing the material benefits thereof. Hence, you should exercise your prudence, judgement and proper care to see that you are making rightful and meaningful use of your intellect and intelligence in your service and profession. In fact, intelligence, *having many connotations holds the key for your career advancement if properly and judiciously harnessed. Ultimately, you will get positive or negative results from the way you utilise your intelligence, the right way or the wrong way.*

> **Note:-**
>
> *Hence, we can conclude that to develop one's personality completely, one must acquire the ability to apply one's knowledge and skills in the most appropriate manner, and this alone is known as 'Intelligence'.*

CHAPTER - 8

MEMORY, LEARNING WILL & CREATIVE POWER OF YOUR PERSONALITY

> **Abstract**
>
> Memory, learning will and creative power are distinct intellectual features of your
>
> scope of progress and advancement in life unless you adopt these skills in your service career. Your memory is the Divine gift given to you at the time of your birth. So, it is entirely your responsibility to develop and make its maximum use in your career. Learning is a continuous process and lifelong experience. It is a pathway to gain knowledge for achieving your advanced career. It is an endless exercise for upgrading your knowledge and wisdom. Creative power is a vast storehouse of the wisdom of the past, understanding of the present and vision of the future. Creative power enables you to create new things, new procedures, techniques, discover new practices and
>
> become valuable assets of your personality in making substantial contribution to your organisation and to your personal career growth as well.

General

intellect and talent domain of your personality. They are responsible in enhancing quality

assets. Besides, you are able to achieve enrichment, empowerment and enlightenment in your life. These aspects will be comprehensively dealt in this chapter.

MEMORY

Relation

Memory of a person and his personality are intimately related with each other because his learning capacity and uptake of skills depend on his memory and grasping and absorbing abilities. Every person is endowed with the memory which enables him to remember innumerable things in his life. Animals too have the memory that makes them to have

man's memory is expansive, expressive

touches and eats. These are basically the main functions of his sense organs.

Brain-Mind-Memory Operation

Human memory is an integral part of the brain. Whatever the sense organs perceive, they are received in the form of signals which the brain passes to the memory for storage. Now, memory is a simple storehouse of information, data, images, impression, numbers, names etc. and it stores whatever is passed to it. But, brain and mind control and decide what type of information should be stored in your memory. As you have passed through your childhood, whatever you have seen and perceived, you have formed the opinion and impression that are directly stored in your memory. As you grow and you start thinking, there is an internal verification and validation network and only that data is stored in your memory which is cleared by your mind through this validation network for relevancy of storage. In this respect, refer to a typical *Brain-Mind-Memory representative network* simulating computer analogy as given in the chapter 4 of my book on ***Personality Development and Career Management** published by S. Chand & Company New Delhi*.

Types of Memory

In a general sense, the memory is associated with your capacity to remember and reproduce whatever you have seen, heard and read. It could be names, places, events, songs, jokes, dialogs, poems etc. Your capacity and efficiency to recollect and reproduce the events becomes the indicator of your memory being described as :-

    (a) *Sharp memory*, also called *photographic memory*.

    (b) *Good memory*

    (c) *Average memory*

    (d) *Poor memory*

Now, the human memory is associated with the response factor. As a result, it depends upon how your memory responds, grasps, assimilate and reproduce. This composite process finally determines the quality and capacity of your memory and has consequently the direct bearing on your learning process. If your memory is weak, then even if your response is good, you will not be able to express and reproduce. Eventually, it sets a limit on the capacity and retention of your memory.

Contribution and Role of Memory

There are certain valid questions about the relationship of memory with your personality as under :-

    (a) What is the contribution of the memory to your personality?

    (b) How does it help you to improve your personality?

    (c) What effective role does it play in projecting your personality?

Well, let us take an example. You as the head of your organisation or commanding officer of a unit meet someone who belonged to your organisation and served with you as your subordinate. You are now meeting him after a long time. As you handshake and address him by his first name and further enquire about his family and children, he is definitely surprised and moved by seeing such a personal touch in your meeting with him. So, your sharp memory has created an impact of personal touch and attachment that he will remember you forever. Take a look at another example from the industry in which a General Manager meets his worker and addresses him by his first name. This small act of your memory creates on him the positive impact of personal touch. As a result, the worker feels affinity, attachment and loyalty to his head and the organisation for which he gets a sense of belonging. So, this reveals the power of your memory that enables you to establish personal relation and rapport with your subordinates and workers.

Here is a situation in which you are conducting very important meeting and discussing the company's policy and objectives along with the financial status, order position and estimated cash-flow. Suddenly, you get bog down and you grapple with certain data for supporting your argument. At this stage, your staff member rises and rattles out relevant data along with proper reference in support of your arguments. Your sudden reaction is to look at him and feel obliged for help given to you in the time of extreme need. You of course proceed and successfully complete the task. Now, how will you look at your staff member and the service he rendered to you at the right time of your need by virtue of his sharp memory. Naturally, his staff member gets kudos and good remarks in his confidential report that will help him for promotion. Such examples are numerous where either your memory or staff member's memory play crucially   significant role. As a result, the following benefits are accrued :-

    (a) Personal relations and rapport
    (b) Cordial relations with attachment and belonging
    (c) Loyalty and affinity
    (d) Assistance and guidance in critical situations
    (e) Involvement in administration
    (f) Job satisfaction

The above are the important aspects of your personality and enhance the glory of your self-image.

Improvement of Memory

Memory plays an important role in each and every aspect of your career and life. It substantially contributes to improve your performance and glorifies your role. When a child memorises a lecture or a song and delivers forcefully, he or she is complimented. When a person memorises a speech and delivers forcefully, he receives appreciation and compliments. So, the memory of a person becomes his asset for glorifying his personality. Of course, its effectiveness depends upon its *capacity, sharpness* and *retention* and it acts along with other traits of his/her personality. Awareness, initiative, alertness and responsiveness are other attributes which play complementary roles with your memory. Dud memory with superior attributes does not glorify your performance. Similarly, a good memory with inferior qualities is of no use because this asset grossly remains under-utilized. Hence, you really have to harness your memory and try to improve its effectiveness by proper programming and conditioning, as under :-

(a) Develop a good habit pattern of thoughts.
(b) Adopt opinions, advices, statements and beliefs of knowledgeable and competent persons.
(c) Analyse and examine relevance and validity of the events for remembering.
(d) Drop the thoughts and opinion if found irrelevant and immaterial.
(e) Listen to people but decide yourself for ascertaining validity for acceptance.
(f) Recite certain prayers, hymns for giving you power and strength.
(g) Write down the data or take notes or extracts of your interest that easily sink in your memory.
(h) Repeat the readings of the text which you studied one or two times for retention in your memory.
(i) Keep remembering what you memorised while going for a walk.
(j) Brush up occasionally your notes and briefs.

Other measures suggested are as under:-
(a) Have a peaceful and sufficient sleep which can help in memory consolidation.
(b) Have regular physical exercise which increase oxygen supply to the brain and reduces health disorders.
(c) Manage your stressful operations and relax your brain from stress, fatigue and tension by doing meditation and Yogic exercises.
(d) Keep yourself free from bad habits like smoking and alcohol.

Recent research studies have shown that physical regular exercise substantially improves the memory and problem solving skill along with your learning abilities.

Gift of God

It is believed that you are endowed at the time of birth with the memory good or bad, sharp or dud or average. Children display good memory and some extraordinary by boldly giving public performance of songs and dance on stage. As they grow up and start picking up, their thought process becomes active and their concentration suffers. As a result, its effectiveness is generally assessed at the time of annual examinations and performance therein. Now, it is observed that grown up children as well as adults demonstrate qualities of their memories in different proportions and they do derive personal benefits accordingly. It is surprising to see that nobody is aware and conscious of his memory and its influence on his performance. If he does badly, he blames others but not his memory which should have reminded him. So, it is pity that the real role of your memory remains unseen, unrealised and unfelt in your performance. Let us now see the role of your memory in learning skills and creative power.

LEARNING WILL
— A PATHWAY TO KNOWLEDGE AND WISDOM

Learning Factor

This factor pertains to your knowledge, professional skill and expertise which you earn by undergoing proper training classes and self study. In the process, you learn something which you do not know before and later, you want to improve and enhance your knowledge of what you already know before. Now, you can't perform unless you know your profession or the job of your employment. So, your first learning the job and later improving your skill to do it better and better by further learning process becomes an essential activity of your career. And surprisingly, it is a continuous activity as learning is a continuing process. What is required in this phase is that you should know the present level of your skill and knowledge which have earned by virtue of your basic educational and professional qualifications and that determines your standard and reference level for planning a training program for the purpose of updating your knowledge. As you know, there are continuous technological developments and improvements in systems and management techniques and procedures. *What you know today becomes outdated tomorrow.* If you wish to stick to old methods and procedures, it becomes harmful for your existence and survival under the present highly competitive environment. So, *continuous learning and updating your knowledge is not only the responsibility of management but also yours if you want to survive in your career in a dignified and graceful manner in the present volatile market environment.*

Since the management is involved in this corporate world for keeping pace and remaining ahead in the production and marketing fields and maintaining their profit graph up, regular *training programs like tutorials, workshop and seminars* are organised in-house. At the same time, selected persons are sent out on special training outside. Now, you should willingly avail these training facilities for learning and updating your knowledge and skills. In fact, you should come forward and volunteer for such programs as it is in your personal interest for improving your performance and get the better grades. In a way, it is *a reflection on your awareness, keenness, urge and responsiveness for improving your performance and personal standards through continuous learning skill. Thus, you are opening the way to diversity in your career activities and consequently to your bright promotional prospects to senior and high levels.* Besides, you are able to achieve excellence in your profession thereby bringing creativity and uniqueness in your performance. This becomes a valuable contribution of an employee to his organisation that eventually gets recognised and suitably rewarded.

Learning is a continuous process and also a lifelong experience. The day you stop learning or feels it no more need, you should assume that you have come to the dead end of your career. You will remain out of touch with the modern developments and live in the world of ignorance with the false sense of self-pride, perfection and self-ego.

Types of Learning

There are basically three types of learning skills and it depends upon how you use it in practice and how you derive the benefits from it. This task is entirely left to you. Let us have a look at them as under :_

    (a) *Professional learning*
    (b) *Personal learning*
    (c) *Spiritual learning*

Professional Learning is adopted for improvement of your professional skill which you need for daily working and performance of your duties. Management is responsible to organize training for their selected and deserving employees who are generally deputed outside on special training courses, seminars and workshops. Besides, employees are encouraged to keep themselves updated by giving them some grant for purchase of books and attend in-house lectures or demonstrations which are organized by inviting external experts and specialists. A well equipped library is also made available and remains open even outside office hours.

Personal Learning is generally oriented to personal liking and interest for learning new things and they want to keep abreast with the latest developments, technologies and management techniques. They take their own initiative in looking for latest books and information and make special efforts for their procurement. They allot time from their working schedule to brush up their knowledge and even spend time at home for studying and learning. They convey through their performance the reputation as learned and knowledgeable persons As such, they enjoy the special position, status and respect in the organisation. As a hobby, you read different types of books on literature, novels, current affairs and general knowledge. Thus, you enhance your knowledge base and it becomes useful to you while discussing general topics or initiating discussion on varied topics with different persons. In this way, you improve your skill of inter-personal relationship.

Spiritual Learning is pursued by persons who have religious bent of mind and they look for their own empowerment and enlightenment. They do their normal jobs but their tendency will be to remain detached from professional issues and will do that much which is required and not beyond. These persons will appear self-centered, mature and carefree. They will spend most of their free time in reading religious and theological books and normal discussion will be centered on these subjects and issues.

Now, the next question is How to successfully develop learning skill.

Learning Process

Every one of us is the product of social learning since our childhood. There are four specific steps involved in the learning process as given below :-

    (a) **Drive**. It refers to the motive behind any act. A drive can be either from your within or external forces. Your inner drive refers to your basic needs such as food, shelter, education, love and security. External forces are related to your urge for promotion, recognition, award and prosperity that need changes in your nature such as patience, dedication, integrity, loyalty and resourcefulness.

(b) **Stimulus.** A perceived force which sets your thoughts, feelings and physical action to move in the direction of learning or make you feel need about learning.

(c) **Response**. It is an action that engages you and keeps focused on the external object and draws your attention, thoughts and feeling on it. Thus, it is your reaction to the stimulus forming a mental picture that becomes firmly ingrained in your sub-conscious mind. Incidentally, here memory helps to reproduce your response.

(d) **Application**. This is an application in which whatever you have learnt should be applied to proper use and it should be properly implemented for the betterment of the organisation and its working system. The most important part of this phase is reproduction and its expression in such a way that it is understood by your fellow workers and colleagues.

It should be noted that *learning is a gradual and repetitious process which need your patience, attention, concentration, hard work and total dedication.* The end result is not seen but felt and that too over a long period of time. Of course, you feel quite reinforced within yourself. And *improvement in your feeling self-confident and self-empowered is the direct consequence of learning.*

Development of Learning Will

While effective learning remains the basic function of your keenness, responsiveness, initiative, awareness, concentration and consciousness, you have to struggle and know the methods and techniques which you should adopt for developing your learning skill. You are advised to proceed in the following ways :-

(a) Purchase books of your interest and read them in your spare time. Also recommend such books for procurement by your library authority.

(b) Visit the library of your unit and study the books of your interest. Ensure that your library is well equipped with the latest books, magazines and news papers.

(c) Discuss with your supervisors, senior officials and experienced persons and ask them investigative and intelligent questions so that you gain useful information. Take proper notes and keep records of such informal discussion.

(d) Attend in-house workshops, tutorials and demonstrations which are often organized by your organisation as the in-house training program for you.

(e) Attend seminars and conferences on out station duties voluntarily.

(f) Opt yourself whenever your management looks for detailing someone on outstation special training course.

(g) Avail some short leave for doing a special professional or management course from reputed training establishment like Symbiosis or Indian school of Management Hyderabad or Ahmadabad.

(h) Participate in meetings, group discussion and brain storming sessions as and when organised. Exchange your views and opinion with the others and interact such that your knowledge is updated and you share and broaden your viewpoint.

(i) Adopt a self- development program with emphasis on studies and gaining knowledge like watching selected educational programs on TV.

Responsibility

While it remains your *personal responsibility* to adopt the learning methods and educate yourself, you can always look upon the other effective sources of learning which are your school, college, teachers, elderly persons, parents and your organisation and its staff members where you are serving. All of them provide you facilities for learning and updating your knowledge. In fact, *your employer has more stakes in training you for handling highly skilled and managerial jobs so that he can maximize his production by economizing on manpower and logistics.* Today, it is possible when you can adopt modern equipment, technique, procedures and suitable training modules. So, it is dual responsibility, firstly of the employer/organisation and secondly yours' as an employee who is specially picked up from the available lot. Naturally, *you should make the best use of the opportunity for personal betterment and enrichment of your career prospects.*

Driving Factors for Learning

Notwithstanding as all said above, you should have natural urge for learning and it mainly depends upon your objectives which are driven by your aspirations to become someone in life. It means what you want to become in life such as doctor, engineer, economist, educationist, businessman, industrialist, etc. Then, you have to set the level of your proficiency and rise in that particular profession. If you decide to be an ordinary worker or engineer or mechanic, then your level of learning is mediocre, and your average efforts of learning will suffice. But, if you set the level high like becoming a specialist, top class executive or eminent educationist, or chief engineer then you need high level of professional skill for which you have to do extensive in-depth learning and gain superior professional knowledge and exposure. Hence, setting your objective to a high level drives you to pursue your learning program and keep learning more and more. In the process, your certain positive attributes are commissioned to play very important role in organizing and improving your learning skill and knowledge. Let us see those significant positive attributes which enhance your learning skill and involvement.

Role of Personal Attributes in Learning

It is evident that your certain positive attributes indirectly play the significant role in the entire process of learning. You remain the sole beneficiary from the learning process and its program since your promotional prospects tremendously improves as well as your personal reputation as a professional and specialized person goes around thereby improving your chances for diversifying your career in different fields. In the entire learning process, you remain at the central stage for responding to different training programs. Obviously, your success in the learning process depends upon your certain positive attributes such as :-

    (a) Keenness and urge

    (b) Drive and motivation

    (c) Willingness and will power

    (d) Initiative, awareness and determination

    (e) Responsiveness and concentration

    (f) Vision and foresight

    (g) Hard work and dedication

    (h) Humility and politeness

    (i) Adaptability to different training environments and outstation facilities

    (j) Sharing and cooperation

Incidentally, responses of individuals to the same learning program and environment will vary over a wide range because of the personal attributes as listed above and their different levels as present in human beings. Personal attributes remain at the root for displaying different responses and they certainly make the difference for developing and adopting different learning skills.

CREATIVE POWER

Meaning

It is defined as the making of new or rearranging of the old things in a new way so as to give it a new form. Thus, it represents the activation of human potential and the creative energy of your sub-conscious mind which is a vast storehouse of the wisdom of the past, understanding of the present and vision of the future. You are therefore able to create new thoughts about any challenging thing and develop artistic, scholarly or professional talent for achieving specific goals which you feel that they are meaningful and important to you. Thus, creativity is a thinking exercise and it is focused at developing mental skill for generating new ideas that may be more useful than the old ones.

Creativity is an ability given to us at birth. It can't be lost but it goes into hiding due to various reasons and lies dormant inside us for lack of use. You have to tap your abilities and develop them for using in a purposeful manner. It requires your persistent, focused concentration, positive attitude and self-confidence in believing existence of other possibilities.

Development of Creative Power

Since the creative power revolves round the concept of creating new things or arranging old things in a new order, you should learn to produce new ideas by continuously thinking over the problem and visualizing different solutions and alternatives. In this respect, you should ask the following specific questions to yourself as under :-

(a) Is there a possibility of different solutions?
(b) Is there any alternative way of approach to the problem?
(c) Have I considered the problem in totality or left its loose ends?
(d) Am I on the right path of thinking for the alternative?
(e) Have I mustered all my intelligence, imagination, knowledge and wisdom in my creative thinking?
(f) Have I totally shade off my rigid, insecure, inflexible attitude and thinking?

These questions are aimed at removing any cobweb and misconceptions from your mind and totally making it free for positive thinking in a free style mode. Now, you can take the following steps in developing your creative power :-

(a) Identify the problems or issues and imagine its scope, And be sure about the end objectives you wish to achieve after solving the problem. Think of the form in which you wish to have a solution.

(b) Write down the specific problem and register it on your mental screen and sub-conscious mind for searching its solution. In this way, you address your inner faculties and put them in motion for thinking.

(c) Be patient and don't get upset for not being creative to find solution. Get back to your home and relax. Keep a pad and pencil on your bedside table. Before going to bed, think of the problem by looking deep into the blank space of the cosmos and deeply ponder. In case you fail, it may strike you the next day after comfortable sleep in the toilet while pondering and visualizing the problem. This is my personal experience.

(d) Adopt the brainstorming method in which two or three separate meetings could be held with four to six persons for a period of thirty to forty five minutes. In the first meeting, think of the problems and generate many problem solving options as possible. Then, solicit the ideas from group members by encouraging discussion for getting free flow of different ideas and suggestions. At the end of the meeting, evaluation is carried out on the basis of the cost-benefit ratio and the one which receives maximum consents is safely adopted.

(e) Another technique pertains to brain mapping in the sense that you take full advantage of your various mental capacities which are related to visual, intuitive, logical and analytical faculties of your brain. It is based on perception versus reality approach in which your brain considers all possible solutions and their viabilities. You finally exert your judgment and make up your mind for the one meeting almost all the conditions.

(f) Expose yourself to as many divergent people under different situations and discuss the issue with them along with your searching questions and doubts. Get their ideas and opinions in a random manner without any preconception. Examine the merit of their solutions with your analytical mind and ascertain its validity and viability. Here, you can read in between the lines too.

(g) Read the though-provoking books, meet interesting and wise people, attend lectures and speeches and engage in meaningful conversations.

(h) Be inquisitive, curious and always searching for new ideas and solutions.

Use of One's Creative Power

Creative power is basically an in-born faculty in you. It is your personal art and power. It is normally demonstrated in your interest areas and hobbies. Research and development activity is another area of your creativity. It is also manifested in your intelligent discussion and interaction with your colleagues. While discussing in a crucial meeting when the people get stuck and come to a dead end, you can pull them out by your intelligent intervention and offer the creative solution. There is enough scope for using your creative power in an organisation where you can introduce new innovative techniques and procedures in different branches of your organisation. Management always looks for a creative person and makes his best use for problem solving. As such, he enjoys a special respectful position and is always held in high esteem. *Remember that there is no dearth of problems in an organisation and there is always a search and demand for a creative person. Now, if you are a creative person, it is entirely up to you how best you can exploit your power to your best advantage as well as to the best interest of the organisation.*

Concluding Remarks

We have seen the role of the memory and learning will in enhancing the quality of your personality. Both are instrumental in raising the effectiveness and glory of your personality to a higher level. In fact, your personality becomes distinguished and glorified in the eyes of your senior officials since it becomes an asset to their organisation in resolving their problems and thereby making distinct contribution towards its stability, growth and reputation. They also become your personal asset in consolidating your position in the hierarchy of your organisation and earning high esteem and better career prospects. You no more remain a static person in your career which eventually gets momentum, boost and diversity. Thus, you become the direct beneficiary from them as you are placed ahead of others and the chances of winning success become bright in your career.

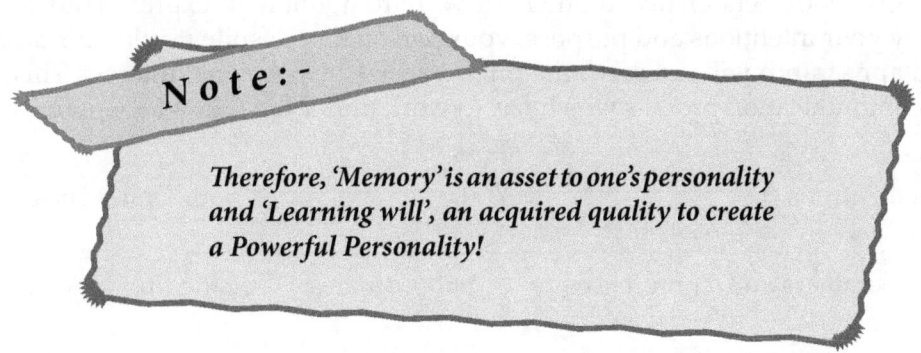

Note:-

Therefore, 'Memory' is an asset to one's personality and 'Learning will', an acquired quality to create a Powerful Personality!

CHAPTER - 9

COMMUNICATION SKILLS

Abstract

Communication skill is the most important aspect of your personality that determines your interaction, relation and contact with the people within and outside organisation. As a result, you have to deal with various people from different organisations, institutes, industries, corporate business world and also audience on the public platform. You have syour proposals in the convincing manner. For this

expression. Your command on oratory, quality of your loud and clear expression

physical drawbacks of your outer personality are overlooked by your excellent communication skill and its expressive power. Communication skill is the only means for you to convey to the public about your research and investigative work otherwise you remain an unknown, obscure, unconnected and unnoticed person despite your high class work and remain deprived of public recognition, award and

personality.

Role

The communication skill is very important part of your personality because it conveys various aspects of your inner personality to outside world. It also becomes a vehicle for expressing your personality to others. If you are not able to express your thoughts and convey your intentions and purpose, your personality despite its pleasant structure, grace and appearance will not serve the public, social and personal interest. This skill is part of a communication process which has to work under the following environment :-

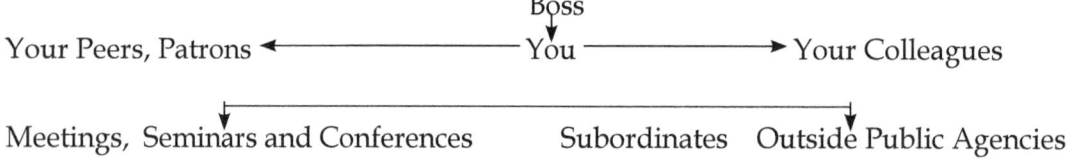

It is evident that you as an active member of an organisation and its departments/ section are required to work and form relations with various functionaries who have different backgrounds, values, styles, cultures, expectations and responsibilities. Communication is the only means by which you are able to contact, transfer information and establish relations with others who are working under the same environment. At the same time, the persons who belong to sales, logistics, finance and administrative departments are required to deal with the people outside their organisation very often on various accounts and regularly submit reports and returns. So, an organisation has to always keep the communication channel open within and outside for effectively carrying out operational, commercial and administrative activities.

Types of Communications

Basically, there are two types of communications as under :-

(a) *Interpersonal Communication Skill*
(b) *General Communication Skill*

These basic two types of communication skills are discussed in the succeeding two parts

PART - ONE
Interpersonal Communication Skill

Scope

What is the scope of Interpersonal Communication Skill and how is the subject related to your personality? To start with, these are relevant questions because this subject basically appears to be part of a wide spectrum of Communication Skills and yet it is surprisingly projected as a separate topic. Obviously, its scope becomes limited to dealing with small groups of persons at personal level in an interactive mode with the primary purpose of making them feel good and at ease. When it is a small level interaction and interactive dialog, *your personality definitely plays a significant role in attaching two parties in a special link for transferring their thoughts, information, views and opinions in a free and frank manner.* Hence, interpersonal skill plays an effective role at the personal level where two parties meet and informally talk together and exchange their views and information in an interactive mode thereby paving the way to establish a communicative link of personal rapport for transferring information.

Requirement

You work in small groups, teams or as a part of section, department or company. You work in different roles like a worker, supervisor or manager. You are often the head of a small unit, section or department and eventually become its leader. As a result, you deal with your persons as colleagues, subordinates or senior or junior executive or manager for getting work done from them. In the process while you are dealing with them, you have to communicate with them, talk to them and discuss, pass on instructions and directions and get the feedback reports. Now the questions are :- –

(a) **How effectively and successfully will you do this job?**
(b) **Is there any scientific process?**

(c) Is it linked with your personality for establishing relations?

(d) If so, how is it and in what form?

These are very important and relevant questions and their answers are found in the art of interpersonal skills.

In a way, *interpersonal skill is basically an art of establishing a communicative relationship with another person or persons and making him or them feel good and at ease.* It involves a process of sharing ego-related traits and needs that eventually motivate and influence other persons effectively and in a positive and predictable way. In fact, *interpersonal skill is intended to enhance individual confidence and self-respect and allow persons to perform at their high level and in the process experience the positive feelings of high self-worth and high self-esteem that are naturally associated with any person and his accomplishments. An individual of whatever hue wish to feel important that eventually becomes a driving force in him.* As a result, interpersonal skill offers you the key of largely going through personal dealings and issues with other persons that finally make your communication and contact meaningful and productive.

Interpersonal skill is based on the fact that other persons are very important and you want to experience certain things from them. From family members, you want affection, cooperation and support. From employees, you want cooperation, loyalty and maximum work output. From employers, you want encouragement, recognition and fair compensation for your sincere and dedicated work.

Interpersonal skill is one of the most important qualities, required in the corporate world that pertains to your capacity and ability to get along with the people of different types and potentials. There are innumerable examples of individuals who are supervisors, managers or heads of large organisations or industries, not because of their professional competence but because of their abilities to deal with the people and get the best services from them. In this respect, there is a new criteria emerging that pertains to the significant role of interpersonal skill, played in the careers of eminent and empowered professional managers who have been successful to reach the top levels. They emphatically point out that *those who consistently demonstrate an ability to achieve results with and through other people tend to be promoted to high levels commensurate with their proven performance and competence.*

Code of Conduct for Interpersonal Skills – Process for Dealing

Now, the question is how to go round and achieve it. It is well known that the *recognition is the deepest craving in human nature that is related to his ego of feeling important.* You should therefore follow for interpersonal skill a code of conduct which demonstrates your sufficient courtesy, patience, politeness, gentleness and interest in initiating a dialog with them. The code of conduct consists of the following steps :-

(a) **Be alert**. You should be alert and look for an opportunity to praise or compliment for act of accomplishment by others.

(b) **Be enthusiastic.** You should show sufficient interest in your dealing with others. Show that you are always happy to meet them, handshake with a smile and a few nice words.

(c) **Be available.** Never say I am busy and never try to avoid meeting even your casual friends or visitors. Encourage for informal meetings and show that you are pleased to meet them. *Your gesture of meeting a visitor even for a moment out of your busy engagement will be highly appreciated and deeply commended for your greatness and generosity.*

(d) **Be attentive.** Show your interest and carefully observe their reaction, statement, expression, body language and habits.

(e) **Be appreciative.** People crave appreciation for their works, statements, behaviour and expression. It raises their ego, self image and they feel encouraged to talk to you freely and frankly.

(f) **Be approving.** Others look forward to you to approve their efforts, pursuit or endeavor often in the face of adversity. It leads to feel them confident and look up to you for support and appreciation.

(g) **Be accepting.** Accept others what they are. Accept as they dress, behave, and voice their views, ideas and opinion in their own manner. Once you accept, they get strength and courage to change for better if you advise.

(h) **Be affirming**. You should laud where credit is due and be cautious in criticising.

(i) **Be discreet**. Discretion is the better part of reading people and keeping to yourself what you have thought and learnt about them. You should be careful in your comments and gentle in expressing your disapproval.

(j) **Be a friend.** You must show your friendly attitude and behaviour that encourages others to behave in a friendly manner.

"It should be noted that these are basically indirect positive traits of your personality which play a significant role in the art of your intercommunication skills."

Importance of Effective Listening

Listening is a vital part of interpersonal communication process. You should have the patience to listen to the people carefully if you don't wish to miss information of your interaction which could be of critical importance to you later. As a leader, you must cultivate patience and keenness to listen to your team members. At times, vital piece of information comes out in casual listening informally to their views or by your deliberate questing during the process of listening. Recent studies have shown that you spend 30 % time in talking and 45 % time in listening. So, this indicates critical importance of effective listening.

Art of Listening

So, the most important step in the interpersonal skill is listening to others. It plays the key role in the interpersonal skill where you seize the first opportunity to let other person to talk and you listen to him attentively. It is also treated as a courteous and graceful gesture as you treat a person with a human face of honour and regard. *Active listening is an effective mental skill.* It requires keen concentration and attention to what others are saying. So before you start the listening process, you should ensure that :_

    (a) **You have enough patience, politeness and gracefulness.**
    (b) **You should be calm and composed while listening.**
    (c) **You make the person relaxed and composed.**
    (d) **You shouldn't provoke anyone initially.**
    (e) **You understand the person's background and environment from where he/she is coming.**
    (f) **You appreciate his language, tone, loudness and don't adversely comment on it.**

With these preliminary steps, you create a friendly atmosphere and demonstrate that you are really an interested and privileged party to talk to the person and keen to know the person's views. Now, let us consider the elements of the listening process

Elements of Listening Process

Listening Process in the context of interpersonal skills involves the following activities :

    (a) **Sensing.** It involves physical hearing and taking mental note of is being spoken. It is possible to have interruption while you are hearing and there may be digression. However, you should maintain your focus on sensing process.

    (b) **Interpreting.** The process of interpreting deals with decoding the information and gives meaning to it while keeping in view the purpose or motive of the person as he talks and gives you information.

    (c) **Perceiving.** Interpretation leads to perception of the criticality of issues or possible solution or some creative instinct in a logical and rational manner. *Perception is loosely called the sixth sense or the sense of reading in between the lines while interpreting the information.* Eventually, it becomes the valuable quality of a person which is inborn and later developed from his art of good listening.

    (d) **Responding.** This function pertains to keeping eye contact and acknowledging the message by reacting to the speaker. You need to respond to the speaker appropriately by some action such as shaking your head in acknowledgment or eyeball movement or some hand movement. This response of your body posture encourages the speaker and assures him about your continued interest and focus of your attention on him throughout.

    Now, you are switching your role to become an active listener by taking the following steps while listening.

Systematic Approach for Effective Listening

As a part of the systematic approach, you should proceed to adopt the following steps for facilitating effective your listening :

(a) Allow other person to give vent to his feelings and thoughts.

(b) Allow him to get relaxed and feel privileged for talking to you

(c) Identify the topics of his interest and initiate discussion by politely asking his views. .

(d) Show that you are earnestly interested and keen to listen to him.

(e) Allow him to pause, think and build his confidence while expressing his views and thoughts.

(f) Don't interrupt and don't show your disapproval on his views.

(g) Ask a few questions while listening in order to indicate your keen interest in discussion with him.

(h) Avoid criticism or negative comments. Also tolerate his native or fowl language.

(i) Be patient, gentle and composed while listening to him.

(j) Ask pointed questions to seek or extract information of your interest.

(k) Nod often, lean forward and look into his eyes thereby showing your keenness in discussion.

(l) Keep your body movements and body language under control whenever you disagree with his views and opinions.

(m) Resist any external diversion or distraction.

(n) Finally, say thank you and appreciate him for sparing time for discussion with you.

This systematic approach to effective listening is right when you want to discuss with someone from whom you are interested to seek specific information or you wish to find out the scope for an solution or just discuss casually and informally. Here, you draw a person in discussion in an informal way. You may also like to discuss formally when you invite a person to your office. You may hold a group discussion with more than one person and procedure remains the same.

Talking to A Disturbed Person

As a head or manager, you have to deal with a person who is mentally disturbed and unhappy with the administrative set up which he believes has not given him justice. There are many reasons for such a situation to occur because of the administrative, operational and managerial system that may cause delays or denial of dues in personal matters. So, when a person is found disturbed, it must have caused on any one of the following accounts :-

(a) Non selection to the next rank by the departmental promotion board.

(b) Denial of casual or annual leave on your application.
(c) Delay in disposal of legitimate financial bills.
(d) Denial of loans, allowances or certain facilities which are deemed to be entitled.
(e) Domestic reasons of different nature that has affected his courage, moral and mental peace.
(f) Financial problems or goof up which creates mental worries.

A person under categories (a), (b), (c) and (d) feels aggrieved and he carries grievance and a feeling of grave injustice on his mind. So, he wants to know the cause and also redress. So, this person seeks an interview with you and he is given the time of appointment. The person enters your office at the appointed time and looks for your permission to speak. Now, you should make him comfortable in the chair and show that you are ready to listen to him. You should give him patient hearing without interruption and try to fully understand his case. You may ask a few questions for clarifying the issue. You should show personal interest in his case and give him confidence that he would certainly get proper redress. Your patient and effective listening makes all the difference in bridging the gap between an employee and the management through your interpersonal skill.

There is another way of handling such a disturbed person. During your routine visits or if you come to know of such a person from your team or group or section who is disturbed, you call him or go to meet him and earnestly and affectionately enquire about the cause of his disturbance. Your sympathetic, personal approach and your readiness to listen to him make a lot of difference to him to feel relief and relaxed. When you initiate discussion on his grievance, you should be sympathetic and a bit appreciative of the genuineness of his grievance. You should explain the reasons only after giving him patient listening and fully understanding his case. Your effective listening to his grievance relieves him of the mental pressure and it is a half win of the battle for you from your interpersonal skill of effective listening.

PART - TWO
General Communication Skills

Types

Generally, there are three types of general communication :
(a) Interpersonal Verbal or Oral Communication
(b) Written Communication (with the recent addition of *E-MAIL*)
(c) Public Speaking or Address

These types of communication take place within an organisation called intra-communication through the inter office note (ION) as well as with the outside agencies through official letters called inter-communication letter with a proper reference and file numbers for record purpose. Body language and Para-language can't be considered part of communication because they constitute visible reaction which occurs as the consequence of direct communication in the form of dialog, discussion or negotiation.

Written communication is used to convey the rules, regulations, procedures, policy matters, financial balance sheets, personal and administrative business matters of which record has to be maintained for reference and processing for various purposes like negotiations, interviews, promotion boards and audit. This written communication is brief to the point with brief context and is given in clear terms without any ambiguity. It is given in the form of memos, orders, briefs, job requirements, reports and returns. This communication is addressed to a specific action addressee which may be an individual or department or specific outside agency with copies to non-action addressees for information.

Verbal or oral communication is often used to convey the orders, instructions and directions to employees on day to day basis for execution. It is also used for briefing the staff members of a special mission or project. Besides, it is effectively used for giving professional presentation and for addressing a special dedicated audience on topics of public interest. So, it becomes a part of lecture, talk, presentation, speech, briefing, address, discourse, negotiation and group discussion.

Communication Process

This process covers the following areas of questions and purpose associated with them :-

(a) **Why** – *Reason* for a communication. Spell out the specific purpose or objective.

(b) **What** -- *Contents,* pertaining to the intended message which is targeted to a particular recipient.

(c) **How** --- *Means* that the channel used to convey the text of communication over the media which could be telephone, post, Fax, E-Mail.

(d) **Where** -- *Place* from the communication is originated and its destination where it is received.

(e) **When** ---*Time* when the communication takes place and how long it exists.

A communicator needs to properly understand the mechanics and modality of a communication process as briefly stated above through the pertinent questions so as to constitute a *whole communication for really becoming effective and meaningful.*

Platform for Communication

Your communication skill comes to play a very important role when you have to address a function, a group of persons, deliver a key note address as a guest speaker or chief guest. You are also required to participate in office meetings, group or panel discussions, brain storming sessions and seminars and do the public speaking. This is an occasion you use for conveying your thoughts, views, proposals, plans to your senior and subordinates for improvement of the in-house functions and operations and optimum utilisation of the resources and manpower. You also use this platform in order to demonstrate your knowledge, experience, wisdom, working skills and vision and convey to the people or audience your diligence, depth of analytical and evaluation skills and a deep sense of public service and responsibility. Through your communication skills, you try to project your image and high domain of personality as a learned and experienced person in the professional field with your commitment and dedication to the public interest in general and your organisation in particular. *In fact, communication is the only way and office or public is the only platform which offers opportunities when you can make maximum use of your communication skill for creating favorable impression and awareness about your work style, professional wisdom, management and learning skills* and eventually, gain credit and publicity for your career prospects.

So, *the communication skill offers a means to focus all the efforts, talent and creative energy of your personality for achieving valued goals and objectives consistent with the organisation's well- being as well as offering opportunities for career advancement.*

Becoming An Effective Verbal Communicator

Now, the question is - *How to become an effective communicator?* What steps should be taken and what proper guidelines should be followed? These are comprehensively given below :-

1. Be clear about the purpose of your subject of talk. Understand its objective and state it in specific and clear form.
2. Collect all relevant information connected with the subject along with data and put it under different group headings and paragraphs with important points and words sidelined and marked in red ink.
3. Know the quality of audience or group, level of their receptivity, etc. Ascertain whether they are professional or general type and are they interested in listening to you.
4. Use certain phrases, specific sentences and examples with little humour in order to clarify and emphasise your point.
5. Memorise your speech. Look casually at your notes but always look straight at your audience.
6. Use proper modulation in your voice and delivery. Support it by proper movements of your hands and body, while conveying your emphasis on certain part of your speech.
7. Look at certain selected persons from the audience and see their reactions by nodding, staring or head movements.
8. Maintain cheerfulness and smile on your face. Show your enthusiasm, energy and interest with positive approach.
9. Be time-conscious and deliver your speech within the stipulated period with little variation. A long speech becomes boring for the audience.
10. Use presentation aids such as *projector, slides* accompanied by a *pleasant background sound.*
11. Practise and observe the quality of your voice. Remove any defect like huskiness, long pauses, loudness, etc.

12. Demonstrate your confidence, logic and conviction while delivering the speech.
13. Before concluding your speech, you should summarize the salient points of your speech.
14. At the end of speech, you should ask the audience to shoot some questions and you should politely answer them.
15. Before you close your speech, don't forget to say thank you for giving you an opportunity to express your views on this platform.

It is pointed out that this is the standard pattern of guidelines which are applicable to any type of speech, address, talk or presentation. Its duration may vary from a few minutes to an hour or hour and half depending upon its scope, length and purpose. This will be an invariably in-house address with an audience strength varying widely over the numbers for attendance. In fact, you should not take any notice and bother about the strength of the audience and your delivery and enthusiasm should remain unchanged.

When you want to communicate in a meeting or participate in a group discussion, your approach is little different and you should follow a little different technique, such as given below :-

(a) It is a gathering for interaction among the members. So, everyone should get an opportunity to express and discuss.
(b) All members are equally competent and prepared. So, you should have patience, regards and respect for them and their views.
(c) Even when you disagree or disapprove, you should be polite and courteous while expressing your viewpoints. Never express your disapproval bluntly in harsh language.
(d) Cooperate with the members by supporting their views and strengthening their arguments.
(e) Keep the tone of discussion soft, low and gentle. Exchange views in amiable and peaceful manner.
(f) Avoid feelings of any heart-burning or ill feelings from any inadvertent remarks.
(g) Encourage members to come out freely and frankly about their views and opinions.
(h) Avoid any personal remarks or criticisms on company policies and operations. Also avoid petty politics.
(i) Keep the constraints of time in mind and give every one chance to speak and express.
(j) Avoid the domineering attitude and behaviour by any member in a meeting.
(k) Avoid worthless and meaningless discussions and stick to the point and objective of the meeting.

(l) Say frankly NO if you do not know or don't have the information or knowledge but don't waste time in yapping unnecessarily.

(m) Before concluding the session, you must summarise the deliberations and evaluate how far the objective of the meeting has been met. List out the points of disapproval or descent which may need more discussions and further meetings.

Well, for becoming a good communicator, you should deeply prepare with focus on the objectives of your communication. You may revise by meticulously going through it. You should practice when you have to deliver a formal speech or talk before an audience. *Remember that your thorough preparation of the subject, memorizing it and practicing for delivery give you sufficient self-confidence, courage and boldness. At the same time, it is your self confidence and boldness in expression that make a lot of difference in creating impression of your personality on the audience*

Language and Style

You are generally using English or national language for communication. It is good to observe rules of grammar and correct words while expressing and presenting the subject. But at the same time, you should not be over cautious and too conscious. You remain natural and normal and concentrate on the full text of the subject. In this respect, I would like to quote my personal experience. When I wrote my first book on **Introspection and Self Assessment** and gave it to one of the publishers, he commented so adversely on my language and use of the words like ' we and you ' that I got immensely demoralized. Later in the course of reading several books I came across the one in which the Canadian reputed author stated categorically in the preface that *it is the prerogative of the author to use the language the way he likes so long as he conveys his thoughts in the most natural form.* So far use of the words like we and you are concerned, it is his discretion and style to whom he wants to address while emphasizing his points. This approach of the English author relieved me a lot from my tension of not knowing proper English as deemed by the publisher.

It does not mean that you should not follow grammar or use of proper words in your expression. You should take precautions to check that the sentences are properly and correctly worded and expressed. But, you should not get bog down about niceties and articulations of sentences and words and waste your time so long as you are satisfied that you are able to clearly convey your objective and intention. And there lies your communication skill.

Public Speaking

In the public speaking, you address to a large group of people who collect at an appointed place for listening to you. Here, you get an opportunity to directly talk to the people and covey your thoughts, views, opinion in a systematic form and manner. You have prepared your message, thoughts and views and you want to convey them so that they appreciate for receiving valuable information from you. You also wish to inform the public about certain issues and present their analysis and impact on the public living. Thus, you get a public platform where you establish a direct link with the public and address them in such a way that they swing to think like you, look into your views and form a favorable opinion about you. This platform is generally used by the guest speakers and political party leaders for canvassing about their party ideologies and swinging the public opinion in their favor. Thus, it is highly important for you because :-

(a) You talk face to face with the people who gather collectively for listening to you.
(b) You get wide publicity, visibility and reach out
(c) Your public image is improved.
(d) You are looked upon as a highly learned, knowledgeable and professional person.
(e) You earn a good reputation for your professional and personal competence.
(f) Your personality gets a boost in the public eye
(g) It helps you to earn good rapport from your superiors.

The Art of Expression

Pubic speaking is definitely an art. It is really a *technique for presenting your thoughts, views and investigative and analytical work*. In fact, it forms a *part of mass communication* system where you address a group of people assembled as a mass to listen to you. Expression and articulate communication are the essential part of the public speaking. Here, expression plays the key role and is the fundamental ingredient of the art of speaking. *You may be a learned person. You have worked hard on the project and succeeded. You know a lot of things. Now, what is the use if you are not able to express your knowledge in clear, consistent, forceful and fluent form to an audience. So, expression goes hand in hand with the public speaking for creating a strong favorable impact.*

Once it is considered an art, it is treated as a natural gift. You possess a flair for public speaking. Once it is located in you as it is normally done while interviewing in the Service Selection Board, it can be developed by proper training and practice. What is required to do is to prepare your text for speech and memorize it. Once it is memorized, you start practicing for delivery. In this respect, you are advised to stand before the mirror and you start addressing to your image in the mirror. While speaking out, you observe movements of your hand, head and expression on your face. If you find them awkward, you correct them. If you find nervousness on your face, you should feel bold and you have a faith in your well preparation. You may go a step further and record a part of your speech on a tape recorder. Once it is over, you replay and observe the tonal quality, loudness, clarity and pause. If you find defects or if you are not happy with its quality, you may take necessary corrective steps and improve upon the delivery of speech.

Here, I want to emphasise the point that *the art of expression becomes your biggest valuable asset. When you begin to speak on the subject and express in a forceful manner with powerful flow and throw, you carry the members of the conference with you and create on them tremendous impression about your personality and its image.* You establish your unique reputation as a public speaker. As a result, you are often called most of the times to conduct the proceedings of the conference and also invited as guest speaker or for delivering the key note address. Thus, by your sheer oratorical skill, you are able to create a special respectable and remarkable position for yourself. *Remember here that nobody bothers about external part of your personality, nobody takes note of your appearance but they respectfully look at you because of the richness of your inner qualities to which the skill of your oratory gives proper vent and make you a public man.*

Concluding Remarks

Communication is a very important tool in establishing official, social and personal contacts and relations with staff, team members, subordinates, friends, neighbours and others. It is basically an art with a psychological impact and it needs to be gradually and skillfully developed. Your patience, calmness and persistence make a lot of difference in developing everlasting relations. *Your listening habit and skill plays significant role in making your communication effective, productive and result-oriented. You become the real boss and leader of your department mainly due to your effective and impressive communication skill.* In that case, certain negative aspects of your outer personality are glossed over because you are able to impress and motivate the people with your superior communication skill. The same is true when you address the people in public audience or whenever you participate in discussions or meetings. *Remember that you will always carry the members with you by your eloquence and powerful expression for driving the points of your interest.*

The art of public speaking is an effective means for projecting your personality. Nobody bothers about your look or dress if you are able to deliver a speech in a forceful manner and produce the impact. Oratory is the biggest asset of the mass leaders because they create an impact on the public audience. Professional and managerial persons are often required to present their works and this art of public speaking is the one that can give them wide publicity for their works. Hence, *the power of your expression and readiness to boldly communicate with the audience becomes the key factor of your personality in enabling you to earn proper publicity, recognition and public respect.* .

> **Note:-**
>
> *There are various steps to develop good communication skills, such as: Know What to Convey, Gave Courage to Speak What You Think, Practice, Make Eye Contact, Engage Your Audience, Use Gestures, Be Aware of What Your Body is Saying, Show Constructive Attitudes and Beliefs, etc.*

CHAPTER - 10

LEADERSHIP ASPECTS OF YOUR PERSONALITY

> **Abstract**
>
> objectives of your organisation. You lead a small or large group of personnel under
>
> needs many important positive qualities in your personality for performing a number of important functional tasks and executing responsibilities towards the management and your group members. Leadership is an important aspect of your personality for demonstrating your planning, organizing, administering and executing abilities and potential with focus on achieving an objective within the scheduled time of completion. Leadership has become an important criterion for selection of the candidates for
>
> for their assessment to higher ranks during their service periods.

Concept of a Leader

Every body is a leader in his way. The head of a family is a leader of the family. Every team or a small group has a nominated leader. Every department or division has a head who becomes the leader of his subordinates and staff members. So, every project or a mission or an organisation, small or big has a leader who is appointed and is responsible for performance and discipline of his team/group/project/mission. In fact, no organisation or industry or department can exist without having a head as its leader on the top position and middle functional levels who are called senior or high level managers.

a person who heads an organisation leads, directs, supervises and ensures

So, he remains exclusively responsible and accountable for executing the task and achieving

for executing a job with the constraint of time and resources which becomes the essence for assessing his executive capabilities and leadership qualities.

Specific Aspects of Leadership

Now, there are a few essential and significant aspects of leadership as under:_
- (a) **A specified task**
- (b) **Exclusive responsibility**
- (c) **Management of resources and manpower**
- (d) **Time of completion or delivery**
- (e) **Command, control and discipline while leading**
- (f) **Relations while working together as a team**
- (g) **Facing risks and challenges**

Scope of Responsibility

Let us take a look at the scope of his/her exclusive responsibility. It is wide and covers a large spectrum of management. Briefly it is projected in threefold ways as under :-
- (a) Towards his superiors who has nominated him as the leader.
- (b) Towards his team members for leading them with adequate resources for accomplishing the assigned job.
- (c) Towards discipline, care and welfare of his team members.

So, a leader is a person who is sandwiched between two echelons, one on the top as his superior officials to whom he is responsible for accomplishment and below his subordinates and staff members through whom he has to accomplish the job. So, there are two important key factors which are related as under :
- (a) One is related to prove to his superior officials or management that he is fully competent to execute the job and lead his team in a successful way.
- (b) Second is related to his team members and subordinates that he is fully qualified and confident to lead them for accomplishment of the task.

Principles of Leadership

A leader while leading his team members has to follow certain principles as given below:-
- (a) Follow the rules, regulations and procedure.
- (b) Acquaint yourself fully to know the objective of leadership.
- (c) Don't question your superior authority or management on nominating you as a leader.
- (d) Focus your attention on the objective and fully understand from all angles like size, scope, quality, time constraint, resource requirement, etc.
- (e) Be honest, sincere and truthful while assessing your capabilities and competence for executing the job. In fact, this is required to anticipate bottlenecks and bid for additional resources if so required.

(f) Follow equality, secularity with no caste, gender and religion bias and prejudice.
(g) Maintain self-image and self-esteem while dealing with your team members.
(h) Maintain the sense and spirit of duty, responsibility and commitment.
(i) Keep yourself and your team members well informed and updated with latest information, techniques and skills.
(j) Stay away from in-house politics and avoid criticism and confrontation.
(k) Follow ethics, traditions, code of conduct, etiquettes and morality.
(l) Observe time management and remain conscious of the time schedule for completion.
(m) Seek timely advice of your superiors whenever in doubt or trouble. Keep them informed about the progress and appraise them about any anticipated bottleneck or hardship.
(n) Stay away from flattery, false self pride and eulogy from your team members.

Awareness

Besides following the above stated principles of leadership, you have to remain aware about :-

(a) Professional cultures and traditions
(b) Self-Physical fitness and health and well-being of your team members and their families
(c) Habits, behaviour, conduct and manners of your team members
(d) Resource and logistic support and position
(e) Level of professional skills and application of your team members
(f) Religious, ethical and egoistic sensitivities and sensibilities of your team members
(g) Continuous drive and motivation required for forcefully advancing towards objectives

Commitments of Leadership

A leadership is distinctly committed in four layers of its responsibilities as under :-

(a) **First organisational layer** means towards his superior authorities who has appointed him as the leader with full faith and trust in him. Consequently, he becomes responsible and accountable to them for execution of the task.
(b) **Second professional layer** means towards his profession and performance with full knowledge about execution, evaluation, feedback and consolidation of the accomplishment.
(c) **Third organising and administering layer** means provision of adequate resources, logistics and manpower and their judicious and tactful deployment

with respect to the threats and opportunities, risks and challenges as perceived by him on the ground.

(d) **Fourth managerial layer** means skill in ensuring team spirit, cooperation, coordination and high moral among his team members throughout execution period.

It is quite evident from the above that a leadership has multi-dimensional responsibilities and commitments with wide scope and range.

Positive Attributes of a Leader

A person who is nominated or selected to lead should essentially possess the following positive attributes :

(a) Professional competence
(b) Initiative and awareness
(c) Commitment, dedication and involvement
(d) Strong will power, firmness and vision
(e) Decisiveness, determination and stability
(f) Loyalty and integrity
(g) Drive and motivation
(h) Enterprising spirit, boldness and courage for facing risks and challenges
(i) Flexibility and adaptability
(j) Command over powerful expression with clarity and loudness
(k) Communicating and oratorical skills with team members
(l) Honesty, gentleness, patience and toughness
(m) Time sense and consciousness
(n) Temperamental balance, calmness and composed posture
(o) Fairness, uprightness, unbiased and unprejudiced
(p) A good effective listener to get proper feedback for monitoring

Besides having the above leadership-oriented attributes, there is a need to have the following abilities and capabilities :

(a) Planning and organising skills
(b) Command and control over the job and its progress
(c) Delegation of responsibilities to different team members
(d) Organise a proper feedback network for getting timely inputs and intelligence
(e) Briefing team members for keeping them informed about the objectives, approach, time schedule and resource positions
(f) Judicious allocation and application of manpower and resources
(g) Promote proper cooperation and coordination among team members

(h) Maintain the high moral and spirit of team members by giving pep talks
(i) Evaluation of the results from the cost-benefit point of view

Ethics, Values and Etiquettes

It is an unwritten code of conduct which involves following certain ethics, values and etiquettes by a leader. When you judiciously follow them, you get an edge in your style, conduct, modality and you are effectively able to exercise your moral authority and control on your team members. Hence, these factors are given below :-

(a) Treat your team members with respect and dignity.
(b) Give your undivided attention to your team member or subordinate when he comes for seeking your advice or clarification.
(c) Be punctual to all meetings which you attend as a leader.
(d) Attend social functions whenever invited
(e) Don't disturb others when they are engaged in work.
(f) Never fire or criticise your subordinate in other's presence.
(g) Avoid discussion on sensitive subjects and personal matters.
(h) Show respect to your seniors and elders.
(i) Maintain equality of gender, caste, creed and religion.
(j) Be careful with your humour and critical remarks.
(k) Be open, humble and receptive to new ideas and suggestions.
(l) Offer gratitude for patronage, assistance and positive advice.

"Incidentally, these are all important positive attributes and abilities of your personality which are identified for you to become an effective, responsible and trusted leader in any organisation".

Key Factors for an Effective Leadership

If you want to be an effective leader and successfully accomplish the assigned task with grace, dignity, trust and distinction, you should observe and keep in mind the following key factors :-

(a) Professional skills, knowledge and full competence.
(b) Creative and innovative spirit and urge.
(c) Human relationship with staff members for motivation, team spirit and coordination.
(d) Management skills for planning, organising and administering purpose.
(e) Interpersonal and communicating skills for exercising effective command, control and execution.
(f) Adherence to values, principles and ethics for exercising moral control and maintaining a high moral.

(g) Cooperation, coordination, monitoring and feedback for making timely course of corrections.
(h) Flexibility, adaptability and openness in approach and dealings.
(i) Focus on updating knowledge, skills, training and priorities of work.
(j) Physical fitness, boldness, courage and adventurous spirit.
(k) Drive, initiative and motivation by setting personal example in performance, honesty, morality and adaptability.

Different Styles of Leadership

There are different manners and styles for exercising leadership. It depends upon different cultures, training and attitude of a person who is selected or picked up from available lots of personnel, etc. Let us see different modalities for exercising leadership as under :-

(a) **A strong assertive leader with conviction.** He focuses on his leadership and objective and is totally self reliant and confident without needing any guidance and advice after initial briefing. He is clear, straightforward, forceful and demanding from his team members. Such persons are stickler for discipline, command and control over their team activities.

(b) **A moderate accommodative and adaptive leader with flexible and listening approach but decisive of his own way.** He is not rigid but amenable to suggestions. He remains in touch with his members and carefully listens to their views. In fact, he invites them to voice their opinions and deeply deliberate over them. He is cordial, amiable and polite with an accommodative approach. But, this leader takes his own decision and adheres to it.

(c) **A self-eulogist, proud, esteemed leader with high self-image and projection.** He is an introvert type with focus of his attention on himself. He talks much of his past achievements and has formed his opinion. He takes the credit for his leadership and accomplishment without sharing it with his team members. He remains self-centric and self-focused with the least regards even for his senior officials.

(d) **A dependable, non-committal, soft, indecisive leader with a flair for listening to others and then deciding.** This generally happens when a person is new to a job and does not have adequate experience but the leadership is suddenly thrust on him by virtue of his cadre and qualifications.

Incidentally, this style and manner of exercising leadership depends upon the positive and certain negative attributes possessed by a person. In this respect, a leadership with the style and manner as stated at serial (b) is preferred compared to the one stated at serial (a). The type of leadership stated at serial (c) and (d) will be damaging to an organisation as such leaders will prove to be incompetent for leading an organisation in the present fast moving highly competitive world.

Response and Obligations

Now, it is not leadership alone which can singularly produce success but it needs all round efforts of team members to support and perform under the leadership. The team members also have the stake in the success which is finally treated and projected as success of the entire team/group under the unique leadership. So, in this respect when team members share and bask under the glory of success, they have certain duties and obligations towards leadership as given below :-

    (a) **Understand clearly commands and instructions.**
    (b) **Remain attentive and alert, while briefing is done by the leader.**
    (c) **Extend wholehearted support and cooperation to leadership**
    (d) **Never question the authority of the leader.**
    (e) **Focus your attention and energies on the duties, specifically assigned to you.**
    (f) **Report to your leader about the progress and final completion of the work. Seek advice if encountered with a problem.**
    (g) **Maintain proper discipline and cordial relations with your colleagues.**
    (h) **Discourage the spirit of competition as an individual and up-man-ship.**

Selection of a Leader

Every organisation, institution and industry has a *promotion policy*. Selection of persons for higher ranks is made through this process on the basis of their annual confidential performance reports and recommendations. Now, when a person is to be selected for heading a section, company, department or division, the promotion board mainly examines the leadership qualities as reflected in his dossier. So, performance of a person is verified in view of his leadership qualities. Now, leadership criteria are specified for different ranks and posts like manager, senior manager, deputy general manager, etc and their placement as heads. It is evident from this normal process that your basic attribute profile with highlight and emphasis on your leadership attributes becomes the primary document as prepared and presented by your senior officials along with their recommendations.

Role of Training in Leadership

It is said that leaders are born. There is no doubt as they are born with a bundle of positive attributes. Now, the strengths of these positive attributes as possessed by an individual vary over a very wide range from person to person. Those who possess leadership related positive attributes with high levels of strength, eventually become mass leaders in social or political fields. They start showing symptoms of their *leadership qualities right from their early adulthood in various activities like school, college, community, games, agitations, movements, processions, etc.* They participate in various activities and perform the leading role. Whenever and wherever, there is a strike or protest march, these types of persons will be there to lead and present their issues before the concerned authorities in a forceful manner with a fiery delivery of speech. Since they are the born leaders like *Mahatma Gandhi, Jawaharlal Nehru, Lal Bahadur Shastri, Indira Gandhi* and so on, no formal or informal training is required by them. Circumstances as existed that time forced them to come out by their inner forceful leadership qualities and lent their leadership for the public cause and later became their mass leaders. ***The most significant asset of these leaders is their oratory and expression of their thoughts, views, opinion and concern with conviction in fiery and forceful manner. Here, the physical personality takes a back seat and his inner personality in the form of his powerful expression becomes dominating.***

There is of course a separate general case of leadership that is normally required to lead at different levels of organisations, institutions, industries, corporations, defence forces, etc. Selection of the heads is normally made through the departmental promotions as well as open advertisements by the selection committees. Officers are selected by the Service Selection Boards at the initial stage. In this process, efforts are focussed on observing their leadership qualities by subjecting them to various field tests. Once selected and placed, it becomes the responsibility of an organisation to train them properly in order to suit to leadership needs of their respective organisations at various levels.

There are special training schools, colleges and centers which offer composite training packages and modules for management training with emphasis on leadership. Reputed industries like ***Tata, Reliance, Birla*** have jointly or severely established industrial management schools where the young executives are given rigorous training for grooming as leaders for working in their companies at various lead roles. Now, what happens when such training is given to a young executive who has the leadership qualities but they were lying low in an inactivated form. ***With an intensive exposure to the proper training under packaged program, his leadership attributes are activated to higher levels according to the response given by him.*** As a result, all of them are not going to become big leaders but ***their leadership caliber, acumen and capability will vary according to their response levels and the extent to which these attributes are activated.*** Thus, you will find a wide difference in performance of these leaders. So, ***some may reach top levels, some may stay at middle levels and some will fade out at low levels.***

Objective of Excellence- Special Role of Leadership

This factor is generally associated with the responsibility charter of leadership. It means that excellent performance and its accomplishment should always be focus of a leader while leading his team or group for achieving the objectives. He should always remain conscious and aware about achievement of the quality and excellence in his performance. It has become need of the day for survival in this competitive environment with a large number of competitors trying to grab the market for their products.

Every leader works hard with dedication and honesty but he is not able to achieve excellence because this factor is judged and assessed by a group of the costumers who act as the third interested party. A leader may produce the product as per the qualitative standards as laid down but its acceptance as an excellent product is left to the choice of the costumers if multiple products are available in the market. Hence, **excellence is a concept related to**

the quality which depends upon perception, judgment and assessment of the users. So far as the leader is considered for his responsibility for ensuring excellence, he has *to adhere to certain principles, adopt a modern work culture and appraise his staff members about the competitive market position and costumers' expectations.* So, targeting for excellence is a complex issue and has to be handled and resolved by a leader in consultation with his staff members after considering manpower, resource position and capital investment. In this respect, certain guidelines are given below for compliance:-

(a) Maintain desire, enthusiasm and passion for doing and producing work of top quality and excellence.

(b) Have positive visualisation and expectations by harnessing cooperation and imagination of your staff members.

(c) Create an energetic and conducive working environment for others to offer their best outputs.

(d) Arrange meetings and sessions in a relaxed and tension free conditions and encourage them for suggestions and views.

(e) Center your thoughts and keep focus on excellent performance.

(f) Develop creativity of your staff members by increasing their imagination, perception, attention and thinking power through proper training, exposure, visuals and handsome rewards.

(g) Maintain balance in your personal work style and domestic commitments with a view to keep your thinking and creative power active and working without any stress and strain.

(h) Arrange resources, tools, equipment, skills for ensuring quality performance and work output.

(i) Arrange the dialog with your costumers and get a feedback on their expectations about the quality and its excellence.

(j) Keep an eye on the market and availability of products and their quality standards.

(k) Consider finally the financial aspect, resource and capital position and then work your strategy for producing an economically viable product with market oriented quality and excellence.

It should be noted that the concept of excellence should not be open-ended, but it should have the practical constraints of what is possible and what could be achievable with the available resources and manpower. Your concept of excellence should also be governed by the market demand, competitive galore and public expectations. There is no point in keeping your concept of excellence too high without considering the need of the day. *So, it should be noted that excellence is not an act but it should be encouraged by the leader as a habit in his performance.*

Concluding Remarks

An extensive and exhaustive scope of leadership and about its various aspects is adequately covered in this chapter. Every one of us is born with leadership qualities which are displayed at various levels at a later stage in our life. At a small level, the head of a family conducts his family. Now, it depends upon his leadership qualities as required at that level to keep the family well organised and united or brake in small units. The requirement of leadership qualities increases as the level of organisation grows up. The leadership qualities also become evident in seizing the right opportunities at the right time and exploiting it to the fullest advantage. They display their talents, intuitions, abilities and sense of timing in various fields of leadership and come up of their own when demanded. *Remember that leadership is not chance nor an accident. You can't make any person a leader and even force on him leadership, it is not effective and productive and even remains limited to a small field.*

Note:-

Remember that it is the strong, visionary and unshakable leadership that make a difference to turn the tide from defeat to victory, failure to success or loss to gain in highly critical condition.

CHAPTER - 11

FORMING RELATIONS WITH PEOPLE

Abstract

Relation and behaviour are the means for connecting you with different classes of people from the outside world. You are brought in the mainstream of *public relations and contact*. In fact, establishing relations and winning friends become an art which needs special skill, patience and motive. There are different types of relationship and each needs different skills and motives whenever you wish to form. Winning

networking and public relation (PR) work. People from sales, marketing and human resource department need this specialised art and they should skilfully develop it. In this respect, the book written on the subject by Dale Carnegie is famous but

applying to our people, business and corporate world.

Important Role

Relationship and behaviour play very important role in connecting you to the people around you. To be able to do the best and win success in your personal and professional life, you need the support and cooperation of other people at every stage. You can't just act and perform alone and single handedly and can't function in isolation of a team, group, section or department of any organisation. You are employed to work on the job

you are invariably and essentially part of a group of persons who are working together

the head of a section or small group or team. Irrespective of what you are, *you have to interact at every stage and perform your role as a worker, supervisor, executive, manager*

While dealing with other persons, your relation and behaviour with them become the reckoning factor which is treated as an essential part of your managerial skill. Others look at it as a human resource issue. Now, the relations and behaviour depend upon your nature, behaviour, mindset, conduct, manners and skill. So, they indirectly depend upon your personal attributes of both positive and negative types which are an integral part of your personality. It is enough to focus attention on these issues so that *you get another equally important picture of your personality in forming friendship, relationship, bonds, attachment, team spirit and involvement. Of course, they are based on how much you love, care, interact, listen and carry your people with you in peace and difficult situations.*

The Art of Relationship

Relationship is essentially a two way traffic which is similar to require clapping by both hands. *It is basically built on mutual trust, liking and desire from both sides.* If one party lacks in liking and does not desire to have friendship, obviously you just can't have relation with them. You can't thrust relation on them and form it against their wishes. So, *it becomes an art in which you create the need and interest of the other party in having relation with you.* You have to channel your efforts in such a way that you create a desire in a person who senses the need and interest of his organisation in forming business or personal relation with you. In the on-going process, you create mutual regard, trust and confidence in your relations and both of you onwards become mutually dependent *that leads to development of healthy relationship.*

As far as your team or group is concerned, you have to talk to them and share your thoughts, feelings, experience and knowledge with them. With them, your relationship is continuous and dynamically interactive. Your working together becomes an art or technique in ensuring their engagement, support and cooperation for achievement of the mission target as specified. It is the trust of the members of your team in your leadership and your confidence in your team members' support, cooperation and commitment that becomes important indicators of good relationship which *becomes the backbone of your personality for winning success under critical conditions.*

There is always a mutual understanding with the spirit of give and take in any relation and strong relationship is built on this principle. By giving openly and freely to others' way of thinking and needs, you will be able to receive what you want in return. It means that *you can't be a lone beneficiary in a relation. This is the essence of human relationship and the role played by your personality in bridging the inter-human relation gap.*

Types of Relations

Formation of relationship depends upon your purpose which is classified as under :-

    (a) Professional relation
    (b) Business relation
    (c) Friendly relation
    (d) Traditional relation
    (e) Personal relation

Professional relation is formed by the virtue of you being an employee and you are required to perform alone or in a group with assistance from others. You are tied down to perform a specific job and you have to interact with others in an official manner according *to a code of official conduct.* Hence, the relation so formed is professional and official which may turn in personal relation depending upon the liking and desire of both the parties.

Business relation is temporary in nature and is formed by motivation to do a business as a customer or client. Here, a business deal is negotiated and executed within a certain time period. Hence, the business relation lasts for the duration of the business and may or may not last beyond its completion. There is a mutual trust and give and take spirit in the series of meetings and negotiations before the deal is finalized. In fact, *give and take principle is very important in early finalizing the deal and becomes the key factor for ensuring future growth of business and extending business relations.*

Friendly relation is informal between two persons with the primary purpose of helping each other in a difficult time. This relation is built on the basis of understanding, trust and comradeship. It is a friendly gesture of helping each other without specifically asking for it. You meet a person in a conference or seminar and exchange views in an informal friendly manner. You develop liking for each other and continue thereafter in the form of exchanging greetings, best wishes through E-Mail. Thus, you form a networking of friends which you keep active and you don't know when it comes to your help in future.

Traditional relation is formed by virtue of your traditions like marriage in which young members are tied in married relation which stays for the whole of their life. Initially, such relation appears to be forceful and is created by the tradition of marriage. But, once they live together, this relation is changed to mutual trust, liking, affection and personal bond. There are other relations like in rural panchayat bodies, religious confluence where people of different regions, sects come to gather for meeting and deliberations. This is a cordial amicable relation formed with common objective to resolve the issues.

Personal relation is little different and delicate. It takes time to form this relation but once it is formed, it is of permanent nature. This relation is the culmination of the above types of relation. It depends upon many factors such as mutual regards, understanding, trust, cooperation, liking with a deep sense of togetherness, affection and attachment. It takes time to develop this relation. It is not known what clicks but when it clicks, the process is non-stoppable and it ends in forming lasting relation. You maintain this relationship by social callings, visits, attending social functions and frequent telephone calls. Incidentally in this relation, family members are drawn and participate in social gatherings.

HOW TO MAKE FRIENDS

Motive for Making Friendship

To start with, there is a question.

Why do you want to make a friend?

What is your objective and interest in forming friendship with a person who is not known to you and you don't know whether he is equally interested?

In this respect, I would like to quote my personal experience. While doing my regular exercise in a garden, I used to see a person well dressed in white attire with polished black shoes. He came daily for walk in the garden. He walked slightly bent but in an impressive manner. He did not talk to anybody and after his walking, he used to sit quietly. Being always well dressed in white and his impressive look, I thought that he might be just a retired judge or a very high ranking Government official. Over the period, it aroused my curiosity and one day while he was passing by my side, I hallowed him by saying Good Morning and slightly moved to shake hand after introducing myself that I am Col Onkar. He wished back to me and said I am Sudheer. Then, I enquired whether you are in service or retired. He said that he had retired one year back. I asked from which department. He replied that he retired from a College as a Professor and Head of the Department. With these few words, he walked away saying thank You. He did not bother to ask me who I was and where did live. Since he walked away without proceeding further, it was evident to me that he considered himself too big to talk to me and reciprocated to me just because I called him. Now, can you win such a person who happened to be :-

    (a) Egoistic and having too high a sense of Self-image about being Professor.
    (b) Feeling a sense of superiority in status.
    (c) Suspecting someone who talks to him first below his status.
    (d) Likes to be not disturbed and want to enjoy his loneliness.
    (e) Not social and reveal no interest in developing social contact.
    (f) Frown to form relation with an unknown person.

Now, if you come across such a person, even being well educated, you can't form friendship or extend a hand of friendship unless he should equally feel the urge and he should not consider himself too high and other person too low in status. On the occasion of such casual meeting, you can't go out of the way to win and influence him unless you have a specific interest and objective in your mind.

Since the word how to make a friend is used, you can form friendship with a likeminded and willing person. It happens that other person may not reciprocate to your initiative. Now, you can be persuasive and persistence in your approach and efforts. But, *this can happen only when " You should have specific interest, motive and objective.* "Having just a social purpose of forming friendship with a particular person will not work and yield any positive result. So, *you have to target a person and focus on him with your specific interest and purpose.* You may not succeed in the first attempt but you will definitely succeed with repeated efforts and pursuance. In the above example, since I did not have any purpose and interest, I did not pursue the case.

Personal Approach for Making Friendship

As said earlier, the task of making friendship is basically a two way affair and its key lies in your abilities to form relation and maintain it. There is a give and take principle in a friendship in the sense that one should not stick to his way of thinking and believing that his views are right. So, when you look out for making friendship, you should be clear about your expectations and purpose. Once you are clear in your mind about the type of friends, you should then proceed to look around for seeking them. Now, the question is how to match their expectations from both sides and how to bring them together. One of the parities has to take initiative to start the dialog. So, you may proceed in this respect by adopting the following approach :-

1. Dress neatly and properly.
2. Assume your appearance so that you look friendly and trustworthy.
3. Control your unnecessary body and hand movements and irritable habit if any.
4. Walk gracefully and in dignified manner. Conduct yourself in an impressive manner.
5. Look around with proper eyeball movements and don't show much interest in any particular thing.
6. Wish ' Hallow ' with a smile to a particular person whom you are interested to form friendship.
7. Address him by name and initiate dialog by saying *'How are you '*
8. After receiving his response, introduce yourself by saying your name, address and service status. .
9. After getting further response, show your interest by enquiring about his service, native place, parents and present living place.
10. Talk something about his immediate concern, interest and liking about games and hobbies.
11. Ascertain through his talk about his major liking and important interest. .
12. Be a good listener and encourage him to talk about himself.
13. Keep cheerfulness and smile on your face while listening to him.
14. Ask him few questions so as to keep his interest alive in talking and giving you information.
15. Don't get excited by his answers nor criticize him for any undesired remarks.
16. Give your honest and sincere appreciation to his viewpoints and opinion. Also sympathizes for his problems or difficulties and offer your help by saying *'Can I be of some help to you* or say *' May I help you?'*
17. Arouse in him a sufficient desire and eagerness to form friendship with you.

With all these gestures and friendly actions, there is enough indication for extending a hand of friendship to him. You are able to give enough indication for winning his friendship by initially breaking ice and establishing contact. Now, it is entirely up to both parties to proceed further in a friendly manner and carry on the relationship. ***Remember that the most crucial and critical phase is to establish initial contact for which you have to take proper steps for making friendship.*** Useful and meaningful relationship is possible only when the other party is equally eager and you have to initiate such action so as to create his interest and desire in friendship with you. So, ***it entirely depends upon your nature, temperament, attitude, interest and significantly on your skill for taking above steps and finally winning the friendship. This is how your personality plays a significant role in making friendship for you as desired.***

Forming Relations or a Relationship

The next step after making a friend is to form a relation with him. This relation is either temporary or permanent and it depends upon how you wish to develop contact further. This friendship is extended to the meetings of the family members on special occasions such as religious, social or personal functions. Once the family members are involved in your friendship, it leads to form lasting bond of relation with mutual trust, regards and cordiality. Apart from occasional meetings outside, you commence to call on homes on formal or informal occasions. Thus, it is possible to progressively strengthen the initial contact of friendship into an everlasting relation. You follow an unwritten principle of give and take in this relation without any expectation and the relationship remains based on affection, respect and trust from both side. In this relation, you avoid discussing controversial subjects, issues and refrain from taking a personal dig. You also need to avoid arguments which may cause hard-burning and you should stop them at the right moment. You need to be tolerant to the feelings and sentiments of each other and one of you may have to patiently listen to other's view without any rebuttal. These are certain tricks which are based on my personal experience and you need to follow them if you wish to maintain relation with your friends in your lifetime anywhere. . .

HOW TO IMPRESS PEOPLE

Reasons for Impressing

Why do you want to impress the people? What benefits would you like to derive by impressing a bunch of people? Before answering these questions, it is important to look at the people whom you want to impress. This section of the people may belong to any of the following classes :-

(a) Administrative class who are required to process your personal matters
(b) Customers whom you are selling your products.
(c) Customers with whom you are negotiating business deal.
(d) People from other departments like banks, tax, labor, revenue, health, etc.
(e) People from your own departments like material, finance, administration, etc.
(f) People from political and social sector.
(g) Members of the audit and other committees appointed for your accountability.

Objectives in Impressing

Besides, you want to impress them. But for what purpose? Your objectives in impressing people are enumerated below :-

(a) You want to enhance your Self-image.
(b) You want to earn reputation and recognition as the professional speaker or achiever.
(c) You want to share your knowledge and experience with others and benefit from their queries and doubts.

(d) You want to test and verify your observations and analysis from the experience of the public.

(e) You want to become a leader and champion the social cause for seeking justice.

(f) You want to arouse public awareness and render social service.

(g) You want to become a leader and enter politics. So, you want to test your lung power for eloquence and oratory.

(h) You want to get your job easily done.

Once your objective is clear in your mind, you are really motivated to influence people from the audience. Initially, your contact should start from a small group of persons and may gradually extend to a large audience. Let us consider that you are dealing with a small group of persons and you are tasked on your company's assignment for a specific job. Now, you have to influence such a small group of persons and get your job done. How will you proceed to influence them? Well, you may proceed in the following manner :-

Personal Approach

1. Be well dressed for the occasion. Touch up your appearance and control unnecessary body movements.
2. Conduct yourself in a dignified manner.
3. Prepare your brief thoroughly and carefully along with supporting data and preceding examples. Anticipate questions and doubts. Think of the best line of presentation with emphasis on certain points and your end objectives.
4. When you enter the conference room, wish all the persons present with the best compliments of Good Morning or Good Afternoon as the case may be. Meet every one and shake hand with the expression " How are you Sir ".
5. Initiate a dialog by thanking them for giving you an opportunity to talk to them and sparing time for you from their busy schedule.
6. Be natural and informal in your behaviour and formalities. Observe softness, clarity and pleasantness in your voice and oral expression.
7. Be humble, polite and sincere in your proposition and expectations.
8. Don't criticize or condemn or complain for any delay or lapse from them. In case there is any delay or lapse from your side, tender profuse apology.
9. While presenting your case, arouse the interest of others in your proposal by giving your arguments point by point in a forceful manner.
10. Show your genuine interest in the cause of your case and welfare of your company with due regards to rules and regulations followed by them.
11. Maintain cheerfulness and smile on your face while talking with confidence and conviction.
12. Address a person by name with his rank and be respectful while addressing as ' Sir ' or ' Sahib '

13. Be a good listener and encourage them to talk about their points. Note them carefully, ponder and then reply.
14. Talk in such away as if you are championing the cause in the public interest.
15. While talking, make every one present feel important and treat them respectfully with due regards.
16. If you are wrong or some mistakes occurred, admit frankly and tender apology.
17. Encourage others to ask questions and do talking on the subject. You treat their comments and advice valuable.
18. Give respect and value to the opinion, views and comments from others.
19. Be emphatic and pressing on the noble aspects of your proposal.
20. Dramatize in your expression and hand movements while emphasizing your certain core ideas and issues of your proposal.
21. Gauge the mood and impression of the persons. Watch their reaction for gaining favorable response. Summarize important points of your proposal and highlight impressively those points which pertain to growth potential and public interest for tackling employment problems as your company's humble contribution to national cause.
22. Before closing, thanks them for giving opportunity and listening to him patiently and finally with the humble request for favorable consideration.

The Role of Positive Attributes

It will be seen throughout the entire exercise of making friends and impressing people, that positive attributes of your personality play very significant role in forming different types of relationship. In fact, your personal approach as stated in each case is the manifestation of your various positive attributes. They indirectly motivate you take the initiative and form the relation. Now, what are those positive attributes? These are mentioned below :-

(a) Initiative and keenness
(b) Gentleness and amiability
(c) Calm and composed outlook
(d) Persuasiveness and persistence
(e) Firmness and determination
(f) Openness and flexibility
(g) Eloquence and softness
(h) Adaptability and accommodativeness
(i) Tolerance and patience
(j) Tactfulness and politeness
(k) Honesty and credibility

These positive attributes of your personality are specific to the process of MAKING friends and Impressing people. You are thus able to plead your case before the important people. This is the way *you influence them to your way of thinking.* These are all practical and proven steps and well experienced by the author while sitting on both sides of the table. *Remember that it is entirely your show and test of your personality. You have to tactfully but honestly play the main role. You have to skillfully play your game and keep meticulously kicking the ball and finally score the goal.*

HOW TO MANAGE IN A SPECIFIC CONDITION

Nature of the Situation

This is a ticklish issue and it is basically behavioural in nature. You have to continue to stay in a particular organisation even if you find that :-

(a) Working environment is not congenial and conducive.
(b) Persons whom you have to deal with are not cooperative and friendly.
(c) Boss is autocratic and has no human face towards his employees.
(d) No job satisfaction as there no diversity in employment.
(e) Stagnant situation in growth of career prospects.
(f) Stagnant growth of the organisation.
(g) Changes in your attitude from material to spiritual viewpoint.

There are in fact several reasons that make you feel difficult to carry on in your organisation. But, you can't afford to leave your job and seek employment elsewhere because the job market is tight and depressive. So, the best solution for you is to get along in the same organisation but you must change your attitude and thinking and adopt the following measures to calm down attitude and temperament of your personality. :-

Measures

1. Adopt the positive attitude and positive thinking.
2. Develop your patience, calmness and remain composed and steady.
3. Don't react. Pause and ponder over the situation and allow it to slip of its own without taking its notice.
4. Believe that the happenings are temporary and the bad phase will be over soon.
5. Do your job sincerely, honestly and devotedly. Remain focused on your job.
6. Don't bother about environment as it is out your control. It is better to compromise with it.
7. Keep the contact with your staff or colleagues minimum and restricted to job only.
8. Observe your normal etiquettes and pay your compliments.
9. Don't dabble in personal problems of others nor give any advice unless asked for.
10. Don't give any chance to others to point an accusing finger at you for any slippage.
11. Be happy with your present pay packet and thanks your star and pray the God that you should regularly get your pay packet under the preset meltdown.

12. Extend your whole-hearted cooperation to the efforts of the Management for pulling out your company under presently critical financial conditions.
13. Don't complain or grudge for the present condition. See other side of the situation which appears promising for positive change.
14. Believe that the present situation has a good luck factor which occurs later in the future.

Remember that the *change in your attitude, thinking, outlook and belief makes a great deal of difference in your behaviour and work style and culture.* You control your expectations and adopt the attitude of cooperation, co-existence and spirit of accommodation and togetherness instead of confrontation and noncooperation. *Wisdom lies in swimming with the tide and current of the water flow instead of going against its direction unless severe danger lies ahead. Remember that your best interest lies in your wisdom, positive attitude and thinking and apply the principle of adjustment, accommodation, compromise with the situation and environment and get along rather than wasting your time and energy in opposing, confronting and contradicting it.*

DEALING WITH PEOPLE OF DIFFERENT TYPES

Behaviour and Conduct

This aspect of your personality is part of its behaviour and conduct and eventually inclusive of relation in general. There is nothing specific in this topic except that it needs *to highlight certain behavioural and functional aspects of your personality.* In practice, you have to deal with different types of people from different strata right from your family members to friends to colleagues to subordinates to your seniors in your organisation. At every stage, you deal with a person with different objectives and interest. You approach them under different environment and your reaction is different. Let us see how you should deal with different types of people as under :-

1. With Family Members Need:
    (a) Affection and fondness
    (b) Care and sharing with responsibility
    (c) Respect with regards for parents and elders
    (d) Trust and faithfulness with wife and children.
    (e) Frankness and openness.

2. With Office Staff Members Need:
    (a) Gentleness, politeness and cordiality.
    (b) Mutual respect and regards
    (c) Focus on your work and area of responsibility.
    (d) Avoiding arguments and conflicting topics for discussion.
    (e) Avoiding discussion on in-house politics.
    (f) No complaint against anyone and especially about the management and boss.

(g) Avoiding criticism of any individual and discussion on personal matters

3. With Boss Needs:
(a) Gentleness, politeness and humbleness.
(b) Entry in his office after seeking his permission.
(c) Meeting him with prior appointment only. Otherwise, only when he calls you.
(d) Paying profusely compliments as 'good morning 'or' good afternoon', as applicable.
(e) Never seat in a chair unless he permits you.
(f) Talking briefly to the point and answering those questions he asks.
(g) Be specific in your statement and avoid casualness and vagueness.
(h) Never argue or question his authority. If any doubt, ask his permission to express.
(i) Never say, 'NO' to his instructions or directions or orders on that occasion even if you disagree or you have some reservation. Accept and think over and after a pause or little later, express only after seeking his permission by saying, ' Sir, may I have a point out if you permit '.
(j) Be cheerful and confident and note down in your notebook in his presence.
(k) Avoiding to ask for repetitions.
(l) Asking if anything else 'Sir and say', 'May I leave'.

If you follow the above guidelines, you have no problems dealing with even an autocratic and dictatorial boss.

4. With Friends Need:
(a) Gentleness, politeness and amiably.
(b) Courteousness, gracefulness and informality.
(c) Relaxation and casualness.
(d) Frankness and openness in exchanging views.
(e) Observation of mood of your friend for initiating discussion. Enquire about personal problems or worry if any.
(f) Offer of your help, support and advice whenever need arises.
(g) Avoiding personal remarks and arguments on issues. Avoiding discussion on sensitive matters like religion.
(h) Avoiding interference in personal affairs and issues of your friend.
(i) Maintaining privacy and confidentiality of certain information while discussing.
(j) Following certain moral values and etiquettes in friendship.
(k) Exchanging social visits and drawing family members in your friend circle.

5. With Elderly Persons Need:
You follow all the steps as stated above. Besides, you need to be respectful and careful while

dealing with elderly persons as under :-

   (a) Your respect by touching their feet. This gesture makes a lot of difference to their mood and impression about you.
   (b) Enquiry about their health and well-being.
   (c) Appraisal of your work, service and family members.
   (d) Compliments to their deep knowledge, wisdom and experience and admiration for their contribution and lifetime achievements.
   (e) Appreciation of their services and sacrifices for bringing up their families and their present caring attitude and worries about the youngsters.
   (f) Remembering of good things and valuable advice given to you and how you have been able to come up. So, giving them credit profusely and saying it was all because of their blessings and noble support.
   (g) Praying for their good wishes and blessings for you in future the same way as before and hoping to receive their advice and guidance in future whenever required.
   (h) Avoiding criticizing even if you find their behaviour or remarks irritating or sarcastic.
   (i) Assuring them about your help and support whenever needed. Promise them that you will call on them soon.
   (j) Seeking their permission to depart and seek their blessings by bowing and touching their feet

This is the way you can treat and pay your respects and regards to the elderly persons. What they look for in your approach whether you care them and appreciate their contribution to the family. Your polite gesture of bowing before them and touching their feet changes their mood from isolation and gloominess to cheerfulness and they get assurance about their value and presence. This is really a delicate issue and you must care for their sensitivities and sensibilities of the age factor

NETWORKING

This is the modern requirement of relationship in which you form a network of friends, well-wishers and patrons. These people are well dispersed and placed at different important positions in various organisations, institutes or departments. During the course of your service, you come across them or serve as colleagues in different departments or meet them in seminars or conferences. Now, you maintain this relationship or chance meeting by sending regular greetings of best wishes on the occasions such as New Year day or birthday or wedding anniversary and making occasional courtesy telephone calls especially in a later part of your service. By your gesture, the people remember you and they are somehow impressed about your sincerity, humbleness, gentleness and friendliness. Now, you don't know when an occasion arises in future and you become the beneficiary of your networking with a particular person who extends his helping hand to your case. In this respect, I quote from my personal experience that I was the beneficiary from my networking at a very crucial time of my career. So, I confidently state that networking definitely pays you one day and even if not, you establish a network of well-wishing friends around.

There is a normal complaint from the youth that they don't know the people and they don't have the God Father. They are in fact found unwilling to mix and meet the people. The following drawbacks are observed in their behaviour and attitude :-

(a) Shyness and lack of courage
(b) Lack of initiative and forward approach
(c) Negligence towards visitors, quests
(d) Indifference to attend seminars, conference, lectures
(e) Egoistic and evasive approach
(f) Lack of vision and forward thinking

With this negative approach and attitude, the youth avoid meeting important persons and form acquaintance with them. This tendency is even found among some senior serving persons and they sincerely believe that their work will speak for them. As a result, they remain lonely, aloof and isolated with no one to take care of them under the unforeseen circumstances.

Concluding Remarks

The subject of basically behavioural and relationship nature is comprehensively covered in this chapter. These are personal activities which are based on your psychological, mental and thinking factors. *Your personality plays the key role in making and impressing friends and also in getting along with different class of people. All these activities fall in the domain of communication, public relations, public contact and association. Eventually, they substantially contribute to achievement of your success as an individual or leader or head of the department in any organisation.*

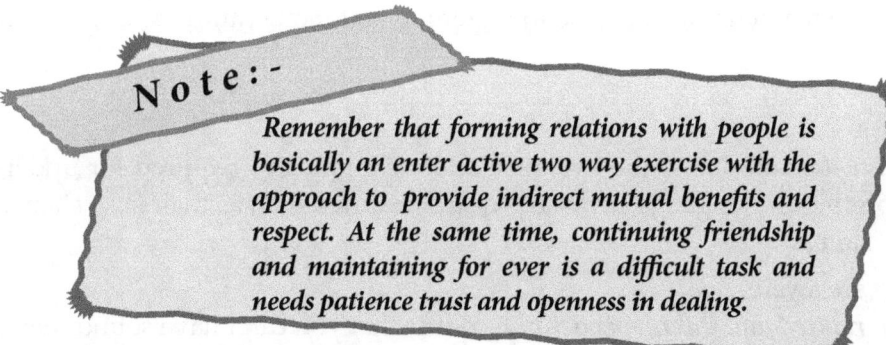

Note:-
Remember that forming relations with people is basically an enter active two way exercise with the approach to provide indirect mutual benefits and respect. At the same time, continuing friendship and maintaining for ever is a difficult task and needs patience trust and openness in dealing.

CHAPTER - 12

HEALTH AND BODY FEATURES OF YOUR PERSONALITY

> **Abstract**
>
> are essential for *state*. The physical health and its appearance is the visible demonstrative aspect of your establishes your unique identity as an individual and distinguishes you from others. Your appearance, body features, movements and conduct determine whether you have the healthy or sick personality. Some of the attributes of your inner personality can be read from your certain body features like head, palm and body movements. Body language has become a modern technique for reading most of your reactions, inner feelings and emotions in business meetings.

General

This chapter deals with the health and body features which belong to the physical domain of your personality. This domain is essential part of your outer personality and establishes your identity in the public. This aspect is visible and seen while functioning and performing. As such, it demonstrates your personality in the physical form. Health of your body plays the key role in maintaining and sustaining tempo and momentum of your personality. *Its*

your mental domain. Now, the expertise and technique are required for understanding and interpreting the language of these physical features such as their size, shape, position and active state. .

As you are aware, *are closely related and interdependent.* It means that you can't have sound mental power have sound health unless you have sound and strong mind. Once, you have both, your chances of achieving success becomes bright. Hence, let us discuss health in the succeeding paragraphs under a separate head.

HEALTH OF YOUR PERSONALITY

Physical Well-being

This factor pertains to the physical characteristics of personality that are evident to us in the form of the physic and body features. It includes your movements, habits and behaviour which are physical activities and visibly observed. Now, their conditions and status make significant difference in giving overall impression and look to your personality. If you are able to properly and effectively function, move and discharge your duties, then it is remarked that you have '*Healthy Personality* '. Otherwise, if your physic is suffering from any ailment or defect, then it is remarked that you have ' *Sick Personality* '.

Indicators of a Healthy Personality

Without going much into the physical structure of your body, let us see the important characteristics of a healthy personality as given below :-

(a) Good physic and health
(b) Proper and flawless movements of body organs such as eyes, ears, hands, nose, etc
(c) Proper body movements, manners and conduct
(d) Reasonable and normal habits
(e) Reasonable display of body language
(f) Smile and cheerfulness on face
(g) Expressive face with proper eyeball movements
(h) Calm and composed posture and outlook
(i) Normal and informal behaviour
(j) Balanced speech and normal hearing
(k) Amiable response and reception
(l) Pleasant expression of ' **Hallow**' on telephone
(m) Normal talking, discussion and response
(n) Social get-together and mix-up
(o) Readiness to offer help and assistance
(p) Exotic and energetic outlook and response

These are general indicators of a healthy personality. Besides, the state of your mind should also be healthy in the sense that your attitude, mindset and thinking should be positive because they create chemical changes in the body that are conducive to form physical health. You directly get the benefit of love, laughter and peace of mind which are the physiological aspects of your personality.

A Positive state of mind has also an indirect effect on healing from an ailment because your will power with mental resolution is enhanced for becoming well and the positively responds to the medicine and care.

Effects of Physical Well-being

When you are physically fit, you enjoy your life. You feel energetic, enthusiastic, keen and active. You show your interest in work and your activism is demonstrated in your performance. In fact, direct result of physical fitness is seen in enhancing level of following attributes of your personality :-

- (a) Endurance and stamina
- (b) Tenacity and robustness
- (c) Tolerance and forbearance
- (d) Focus and Concentration
- (e) Strength and vigour
- (f) Diligence and hard work
- (g) Self-image, Self-esteem and self-control
- (h) Enthusiasm and keenness
- (i) Coolness and calmness
- (j) Initiative and awareness
- (k) Graceful movements and dignified conduct
- (l) Response in learning and training
- (m) Immunity to ailments, illness, depressions, etc.

Method

The most effective way for maintaining your health and physique is to do *regular exercise*. It involves brisk walk with jogging for about an hour preferably in early morning. It should be followed by step by step exercise and a few yogic postures. Ensure that you should sweat profusely. Young persons should do skipping and aerobics that make your muscles strong, flexible and powerful. You should include yogic exercise and meditation in which every part of your body is exercised and worked out. You should also learn to do pranayam which is a breathing exercise that enables you to concentrate and eventually relieves of the mental stress and strain. You should follow a regular schedule of exercise that will certainly keep you fit, energetic and spirited in your work and performance. Here is a word of caution that you should adopt a schedule of exercise according to your age and time available but you should never neglect your health exercise schedule. Besides, you should have nutritious food at regular intervals in a controlled manner without temptation for over-eating due to delicacy of the cooked food. In fact, regular exercise and healthy diet are key factors of your health and keep you ever healthy without getting obesity and over-weight. At the same time, you should avoid over-indulgence in any personal or private activity. While trying to gain and maintain good health, you are advised to have company of good friends and stay away from vices and bad habits. In this way, you are able to conserve your energy and consequently it gets reflected in your cheerfulness and happiness. *This is the only way of keeping good health and physical fitness during your service career and even later after retirement in the advanced age.*

Remember that positive and proactive mind rests in a healthy body. You must think of your health if you want to be a winner in life and regular exercise holds the key for achieving physical well-being.

BODY FEATURES AND APPEARENCE

Body Features

This is a visible outside part of your personality. You are born with the specific body features which have the genetic feature called hereditary relation with your parents and forefathers. These features become your unique physical identity. You are easily identified and recognized by your unique features and their appearance. Your body features become the specific stamp of your personality and you carry it throughout your life. In practice, *these body features give the first impression about your personality and people forms their opinion about you right or wrong, positive or negative, proper or improper. Of course, formation of such an impression depends upon their perception and attitude.* So, let us take a look at your important body features such as head, hand, and general appearance.

Head

This is the most prominent dynamic and impressive part of the body. Its first look gives you sufficient idea about the personality of an individual because it carries specific aura, freshness, liveliness and glamour about his personality. Besides the functional role of each feature like nose, eyes, ears, lips, they remain in a dynamic state. As such, a particular dimension and movement of each feature convey the specific language and impression of your personality. For example, shape, size, movement and colour of your eyes indicate certain personal characteristics such as probing, observing and sensing power, analyzing and judging. Besides, they convey your basic nature whether it is loving, affectionate, crooked, clever, selfish, self-centered, open. In a way, your eyes become the window for looking into your inner self by staring and observing and assess your attitude, mindset, intent and intellectual strength. Your eyes offer you the power of perception and judgment but its grade of assessment depends upon the quality of your eyes. The eyeball movements indicate sharpness of your observation, restlessness, imaginative power and balanced or imbalanced state of your mind. The colour of the eyes indicates health of your constitution.

Nose is the most attractive feature of your personality. Its size, shape, length and width speak a lot about your nature whether it is ambitious, mission oriented, romantic and artistic. Its length, straightness and pointed end offers grace, dignity and glamour to your personality especially ladies.

Forehead is another attractive and impressive feature of your head. It size, shape and width are indicator of the intellectual power of your personality. Your character is read from your forehead. It has Yang and Yin portions marked in the form of lines that indicate the energy level in your intellectual power. A person with a raised, broad forehead and large eyes catches your attention at the first glance in a group or meeting because he looks quite prominent, impressive, scholarly and dignified among others. You start thinking whether he is a scholar, scientist, or high ranking official from the corporate world or government agencies. Such a person is found to fight with the difficult condition and firmly stay on his mission thereby generally giving indication of his leadership qualities.

There are other features like *eyebrows, lips, chin, mouth* and their *size, shape* and position which are other demonstrative features of the head and add grace to your appearance. They all add up to finally make your *personality impressive, graceful* and *attractive*.

Incidentally, there is no significant contribution from other features like *height, size and shape of your body like your head* which dominates and overrules over the drawbacks of your personality from other features if any like low height, fatty structure. Sometimes, negative features of your body are overlooked when you have the impressive forehead and big shinning eyes with forceful power of expression.

BODY LANGUAGE

Meaning in Business Parlance

Body language is a term used for communication using *body movements or gestures* instead of words or expressions. Our body in fact conveys mostly non-verbal impressions along with the words and tones of voice. *It is **basically indirect communication of personal feelings, emotions, attitudes, thoughts through one's body movements, either consciously, etc. or sub-consciously, voluntarily or involuntarily.***

Significance

This feature is specific to your normal body movements in the most natural and involuntary form. They send and receive non-verbal signals all the time. These signals have assumed a lot of significance in the corporate world because they carry unspoken *meaning, loaded with verbal expressions, reactions, impressions and mental thought processes*. In fact, **they are actuated from your inner attributes and reflected in the form of your manners and habits which convey specific body language of silent expression and indirectly transmit a specific message to an observer.** Of course, interpretation of the language depends upon the physical, social and cultural context of the situation and ability of other persons.

Understanding body language is the recent technique which has entered the human resource management field and is being used for judging and assessing the people when you see and watch them in your face to face meeting during discussion or interviews. You can simply watch the body movements of the person and sense certain behavioural parameters by your close observations and judgements. You can assess and draw your conclusion from such physical movements of the persons who are totally ignorant and unaware about the signals transmitted by their movements and decoded by the other party whom they are encountering in a meeting or dialogue or interview.

This technique is now being adopted by the interview boards for assessing certain attributes of your personality. It is combined with the personality test and seen in totality. As the candidate enters and interview starts, members of the board observe his personality and body movements and start decoding the body language. The candidates are totally unaware about their own movements which may be natural or deliberate and caused consciously or sub-consciously by the interaction during the interview.

Types of Body Language

This language conveys different types of feelings, emotions and thoughts as under:-

- (a) Aggressiveness showing physical threat
- (b) Attentive, involved showing deep interest
- (c) Bored state not showing interest
- (d) Deceptive covering real intention
- (e) Defensive protecting self from adverse situations
- (f) Dominant ruling over others or the situation
- (g) Emotional indicating sensitiveness over the issue/issues
- (h) Relaxed mood showing comfortable position/positions
- (i) Submissive mode/modes showing you yield or agree

In the present context of the competitive environment, you should be aware about this new aspect of your personality. You should keep in mind and remain conscious about it in natural way. This aspect can't be ignored or avoided. While improving your personality and preparing for the interview, you should take this aspect into consideration. These body movements may appear simple and unintentional but mean a lot to those who understand body language. Typical body movements are identified and mentioned below along with their meaning:-

1. Folded arms---- Reflects defensiveness
2. Firm handshake-----Reflects a decisive person
3. Steady eye contact------Reflects openness and trust
4. Passive face avoiding direct eye contact----Shows unbalanced and uncomfortable state of mind
5. Gestures like clenched fist, pointing index finger or hand-----Shows aggressiveness
6. Smile on the face and relaxed state----- Readiness to communicate openly and sincerely
7. Crossing of arms or legs or avoiding direct eye contact, or sitting on the edge of the chair or touching face, nose, ears, chin often ---- Indicates falsehood, wrong and incorrectness in statements
8. Rubbing hands vigorously--- Indicates pleasurable sense of expectations or satisfaction
9. Scratching the head--- Indicates confusion, doubt, uncertainty, etc.
10. Both hands behind the head----- Indicates superiority, confidence and possible arrogance
11. Rubbing of chin--Indicates that your ideas are being given careful consideration or thinking process is on
12. Head resting on hand--- Indicates boredom or fatigue

13. Clenched hands when speaking---- What is being talked or discussed about is frustrating
14. Clenched hands when listening---- The listener is responding negatively
15. Arms folded with thumbs pointing upwards----- Indicates nearly impossible to convince
16. Hands pressed together as in prayer---- A desire to persuade or underline a point gently but firmly

It is pointed out that a few of the visible factors as stated above may make difference to your selection as it depends upon the members to understand their meaning and implications. Body language and its role in interpreting your personality have recently assumed significance because your personality indirectly speaks through body language. It therefore becomes your vehicle for winning the battle for success half-way. It is a physical tool used in a group discussion for dominating over the function. The expression of your feelings or reaction through the body language becomes effective on certain occasions as it acts as a tool for building inter-personal relations in a small group meeting over a coffee table or sitting dinner. You establish friendly contact and relation through your amicable and affectionate gesture and behaviour. In an industry, you can use your body language for motivating, team-building, negotiating and net working.

Concluding Remarks

To conclude, you can't afford to overlook such an important physical portfolio of your personality. It is a highly important, beneficial and fruitful asset of your personality as it has potential to bring a lot of dividends if properly and discreetly used. It is an indirect indicator of hidden treasure of your attributes. This tool does not cause any physical harm but you don't know what harm or damage you cause by hurting the feelings of others from your wrong gestures and body movements. So, you should first understand the language of your different body movements and then master the technique for deriving maximum benefits in interviews and business negotiations.

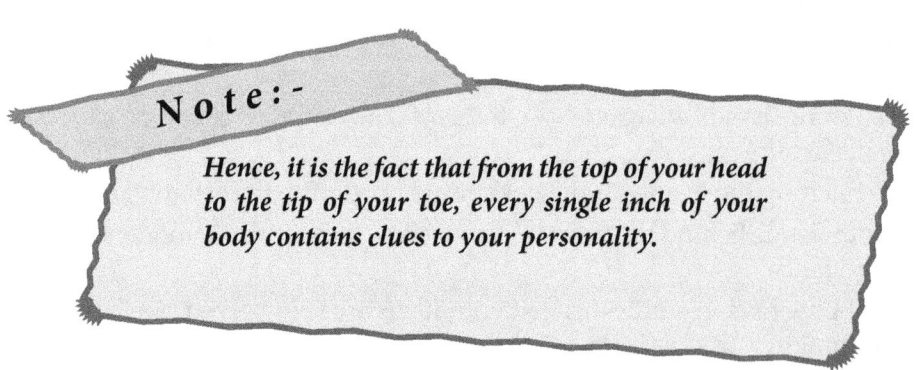

Note:-

Hence, it is the fact that from the top of your head to the tip of your toe, every single inch of your body contains clues to your personality.

CHAPTER - 13

CHARACTER OF YOUR PERSONALITY

> ### Abstract
> Human character is treated as a part of the spiritual domain because it is basically a
>
> improves the quality of your life and earns respect and regard from the public. Because
>
> urge, greed, ego and envy. Your character is seen in complying with certain dictates of prominent positive attributes such as morality, loyalty, integrity, trust, credibility, etc.
>
> leave behind the unique foot print of your personality. The character is also linked with your karma, SANSKARSS and destiny. The character raises your spiritual and moral strength. It is a unique tribute of your personality that silently works in the background for building your image and reputation in the public view.

Scope

and I will focus on its practical applications while working, performing and behaving in your service career. It should become useful and meaningful to you from your career point of view.

and conduct become restrictive and binding but qualitative and meaningful. Since character can't be isolated from your personality in the sense that you have a good character or bad character, your public image and reputation are formed and projected and you are eventually treated with respect and regard by the public.

In fact,

retire from your active service charter or as and when you depart from this world.

Meaning

Character is generally associated with the role played by a person for someone else who happens to be at the centre stage of the drama or cinema. While playing such a role, full efforts are sincerely made to represent the original character and thereby creating the picture of originality.

Although, in this respect, there is total identity with the original person, the focus always remains to project his / her personal characteristics in which major contribution is made by representing his / her nature and character in the most visible, impressive form.

What is being referred in respect of your personality is more or less identical form but it refers to your certain qualities which uniquely identify you as a person from others in nature, behaviour, performance and relations. In the bargain, he is supposed to uphold certain values and principles. He stands firm and determined on his views, remarks and statements. While doing a job, he quietly displays confidence, firmness and restful disposition. *When he deals with his friends, colleagues, he is always respectful, graceful and stays firm to his promise and commitment.* He observes a certain code of conduct in his behaviour, performance and relation.

Such a personal description as given above is for a person who has the character, a genuine one and not representing for somebody else. It remains forever as the part of his personality and he carries it as his valuable precious asset for building his public image which is consequently held in high esteem.

Now, it is evident that *this word character is the conglomerate of certain highly esteemed positive qualities which form his unique individualistic nature for his performance in a specific way in his professional and personal life.* Now, what are those distinct qualities and what are their qualitative implications for qualifying his performance?.

Different Aspects of Character

Let us first consider different aspects of character and how they influence your performance and image. .

1. **Morality.** It means your moral values and behaviour in a moral way. It primarily refers to your behaviour and treatment given to the members of opposite gender, different casts, creed, positions and levels. *It also refers to your ability to stay firm and aloof from temptation and greed and exercise control on your anger, sexual urge and ego.* Your character is seen in observing your promises such as return of loans and favors. All these actions are covered under your moral behaviour and conduct. The most important factor is your commitment to complying and sticking to your words, job, mission and particularly your behaviour towards a person of opposite gender especially young ladies. In fact, it becomes the true test of your character when you treat ladies with honor, respect, regards and don't do any discrimination in work and promotion. Similarly, your commitment and faithfulness to your wife / husband or flirting elsewhere is an important part of your character. In fact, *your character is seen in your ability to control and staying away from five evils i.e. anger, sexual urge, greed, ego and envy.* Your character is measured in the degree of control you exercise on these evils and your personality gets the moral shine accordingly.

2. **Loyalty.** It means willing, faithful, dedicated and devoted attachment and support to a person or an issue or cause or superiors and subordinates. You will display your loyalty to your profession, organisation and its boss. Its scope is extended

to your family members, friends and society. *Loyalty is very important factor of your personal characteristics which determines your commitment, involvement and total responsibility for executing the job assigned to you and your truthful attachment to your superior officials.* In fact, loyalty determines another factor called *dependability*. It means that *loyalty implies dependability of your boss on you and dependability means your loyalty to your boss. So, both factors are interrelated.* It is pointed out that loyalty is a very *important trait factor that directly contributes to the overall productivity of your organisation as well as to you in your personal life. Remember that employers look for loyal persons and you will eventually get suitably rewarded for your loyalty.*

3. **Integrity**. It is another important trait of your character that *determines your ability to remain honest, steadfast, firm and upright against pressure from the evil sources.* It summons your moral strength and power to decide and accept good and justified cause. A person of high integrity will be truthful and have just honest approach in personal and official dealings. *He will not yield to pressure, temptation and corrupt practices and he stands firm and committed to his cherished principles and values. His vision and insight for observing and selecting right and impartial course is spontaneous and genuine. His courage of conviction and integrity to organisation, men you command and country is upheld in high esteem and becomes an important tribute to his character and personality.* In fact, all over and especially in defense services, integrity of high ranking officials matters a lot for keeping the organisational structure and its personnel morally strong and free from corrupt practices. *That is why the most important qualification set for selection of the Head for Central Vigilance Commission is " Impeachable Integrity " as well as it is set for top level officials in other services of Central and State Government.*

4. **Adherence to Values and Principles.** You hold certain values and principles in your behaviour, conduct, relation and performance. You try to adhere and uphold them under all types of circumstances. Thus, *you stay away from illegal, immoral and vicious practices and activities and you steer your way out with upright position and untarnished image.* Your approach and thinking on any issue is positive, clean and unbiased. *You don't like do anything which is immoral, unprincipled and unethical. So, adherence to values and principles becomes the moral strength of your character that takes you through the difficult time and situation.* In the process, you *earn the image and reputation in an organisation as a man of values and principles that becomes unique tribute to your character and personality. Incidentally, your boss or superior officers will think number of times before asking you to do a wrong or illegal job.*

5. **Impartial, Upright and Unbiased Approach.** You equally treat your subordinates, colleagues and friends and make no discrimination on the basis of cast, class, gender, position and level. You don't show your personal interest, bias or relation while deciding the matters before you. In this way, you uphold the rules, regulations and interest of your organisation in high esteem. Thus, you behave

and work in the most transparent manner and never leave a doubt about your impartial and unbiased character.

6. **Truthfulness and Frankness.** Truthfulness means that you speak truth. Your statement is based on facts and truth. You analyze the situation for finding the truth. You standby with a person who speaks truth. Your adherence to the truth under any circumstances earns credit and reputation for you in the public eye. Besides, *you remain at ease, composed and enjoy mental peace and tranquility.* You never show nervousness because you don't need to fabricate stories and find alibis. As a result, you don't carry any stress and tension. As far as frankness is concerned, you are straight forward and transparent in dealings. You don't hide anything and juggle with the facts which you present in a frank and truthful manner.

7. **Trust and Credibility.** This is another trait of your character where you command the trust of your subordinates, colleagues and friends. Your staff reposes trust in you for protecting them from external forces. Credibility means that the people believe in you without any hesitation and questioning. By virtue of your conduct and behaviour, you command credibility from the people for your actions and disposal of cases. It is entirely for you to demonstrate these traits of your character from your deeds, actions, performance and behaviour.

8. **Dependability.** This word implies a person who can be relied upon. It indicates intensity of involvement and consistency in executing the assigned tasks without supervision and willingness to accept additional duties and responsibilities. A dependable person is genuinely conscientious and willing to put additional efforts and time on a given task and ensure that it is honestly, correctly and truthfully done. In fact, dependable persons become an important asset to an organisation and establish an absolute faithful personal link with the boss who takes care of them for suitable awards.

To summarise, the above mentioned character traits are inborn and are referred to as *innate qualities*. They naturally form part of your character oriented personality. They therefore play an important role in giving qualitative and spiritual direction to your life. These are highly valued and demanded character traits from the executives, especially senior and high levels in any organisation, industry, defence and paramilitary services. In fact, your subordinates who display these traits or features are liked and respected by all for their moral and principled support and contributions.

Different Concepts of Character

The word, *'character'* conveys different *meanings* to different *classes of people*. Spiritual people think that every action and thought leaves an impression on our mind. These impressions will determine how you behave at a given moment and how you respond to a given situation. The sum total of all your impressions is what finally determines your character. Accordingly, all actions that you see around and all movements in the human society are simply the display of your thoughts and manifestation of your will and this will is caused by character which is in turn created by your karma. So, *karma and will together determines your character or your character drives your will and karma.* Thus, it displays two way relations. As far as the concept of impressions is concerned, they are formed from *SANSKARS (behavioural advice and teaching)* which you receive from your parents, relatives, friends around and the environment you are living in. They leave a stamp of impression which forms your character. It is then reflected in the form of your habits, actions and performance.

In philosophy, *character is linked with your destiny.* It means that destiny is determined by your character. In this respect, the following couplet is quoted for its significance :-

- Watch your Thoughts for they become Words
- Your Words for they become Actions
- Understand your Actions for they become your Habits
- Study and follow your Habits for they become your Character
- Develop your Character for it becomes your Destiny.

These spiritual and philosophical concepts of human character are complex and difficult to understand by a common man. You are not able to derive much benefit from your career point of view. What you need is the practical concept of the character that is commonly understood and projected in the identifiable form of specific positive attributes of your personal characteristics. Consequently, your character becomes the synergetic force of your certain positive attributes, thereby offering strong moral support, strength and power to your personality. As a result, *your personality gets a unique spiritual and philosophical weightage in a pragmatic manner.* The young generation has to realise the true meaning and importance of character in their life and how it helps them to control and gradually overcome five evils such as anger, sexual urge, greed, temptation, ego and envy as stated before during their service career.

Character *vs* Legacy

Legacy is something which is left behind for someone to remember and respect. A person who is transferred or retires or departs from this world finally leaves some impressions and memories behind for others to recollect and muse over. In the materialistic form, it could be wealth, land, property which don't have any meaning, value and impression in the eyes of the people because they are always doubtful about the ways of earning and amassing wealth. They always look at such persons with scornful view and have no sympathy for them. On the other hand, the people have generally respect for the persons who have character and who demonstrated their character through their performance and dignified conduct. Remember that it is your character that leaves behind everlasting impressions on the mind of the people about your niceties, image, grace, dignity and morality which eventually become guiding principles for others to follow. *It is said that you take your soul forward but leave the footprints of your character behind for others to get inspired and motivated to follow the examples of your good, moral, honest hard work and conduct.*

Time for Significance of Character

Frankly speaking, this word is not much important to your career at an early stage when you join the service and try to settle down on the job. While being a worker, performer, junior supervisor or engineer, you have practically no scope to show your character nor expected from you because you are handling a job of low responsibility. Your focus is on doing your job properly and gain experience for handling senior level jobs.

While you gain more service and assume senior level appointments through progressive promotions and finally become head of a section, group, team, department or later division, your responsibility and accountability tremendously increase along with your executive powers over large resources of manpower, money and materials. While exercising your power for effective and proper utilisation, you are of your own while interacting business with others. This is the time when your character comes to play its effective role in establishing your image, reputation and standing. *The quality of your performance is determined by your honest, hard work, dedication, leadership and social values.* During your executive period, your character plays an indirect silent role while exercising your executive powers over recruitment of manpower, procurement of materials and carrying out promotions of your people in the organisation. Besides, you have to stand against pressure from your superior officials. While discharging your different types of responsibilities, you form your image and establish a unique position in the whole hierarchy of your organisation. *You have to be consciously aware about this important silent and imperceptible domain of your personality*. Ultimately, you will earn high image, esteem and reputation of high integrity because of your positive character. Otherwise, you may indulge in mal-practices and damage your reputation because of your negative character.

Now, as you progressively advance in your service seniority and responsibilities, what should basically matter are *your feelings of self-satisfaction, happiness and peace of mind despite your status and position.* It is sometimes observed that high ranking executives are found disgruntled, disappointed, depressed, disheartened, some disgraced on account of corrupt practices and some unhappy, unsatisfied and left lonely. Had these persons strictly followed the dictates of their character and maintained it throughout their service period, they would not have landed in such a miserable state at the end of their career. They did not realise that the character of a person gives him tremendous mental strength, power and robustness and keeps him away from the bad, unhealthy and immoral practices. In fact, such persons should ponder over their past performance and ascertain whether they have observed and maintained the character in their service periods. So *finally, your happiness, satisfaction and mental peace are linked with your character.*

Role of Character in Promotion to Higher Ranks

As you see around the corruption cases filed against high ranking senior officers at the central and state Government levels, it is observed that these officials have the doubtful character. They could not fight against the evil of greed and temptation. Eventually, they became victim of their poor character as they lacked morality, loyalty and integrity at senior and high levels. That is how *the traits like loyalty, morality and integrity which indicate your basic character have become primary parameters for assessment of their suitability for promotion and selection to the high posts of position and appointment especially in critical areas.* You are aware that there is now the requirement of *"Impeachable Integrity"* for appointments of the heads of the organisations like Central Vigilance Commission (CVC), Central Bureau of Investigation (CBI), judges for high courts and supreme court. You don't suddenly achieve this state of impeachable integrity. You have to go through the successive stages of character evaluation at different levels of your promotion for reaching to the present high esteemed level . *It is your strong character that enables you to pass through the critical stages of your different jobs untarnished, unscratched and unblemished against heavy odds of pressure, temptations and challenges.* You maintain your moral strength and power that spreads around your strong reputation and uncorrupt image which is always held in high esteem. Consequently, your journey through the corridor of power and promotion becomes smooth and uneventful.

Concluding Remarks

While concluding, it is pointed out that *the character raises your spiritual level and moral strength which finally give you genuine pleasure, happiness and mental peace.* After all, these factors can't be earned by tons of money. You may earn name by virtue of your wealth and richness but it is not sustainable nor noticed and recognised by the public if it is not backed by your strong positive character.

It no doubt takes time to realise the fruits of your character but it *silently works in the background for building your image and reputation around.* The real importance of your character is seen from the period of your mid-service onwards when you have rendered sufficient service and achieved sufficient seniority. As a result, you are placed in the post of significant responsibility through a set of promotions. It should be noted that you will easily distinguish persons on the basis of wealth, property but it takes time to distinguish them on the basis of their character.

Now, the importance of your character is seen from the following couplet :-

- **If wealth is lost, nothing is lost**
- **If health is lost, a few things are lost.**
- **If time is lost, something is lost.**
- **But, if character is lost, everything is lost.**

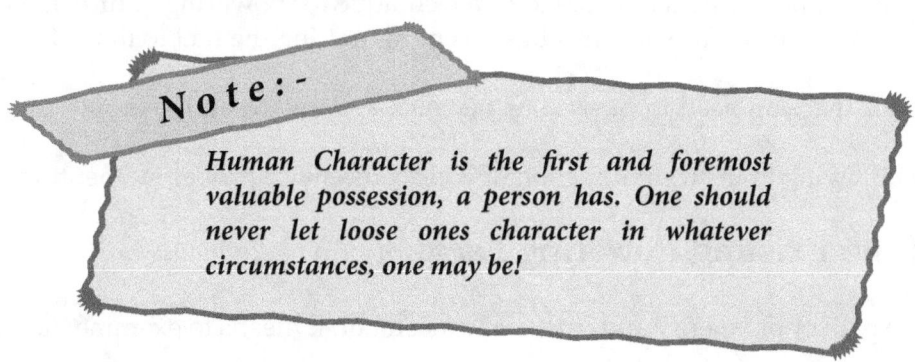

Note:-

Human Character is the first and foremost valuable possession, a person has. One should never let loose ones character in whatever circumstances, one may be!

CHAPTER - 14

EMPOWERING YOUR PERSONALITY

▪Abstract▪

E

pleasure, satisfaction and mental peace. In fact, empowerment focuses on the power of

entirely your desire, willpower and determination for adopting empowerment of your

---

Meaning

empowerment with respect the spiritual aspect of your personality? These are some of the questions and doubts in your mind pertaining to this topic. Let us examine its various aspects in the succeeding paragraphs.

At the onset, empowerment appears to be a technique for powering your personality and give it a push to move forward. It is like an engine getting the fuel to move forward.

What it implies that you need to push your personality forward and it should function

and you keep moving in the right direction of your choice with proper momentum.

Status of the Existing Powering Factors

you along the path of prosperity and career advancement. It means to examine the status of your existing constitutional parameters and ascertain their present grades or strengths with a view to find out whether it is sufficient for powering your personality forward. This exercise is done in the self-introspective mode by adopting the technique of self-assessment and self-appraisal. So, let us examine the status of the following important positive powering traits as under :-

    (a) Setting of a goal / objective / ambition- Have you set up any goal / mission for final achievement?

    (b) Vision- Do you have any forward looking ability with clarity?

    (c) Drive – Do you possess inner force for pushing you forward voluntarily?

    (d) Will-power – Do you have intrinsic desire and how strong is it?

    (e) Motivation – Do you get self-inspiration from within or outside for pushing you forward?

    (f) Focus and Determination – how is your concentration level and do you remain firm on your decision?

    (g) Positive Attitude and Thinking – How do you interact with others ad state of your relationship?

    (h) Responsiveness – How do you react to inputs and feedback and what is your assimilation level?

    (i) Hard work – Your readiness and capacity to work hard and sustain your stamina and tenacity.

Classification for Empowering

These are the specific positive attributes of your personality which determine its state and capacity for pushing it forward in an empowered manner. Now, these attributes are essential and have to be present within you and their present grade or strength will indicate the present status. Accordingly, their present level could be classified as High or Moderate or Poor. Alternatively, *it could be high or average or low. Consequently, your personality could be classified as Highly Powered or Moderately Powered or Poorly Powered.*

After the present state of various powering sources of your personality is revealed, you can effectively undertake the exercise of self-empowerment. It amounts to pushing you from your poorly powered state to moderately powered state or taking moderately powered state to highly powered state and so on. Or, it directs you to focus your efforts on those parameters which need boost from their present poor / average state. So, *there is a slow transformation from one state to another once the basic level of powering factors is measured and established.* In a way, *this exercise enables you to determine amount of your efforts, required for empowering your personality.* Of course, your efforts will depend upon intensity of your desire about the level of empowerment required by you. *This is the only rational and logical way for effectively doing empowerment instead of just listening to general advice and then getting nowhere.*

As stated earlier, the amount of efforts required for empowering will depend upon the present level of powering sources and the intensity of your desire. When you move from poor to the moderate state, you obviously need to put in enormous efforts for improving the strength of the concerned parameters. Now, the basic question is whether a person having poor powering parameters wish to empower his personality. It is generally observed that the persons with poor grade of these attributes have no desire and life mission and they are reconciled to their present state of living. Even among the educated lot of youngsters, you do not find the tendency for causing empowerment of their present personality because they have moderate expectations and aspirations.

Once, you decide to empower your personality because of your intense desire, you have to enhance the speed of various powering parameters so that the exercise of your empowerment move expeditiously in the right direction *with due regard to control on speed and safety.* This precaution is required for making the entire exercise meaningful and successful and you should be able *to keep your engine on the right track and never allow it to jump off the track by reckless driving and enthusiasm for reaching your destination at the earliest.*

Safety Measures

Now, you can think of applying certain safety measures in the form of adopting some norms, such as values and principles. *These safety guards are necessary for keeping your career advance on the right track otherwise you may land up in a state of frustration, disappointment, disgrace and depression despite having achieved high rank, position and fortunes. There are numerous examples of high ranking officials who are found in frustrated, disappointed and lonely state on retirement. They have no friends, get no regards from the society members and receive no help and cooperation from anyone. These people have overlooked code of conduct, duties, obligations and maintained high profile in a distasteful, egoistic, arrogant and unfriendly manner. They might have adopted unfair means and mal-practices during the period of their career advancement.*

Hence, there is a need for you to adopt the *moral values and principles* which will glorify the image of your personality in the public domain. What are those values and principles that will really empower your personality and always keep you on the *glorified track of reputation, happiness and peace.*

Values

Values are general beliefs based on the accepted norms and mode of conduct. These are followed as global tenets that guide action and judgment under variety of favorable and unfavorable situations. Values lay foundation for understanding attitude and perception of a person towards others while working on the job. These values are applicable in various fields like personal, educational, professional, civil society, etc.

The list of such values which may *act as your powerful guide and motivate you to perform highly disciplined and principled career and life activities is given below.* Your performance will certainly get grace and dignity and your personality will eventually get glorified in the public eye.

1. Truthfulness, frankness, straightforwardness
2. Discipline, compliance and obedience
3. Dedication and commitment to work, organisation and subordinates
4. Selfless service, helpfulness and supportive attitude
5. Orgnisational interest, loyalty and integrity
6. Respect for elders, seniors, advisors and persons with knowledge and wisdom
7. Equality of gender, cast, creed and religion
8. Uprightness, fairness and social justice in relations and official dealings
9. Politeness, courtesy, gentleness and humility
10. Care, share and respect for work, tools, machines and workers
11. Urge for knowledge and development of professional and management skills
12. Softness, clarity and firmness in expression and addressing
13. Playfuness, team-spirit and cooperative attitude
14. Conviction in the God and truth
15. Gratitude, appreciation and grace in criticisms

By following the above stated values, the life you lead gets *meaning, dignity, grace* and *quality* and thus become empowered.

Principles

Principles are set guidelines for conducting your life activities according to the rules and procedures which are laid or traditional or conventional. The list of the principles is given below :-

1. Follow the rules, regulations and procedure as laid down by the authorities
2. No questioning of the authority of the management and boss
3. Focus on excellence in performance and quality of job
4. Be honest, sincere and truthful in relationship and dealings
5. Equality, secularity and respectfulness
6. Disposal of work and liabilities dutifully, timely and sincerely without reminder.
7. Continuos learning and updating of professional knowledge
8. Stay away from in-house politics and hostile union activities
9. Stay away from flattery, falsehood and exaggerations
10. Stay away from vices, bad company and corrupt persons

These principles have to do much with your mental, emotional and psychic approach. Whenever you follow values and principles, it indirectly reflects on your positive attributes and their manifestations. Values and principles exercise indirect control on your behaviour, conduct, relation and performance.

Etiquette and Manners

In addition to values and principles, there is a code of social behaviour within a society which is unwritten and self-enforceable. *This code is reflected in your civic sense, morality, convention and traditional practices. They reflect your positive attitude, positive mindset and positive approach while interacting with different types of persons in your daily life.* Since these are related to traditional practices and conventions, it is better to fully understand them and should not follow them blindly without critically examining them for their suitability, usefulness and rationality. Typical etiquette that should generally be observed in your daily personal and official life are given below :-

1. Meet and greet people with 'Hello' and smile on your face.
2. Introduce yourself with a handshake or traditional salutation like NAMASKAR
3. Address a particular fellow politely as 'Sir', 'Mr.' or 'Madam'.
4. Say 'Thank You' if someone does a favour to you.
5. Say sorry if you hurt someone inadvertently.
6. Don't interrupt the speaker and when you wish to, say excuse me and seek permission.
7. Be punctual to attend a function or a meeting or programme.
8. Hold the door open for ladies when you accompany them.
9. Dress properly so as to suit an occasion.
10. Keep your body movements under control while discussing or speaking.

As regards the manners, *they are indicators of your dignified behaviour and civilised conduct. They indicate the strength of your character and not a sign of weakness.* Manners create an everlasting impression on the people you meet. Mannerism makes your personality conducive, effective and graceful. Typical social manners that are identified as good, noble manners are given below :-

1. Say, 'Thank You' for a favour and 'sorry' when mistaken or wronged.
2. Don' talk ill of others.
3. If you are wrong or commit a mistake, accept it gracefully and apologise.
4. Appreciate a person in public and criticise in private.
5. Avoid use of abusive and sarcastic words or remarks or comments during a conversation.
6. Say, 'please' or 'excuse' me if you wish to make a point.
7. Never read the letters or mail of others and don't show interest in others affairs.
8. Whenever guests come to your home, welcome them by opening the door and see them off personally.
9. During parties, take your food along with the guests.

These are the etiquettes and manners which primarily serve the purpose of getting respect and regards from the public and team members. *They indicate your civic sense and strength of your character.* Your personality becomes distinct and impressive when you are complying with the etiquette and manners. In fact, you become confident in projection of your business activities and develop personal rapport with important persons. You receive much credibility and limelight in the corporate world. You create positive impact of your personality and its grooming by virtue of your *enriched and empowered behaviour, conduct and performance* while managing your career.

Concluding Remarks

Empowerment enhances the strength, potential and quality of your personality. It has much to do with your mental, emotional and psychic improvement. There is no doubt about the direct results of your positive attributes which definitely put you on the progressive path of your ambition and achievement of your objectives. *Your personality will not shine and glorify unless it goes through the process of empowerment.*

Empowerment is considered as part of your spiritual domain because you get real peace of mind and happiness by complying with it. You are distinguished from others only on the strength and quality of your personality. *You occupy unique position of dignity and repute in the public eye on the basis of spiritual aspects of your personality. Your word carries the weight and credit.* Your personality is seen as ideal. Thus, *you are able to exercise and leave behind unique impact and impression of your personality on others.*

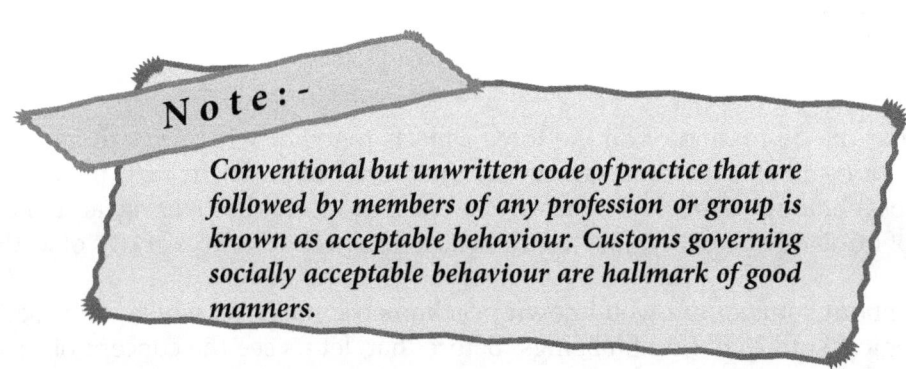

Note:-
Conventional but unwritten code of practice that are followed by members of any profession or group is known as acceptable behaviour. Customs governing socially acceptable behaviour are hallmark of good manners.

CHAPTER - 15

DISCOVERING YOUR PERSONALITY FOR MEASUREMENT & SELF-PROJECTION

Abstract

Discovering your personality and assessing grade of its various characteristics is the most important practical step if you wish to carry out its effective development. It also helps you to project your personality in an impressive and convincing manner thereby highlighting your positive qualities and potential. You can match your personality with the employer's service requirements thereby helping both of you. There are different methods for measuring your personality. Some are of the subjective nature, based on the psychometric testing and some are of objective nature of which one is based on the

out your Self Qualifying Factors. After the exercise of discovering is over, you are in a position to write a realistic and pragmatic report on your personality according to the format given therein. You thus get an objective projection and assessment of your personality and its soft skills which you can effectively use for developing and successfully managing your career.

Approach

conducting the discussion of all the three aspects together whereby you get the whole perspective of all the three aspects in an integrated manner. In fact, in the books of human psychology, there is a concurrent discussion on discovering and measuring aspects of human personality. Just to emphasize the special features of two objectives and

mention about some of the well-known psychometric methods which are based on the psychological studies of human beings. Before that, let us see the concept of measuring personality

Concept of Measuring

Measuring is a method used for knowing the quantitative aspect of any physical entity

parameters or characteristics by grading them in the form of levels for carrying out comparative assessment. In case of human personality, it is not possible to physically weigh its parameters Hence whatever measuring technique is used, it is *aimed at measuring in a subjective manner like saying, very good, good, moderate, poor, none or specifying on a quantitative scale of -4 to 0 to +4 thereby covering the entire range of personal attributes of both positive and negative types.*

Purpose

The primary purpose of measuring is to *evaluate your personality in the public domain* so that :-

(a) Employers can carry out comparative assessment for selection.

(b) You can identify strong and weak points of your personality for enhancing or remedial purpose.

(c) You conduct yourself in a confident, dignified and graceful manner in interviews, seminars and conferences.

(d) You are able to probe the employment market as per your dominant abilities.

(e) You are able to write your bio-data and project yourself in a confident, realistic and effective manner

By measuring personality, you are able to appreciate the fact that people behave and act differently because everyone has different individualistic values and strengths. Thus, *measuring becomes the key technique for unlocking your attributes in a realistic manner so that you are able to undertake the programme of personality development career and business opportunities and professional training programmes accordingly.* Without measuring your personality, any exercise of self-development or career selection and management can be frustrating.

Personality Testing

There are a number of personality testing systems for assessing your personality. They are used to determine personality features, motivation, behaviour, learning and performance styles. These tests are administered in recruitment, screening, training, counseling and development. It is no doubt a highly skilled area and it should be properly conducted, interpreted and assessed by the person who conducts testing operation. Just to assure yourself and avoid possibility of misjudgment, *emphasis is given on self-assessment and self-appraisal process in which you carry out these tests on yourself by self-interrogation.* Keeping this aspect in view, all efforts are made *for projecting this introspective technique in such a way that with a little guidance, you are able to carry out self-testing and self-assessment in an effective and unbiased manner.* Since you are reporting to yourself, you will definitely be realistic and truthful in self-assessment.

Psychometric Tests

These tests are evolved from the psychological viewpoint and are based on the human psychology. As such, they are profusely mentioned in the books on psychology. Some of the popular tests are briefly mentioned below for evaluating psychological background.

Myers-Briggs Type Indicator (MBTI)

This is a personality test based on Carl Jung's theory of psychological traits. It was later modified to project mental outlook structure for identifying human preferences on the basis of human psychology. This test is used in group dynamics, career exploration, employee recruitment, leadership training, marriage counseling and personal development. In this test, the basic factors which are considered for indicating human mental aspect are as under :-

Extroversion (E)	Introversion (I)
Sensing (S)	intuition (N)
Thinking (T)	Feeling (F)
Judging (J)	Perceiving (P)

Combinations are formed as Extraversion/Introversion, Sensing/Intuition, Thinking/Feeling and Judging/Perceiving. As they form two distinct groups each of four factors, total combinations so formed from these two mutually exclusive groups are sixteen, each combination indicating the specific mental aspect of a human being from psychological viewpoint. So, you are able to get sixteen different categories of human beings and you can identify a specific person on the basis of a particular combination as indicated by the test during assessment.

The terms extrovert/introvert refers to the attitude of a person and show how he receives inward energy or flows out his energy. Sensing/Intuition are the perceiving functions for receiving data either from outside or from his sub-conscious mind. Thinking/feeling are judgemental functions and both make rational decision by using data received from above sources. Judging/perceiving reveal the specific attitude and dominance of other factors in a particular combination.

With this brief explanation about the constituent parts of this indicator, there are sixteen unique combinations, each having four letters for giving its own descriptive name, meaning and indicating interaction among them. It finally identifies identity of a person from others in the mental domain of his personality. However, its scope is limited in fully projecting your personality because these are the functional factors of your mental domain from psychological viewpoint and not its traits and characteristics which actually need to be tested and assessed.

16 Personality Factors (16 PF)

16 PF stands for 16 personality factors or source traits that were identified by Raymond Cattell in 1940 as being the main set of factors whereby a person could be classified and identified. These were derived from an analysis of personality describing traits which were eventually reduced to 16 numbers. In this method, the focus is to identify innate characteristics without thinking of their applications. The Cattell's theory asserts that every person possesses a degree of each of the following sixteen traits :-

- Warmth, Reasoning, Emotional Stability, Dominance, Liveliness,
- Rule Consciousness, Social Boldness, Sensitivity, Vigilance, Abstractness,
- Privateness, Apprehension / Apprehensiveness, Openness to Change,
- Perfectionism, Self-Reliance, Tension.

Incidentally, 16 PF is one of the longest standing and most widely used personality testing system and has much wider scope and relevance for measuring human personality in a realistic manner than any other system.

Objective Method

So far, the above methods are based on the studies of psychology and mentioned with a view to highlight the efforts of eminent psychologists for probing and measuring human personality. The methods are used on a large scale because of its psychological background. However on deeply examining, *these methods do not cover a wide spectrum of human attributes of both positive and negative types and project the real strength of human nature, character, behaviour, relation, talent and performance. Besides, they are not objective in projecting the real picture of their soft skills for assessment in the present competitive employment market.*

I propose to offer a different type of approach for discovering a wide range of human traits and projecting them in an objective manner. I have developed two methods for objective projection as under :-

(a) In the form of *introspective questionnaire, for getting psychological insight into your personality that cover* mental, emotional, psychic, intellectual and physical traits of your personality and judging for assessment by grading them on the scale of four levels such as -4, -3, -2, -1, 0, 1, 2, 3, 4 which cover the traits of both positive and negative types.

(b) In the form of **Self Qualifying Factors,** each covering a set of certain attributes in a synergetic form for depicting your *soft skills,* each as a specific quality factor of your personality that is applicable for describing both of positive and negative nature.

The above methods are evolved for measuring personality in such a way that you not only discover your personality but also effectively project it for marketing purpose. Besides, they are realistic in the sense that they are based on your own self-addressed exercise in which you carry your self-assessment and self-appraisal. So, you remain the key player for judgment in these methods and no third party is involved nor you are required to report to any outside agency. So, your self-judgment and assessment are definitely realistic, rational and logical.

Introspective Questionnaire – A Step by Step Approach

In this method, a set of questions under different heads are designed in order to *demonstrate your mental, emotional and intellectual response and action during your performance and*

normal lifetime activities. It is thus possible to determine your attitude, mindset, thinking power and approach in life. Consequently, you set your objectives, vision and views about people around and conduct performance and life activities accordingly. You are advised to carefully study and examine these questions and then state the grade on the basis of a scale -4, -3, -2. -1, 0, 1, 2, 3, 4. This scale covers the entire range of both positive and negative attributes in the form of :-

- **Excellent, very good, good/average, poor or none -- on the positive side**
- **Very frequently, frequently, moderate, seldom or none – on the negative side.**

Remember that 4 is the highest grade on the positive side and -4 is the worst grade on the negative side. You should now judiciously assess your attribute and its grade in the form of its strength, intensity or severity. A step by step approach is given for carrying out progressive assessment. Consequently, you set your objectives and vision and look upon the people and environment around from your perceptions and viewpoints formed thereof.

First Step A – Discover Your Personal Attributes

To start with, take a comprehensive look at your personal nature, character, behaviour in a careful manner and ascertain whether you are :

1. A temperamental person, i.e., you change your mood and react in a tense, irritating and reactive manner when confronted with a difficult situation?
2. An angry person who often loses temper and express your anger in a harsh, loud, Impolite and abusive manner?
3. A warm, lively and cheerful person such that you are caring, sympathetic, concerned, fun loving and energetic towards life?
4. A emotionally stable and adaptive mature person?
5. A socially bold, unhesitating, risk taking, courageous, reformist person?
6. A dominating, forceful, assertive, stubborn and combative person?
7. A person who is open to reasoning, criticism, feedback, remarks and comments and takes in a sportive and educative manner?
8. A judicious, perceptive, sensible, intuitive and forward looking person?
9. A reliable, dependable, resourceful and responsible person?
10. A privacy liking, reserved, shrewd, diplomatic, polished, astute, or forthright, straight, naïve and unpretentious person?
11. An apprehensive, self-doubting, worrying, cautious or casual, complacent and self-satisfied person?
12. A self-controlled, self-driven, conscious person who doesn't need instructions from others?
13. A rule conscious, law abiding, dutiful, conscientious and moralistic person or freelancing, self-indulgent and expedient person?

14. An open to change, flexible, analytical and critical person or traditional, conservative and rigid type person?
15. A practical, task and result oriented person or idealistic, advising, supervising and elusive person?
16. A decisive, firm, focused and independent thinking person or evasive, delaying, casual and dependent person?

Second Step B - Self-Description for Effective Projection

1. A level-headed or idealistic
2. A spontaneous or systematic
3. An open or reflective
4. A factual or conceptual
5. A knowledgeable or understanding
6. An adaptable or organized
7. An expansive or intensive
8. A down-to-earth or imaginative
9. A questioning or questing
10. An enthusiastic or deliberate
11. An all-rounder or deep and specific
12. A reasoned or spirited
13. An open-ended or goal-oriented
14. A straight-forward or reserved
15. A realistic or visionary
16. An ambitious or goal-oriented
17. A service-oriented or value and principled oriented
18. A generous and kind-hearted or reasonable and logical
19. An instinctive or deliberate
20. An emphatic on knowledge or experience and exposure
21. An introvert or extrovert in outlook and approach
22. A sensitive or sensible
23. A thoughtful or cautious
24. Dominative or assertive

Third Step C - Social Interactive Behaviour and Performance

In this step, you are advised to take a close and careful look at your personal behaviour and select from the multiple choices one or two as applicable for your real feelings and reactions.

1. **Whenever anything which you dislike happens, how do you feel?**
(a) Irritated
(b) Disturbed
(c) Awkward
(d) Indifferent

2. **How do you show your displeasure?**
(a) Irritation
(b) Keeping silent and mum
(c) Incoherent body movement
(d) Expressing bad remarks

3. **Do you get angry? How?**
(a) Often
(b) Seldom
(c) Rarely
(d) Not at all

4. **How do you express your anger?**
(a) By shouting
(b) Getting red-faced and making quick eyeball movements
(c) Violent movement of hands and body parts
(d) Expressing abusive words.

5. **When you meet new people, how do you respond?**
(a) Initiate to talk and then listen
(b) Talk as much as listen
(c) Listen more
(d) Wait others to talk and then keenly respond

6. **How do you characterise your approach to life?**
(a) Casual
(b) Serious
(c) Responsible
(d) So-so

7. **How would you like to behave?**
(a) A calm and cool-headed
(b) Patient and logical
(c) Warm and understanding
(d) Quiet and unresponsive

8. **Whenever you see a funeral procession, how do you feel?**
(a) Irritated for causing obstruction

(b) Courteous and bow
(c) Halt and offer prayer for the departed soul
(d) Look other way and pass

9. **What are you good at?**
(a) Focus on the task till done
(b) Shift approach and act
(c) Cross the bridge when it comes
(d) Plan and organize

10. **What type of social life you prefer?**
(a) With many friends and acquaintances
(b) A few persons that you feel close and connected to you
(c) Selected like-minded persons
(d) Family members only or mix of family members and close friends

11. **What type of motive do you have in social life?**
(a) Pleasure and relief
(b) Relaxation and rest
(c) Personal interest
(d) Support and patronage

12. **What type of job do you like better?**
(a) Doing yourself
(b) Supervising
(c) Organizing and managing
(d) Advising and counselling

13. **When you come across a stone on your way, what will you do?**
(a) Overlook and pass
(b) Halt but ignore
(c) Halt, see and pass
(d) Halt, pick up and throw aside

14. **How do you observe a situation?**
(a) Casually and indifferently
(b) Closely and sharply
(c) Deeply and in an involved manner
(d) Lightly and impersonally

15. **How will you take a decision?**
(a) Impulsively of your own

(b) By consulting others
(c) By observing the situation
(d) Instantly and intuitively

16. **How will you deal with your subordinates?**
(a) Cordially and amicably
(b) Friendly and comrade like
(c) Authoritatively and forcefully
(d) Autocratically and dictatorial way

17. **How will you look up to your boss?**
(a) Master and controller
(b) Guide and advisor
(c) Expert and matured
(d) Obstacle and enemy like

18. **How will you look up to your job and performance?**
(a) A source of income and livelihood
(b) Career and prospective ladder
(c) Experience and exposure
(d) Learning and knowledge source.

19. **When you visit a restaurant with your friends and the bill is presented for payment, how do you react?**
(a) Sit unconcerned
(b) Wait for someone to pay
(c) Show your initiative to pay
(d) Snatch the bill for payment

20. **When you receive the call for an important interview but you find your father seriously ill and needs your support, what will you do?**
(a) Hesitant to leave
(b) Request your friends or relatives to take care
(c) Leave straightaway for attending interview
(d) Ignore the interview call and stay for personally caring your father.

21. **When you are given the specific task for timely completion, how will you proceed?**
(a) Take it casually
(b) Complete at your ease and convenience
(c) Complete but will not bother to report
(d) Complete in a responsible manner within time and report completion.

22. **How will you deal with your organisation and its boss?**
(a) Casually and indifferently
(b) Seriously with sense of responsibility
(c) Religiously and spiritually
(d) Devotedly with loyalty and integrity

23. **Suppose you reach the senior, higher and perhaps, the top post in your service career, what will be your priority?**
(a) Focus on the job
(b) Stay and maintain your position
(c) Focus on your personal interest
(d) Relations and togetherness

It should be noted that answers to the above questionnaire reveal and project *true psychic picture of your personality constitution from all points of view. In this step by step approach, you will definitely display your inborn thinking, temperament, intelligence, sense of responsibility, loyalty, adaptability, mindset etc.* In fact, such a self-interrogation process enables you to do true introspection of yourself and carry out self-assessment and self-appraisal sincerely and honestly. Here in this process, you are not answerable to any outside agency but to yourself. It is now entirely up to you to take necessary and timely remedial and corrective steps if you observe any mental, emotional or psychological weaknesses and deficiencies in your personality structure and its organisation. *Such a wise and thoughtful step by step self interrogation for measuring your personality will consequently put you on the progressive and prospective career path.*

You are however advised to conduct this exercise in a careful, unbiased, thoughtful and judicious manner and don't draw any hasty conclusion. In fact, you should take your own time and seek advice from the competent persons whenever in doubt.

Discovering Self-Qualifying Factors (SQF)

This is another effective method for discovering and measuring your personality in the form of your personal characteristics which have functional and operational roles in your nature, character and performance Each Self Qualifying Factor represents a group of your certain personal qualities in a synergetic form and it becomes an indicator of a particular functional factor of your specific nature, character, behaviour or performance. *This method is evolved on the basis of my experience while dealing with personnel of all ranks at junior, senior and high levels. These qualifying factors in fact represent soft skills which are integral part of your personality and are projected in the form of perceptible, identifiable and relevant measurable entities.* They represent specific innate qualitative aspects of your personality. Since you get a different functional and operational outlook of your personality, it becomes an objective assessment of your personality as *it reveals your real strength, weakness, abilities, aptitude and attitude in a realistic manner.*

Another significant advantage which you get in this approach is that most of the needs and expectations of the employers are indirectly reflected in them. There is no need to assess separately as each self qualifying factor is self contained in its meaning, purpose and function. *These self qualifying factors adequately represent your potential, abilities, talent, skills, character traits and performance that convey the qualitative aspects of your inner personality in a truly synergetic form for establishing your specific identity which can be properly and skillfully marketed in the present competitive environment.*

Given Below is a list of 22 Self-Qualifying Factors which represent soft skills of your personality. These are briefly stated in the succeeding paragraphs along with their meanings and functions :

1. Self-Image Factor

It indicates your opinion about your personality, behaviour, conduct, performance and expression. It pertains to your mind and its thinking power to form opinion and impression about yourself and directs your body movements accordingly. It is the result of your thought process which is directed in a particular way because of your strong sense, belief, understanding and concepts that are centred round you.

2. Self-Esteem Factor

It is also called *Self Respect Factor* which projects your pride, ego, dignity, liking, disliking. It indicates your feelings about your behaviour, performance, relations and conduct in your personal as well as public life by virtue of following certain values, principles, etiquette and ethos in life. It represents a group of attributes such as morality, consciousness, sensibility, egoistic, demanding, indulgence, assertiveness and introvert outlook.

3. Self-Tolerance Factor

It indicates capacity to bear up to a certain threshold level that can be improved by proper training, exercise and upbringing. It affects your behaviour, performance and relations whenever specific level is exceeded. It is a group of attributes such as sensitivity, sincerity, maturity, responsiveness, anger and envy.

4. Self-Mindset Factor

It pertains to your mental attitude, approach, outlook and thoughts. It is the direct result of your mental faculties which are activated by slight impulsive act. It is reflected in your behaviour, conduct and performance. It affects your attitude which may be positive or negative, optimistic or pessimistic. It plays significant role in your behaviour and forming relations. It reflects on your temperament, impulsiveness, possessiveness, sociability, cheerfulness and sensitivity.

5. Self-Temperamental Factor

It indicates state of your mind and displays your mood, feelings, temper, anger, passions in visible form. It reflects off balance state of your body and mind. It adversely affects your behaviour, conduct and relations and creates uncertainty and unpleasant situation. It represents a group of attributes such as anger, indifference, restlessness, passions, impatience and sensitivity.

6. Self-Ego Factor

It means how much you show off and think of yourself as the sole contributor and achiever. It is an indication of excessive pride and self esteem. There is an excessive talk about your achievements with little mention of your subordinates or seniors. It is an effort to do self praising and eulogizing. It represents a group of attributes such as self pride, over confidence, arrogance, possessiveness, rudeness and indulgence.

7. Self-Negation Factor

It indicates your attitude of backwardness, conservative and negative outlook and thoughts. It shows unwillingness to change habits and adapt to new way of life style. It indulges in criticizing others for their reforms and changes. Such persons are senile and sulky and create obstruction in progress. It represents a group of qualities such as sulkiness, rigidity, senile attitude, stubbornness, obstinacy, introvert and adamancy.

8. Self-Diligence Factor

It indicates your capacity to work hard steadily, consistently, persistently, sincerely and honestly. It reflects on your stamina to work hard and cope up its rigor. It involves your dedication, devotion and willingness. It represents a group of attributes such as stamina, tenacity, dedication, perseverance and consistency.

9. Self-Intelligence Factor (I.Q.)

It indicates your intelligence level and pertains to your mental process of understanding, comprehension, judgment, reasoning and assimilation. It determines selection of high profile courses and careers and affects your performance in annual examinations. It is a highly significant factor for going through written competitive examinations. It represents a group of attributes such as intellect, responsiveness, initiative, awareness, reasoning, willingness, memory, hardworking and self responsibility.

10. Self-Response Factor

It pertains to your ability to react to a situation willingly and quickly. It indicates your mental awareness and alertness in a positive manner and enables you to store and assimilate information for expression in verbal and written manner. It is responsible for learning and gaining knowledge and wisdom. It improves your professional and management skills and is mainly responsible for your development. It represents a group of attributes such as alertness, awareness, initiative, willingness, hardworking, attentiveness, focus grasp and concentration.

11. Self-Learning Factor

It indicates your knowledge about your service, profession, skills and urges to improve it further. It is a way to gain information and knowledge and comfortably stand in interviews and competitions. It enables to learn new skills and keep updating. It represents a group of attributes such as urge, keenness, ingenuity, responsiveness, vision, adaptability, maturity and hard work.

12. Self-Performance Factor

It indicates functional and action oriented approach and is visible and usually assessed by supervisory officials. It is a self reliant and self oriented activity. It is an individual, group or team act. It is your effective performance which is responsible for your growth. Performance results from a large number of personal attributes such as initiative, hard work, will power, willingness, responsibility, awareness, dedication, team spirit and so on. .

13. Self-Dependability Factor

It means how much you depend upon others to do and complete a job. It forms part of one's character and integrity and stands for credibility and trustworthiness. It indicates your implicit responsibility, faith, involvement and how you are able to generate confidence about your work without supervision. It is a reflection on your attributes such as honesty, loyalty, integrity, dedication, reliability, devotion and credibility.

14. Self-Confidence Factor

It indicates trust and belief in yourself. It reveals your mental power, strength, potential, abilities and talent. It is an important parameter for determining success in your mission and implies your courage, planning skill, moral strength and vision for facing risks and challenges. It is based on many attributes such as hardworking, will power, visionary outlook, positive mindset, courage, awareness, initiative and boldness.

15. Self-Endurance Factor

It indicates your capacity to endure and bear physical stress and strain, hardships without bending or breaking. It reveals your physical fitness and sound health. It determines your physical fitness and mental robustness. It overcomes stress and strain of any hard and laborious mission. It represents your stamina, tenacity, fitness, energy and strength.

16. Self-Time Management Factor

It indicates your awareness and consciousness about time, its usage and management while performing your duties, responsibilities and obligations. It reveals your awareness about completion schedule of your job and responsibility and keeps monitoring progress of activities. Economic use of resources and manpower depends upon managing your time and its control on working-progress. It represents your attributes such as consciousness, vision, foresight, awareness, patience, attentiveness.

17. Self-Business/Entrepreneurship Factor

It is basically a self dependant and self act oriented parameter and pertains to carrying out own business or self service. It enables you to pursue an independent way of life with your efforts and resources. You definitely need an aptitude to do business along with some prior experience and exposure. It represents a group of attributes such as vision, ambition, awareness, responsiveness, patience, persuasiveness calmness, negotiating skill, alertness and decisiveness.

18. Self-Driven Factor

It is basically a self-motivational factor that indicates your sense of doing some meaningful activity of your own. Some proactive forces within you act willingly and push you to act with an urge and keenness. Such persons work without supervision and with an extreme sense of responsibility. It represents a group of attributes such as motivation, urge, responsiveness, keenness, alertness, willingness, will power, creativity, vision, spontaneity.

19. Self-Mission Factor

It indicates your urge, drive and determination to execute an assigned task successfully. It reveals your planning and focused approach with firmness of mind and dedication. It involves team work with cooperative and team spirit. It represents a group of attributes such as drive, firmness, determination, team spirit, cooperation, dedication, foresight and ambition.

20. Self-Leadership Factor

You lead a project / mission or group or team for achievement of the given objective by scheduled time. Leadership carries unique responsibility and accountability for success as well as failure. A leader plans the work and meticulously execute by leading a team of members with full cooperation and team spirit. Leadership includes a very large number of positive attributes.

21. Self-Communication Factor

It is basically a social factor and indicates your relationship and interaction with others and the way you communicate with them. It involves exchange of information, data and work experience and also group discussion, brain storming session. It reflects on your capacity to listen patiently and express verbally and in writing. It represents a group of attributes such as politeness, adaptable, accommodativeness, flexibility, sensibility, responsiveness, sociability and keenness.

22. Self-Organising Factor

It is basically administrative in nature and aims for ascertaining your abilities for organizing events, functions, meetings, sports, ceremony, etc. It involves dealings and interaction with other departments and employing diverse resources. It covers a large scope of activities. It represents a large number of positive attributes which may belong to different qualifying factors

It is observed that these 22 SQF (Self Qualifying Factors) when measured on the scale as stated above *offer you a realistic, distinctly identifiable and measurable picture of yourself. It enables you to know strong and weak areas of your personality.* You can always highlight your strong points or you can take timely corrective actions for overcoming weaknesses in your personality. In fact, this is the main purpose of discovering and measuring your personality so that you can take timely remedial action for correction.

Writing Report on Your Personality

Having discovered and measured various aspects of your personality by using the above stated objective techniques, you are now in a position to write a comprehensive and extensive report on your personality as per the format given in Annexure 1 attached. *Such a report prepared by you reveals your strengths and weaknesses, attitude, tendency, thinking, confidence level, behaviour, performance level and so on.* It closely reflects on your personality and you are able to deeply look into yourself and get the firsthand realistic information through your own efforts. You can proceed for writing a comprehensive personal report .

Now, you have full report before you giving the comprehensive picture of your personality. You can note your strong points and list out drawbacks and weak points of your personality. It is now entirely up to you to draw a comprehensive programme for the development of your personality with emphasis on taking appropriate remedial actions for overcoming and controlling your drawbacks and correcting weak areas. This is how your personal report will effectively serve the objective of your personality development and derive the best advantages thereof.

Concluding Remarks

In this chapter, I have covered three aspects of your personality in the form of discovery, measurement and projection for projecting and self-marketing your personality in the present competitive environment. I have mentioned psychometric methods which are practiced for measuring human personality mainly from psychological viewpoint. Keeping in view their limitations, I have mentioned two objective methods which are based on self-introspective technique for seeking self-assessment and self-appraisal in a realistic and effective manner. In fact, both methods are definitely applicable for discovering and measuring full range of your personality. At the same time, *they give you objective presentation of your soft skills which you have to use for successfully managing your career.*

Remember that there is nothing pious and dignified other than discovering yourself through introspection. Self discovery is the only effective method that enables you to carry out real personality development and successful career management.

> **Note:-**
> *Refer to the Author's book 'DISCOVERING YOUR PERSONALITY FOR MANAGING YOUR CAREER' Published by S. CHAND & COMPANY, NEW DELHI for further details and techniques for discovering the 22 Self-Qualifying Factors as stated above.*

CHAPTER - 16

THE ROLE OF YOUR PERSONALITY IN PUBLIC INTERVIEWS

Abstract

Interview is the only effective method for looking into your personality and testing it for ascertaining its suitability for selection on the job-working of different types. In fact, interview is a means to peep into your personality on the public platform and enable you to

basis of your appearance, manners, conduct, expression and body movements. Then, your inner personality is probed by questioning you on various aspects and efforts are made to ascertain certain important personal characteristics which give demonstration to your soft skills The technique of questioning varies according to the experience and

meticulous expression and proper body movements are the key factors that can enable you to successfully perform in any interview.

Inter-relationship

The act of giving and facing interview is an essential activity of your career. Nowhere, you can get a job or enter a professional career or seek an admission for doing a high level specialized course without giving an interview. Today, interview is the only effective and practical means for selecting suitable candidates especially when there is a huge proliferation of educational institutions. As a result, the number of educated youth is tremendously increasing, but the job market is drastically shrinking thereby making availability of jobs

who could discharge their duties as per his needs and expectations. For this purpose, he or on his behalf his representatives are primarily interested to physically see a candidate and assess his personality for selection. Thus,

giving demonstrative presentation to your personality and assessing its market value from the employment point of view. .

Thus, your personality ironically becomes the saleable commodity in the employment market and holds the passport for crossing the gateway of interview. In a way, interview acts as a screening agent for allowing entry of only eligible candidates into the job / career market. Now, even for seeking admission to specialized professional courses, you have to go through the deep selection process. Hence, *interview has become the powerful medium for demonstrating your personality for proving its suitability and competency.*

Purpose

Here, the main objective of the interview is to physically see a candidate and his personality. It is a face to face meeting for exploring his mind, sentiments, attitude, potential and abilities and establishing his suitability for a particular job. To be specific, the objective is to look into the following aspects of his personality and assess its present grade :-

(a) Mental structure for aptitude, motivation, vision
(b) Emotional status and trends
(c) Psychic behaviour and relation
(d) Intellectual response and expression
(e) Health condition and physical fitness related to stamina, endurance, tenacity for hard working

During interview, above aspects of your personality are more vividly and prominently revealed by intelligent questioning than written testing. Here, access is provided to probe and explore individual's important qualities, mindset and behaviour. The written test reveals only intellectual abilities of a person while in the interview, various behavioural aspects such as initiative, self-confidence, mental alertness, tact, drive, adaptability depth of knowledge and leadership are revealed in a physical and conclusive manner. These are personality traits and they are evaluated by the interviewing persons. At the initial stage, *there is no other effective means for testing and assessing the personality and its qualities except the bio-data. That is why the interview has essentially become a public platform for the purpose of selection in an open and transparent manner.*

Job Classification for an Interview

The nature, structure, level and modalities of an interview depend upon the classification of jobs. Now, a job is classified as under :-

(a) On the job working at the base level like a clerk, teacher, mechanic, driver, fitter, operator, etc.
(b) Supervisory/superintending level
(c) Executive level
(d) Managerial level
(e) Departmental/ Divisional head at senior and high management levels
(f) Top management level

Accordingly, there are two types of interviews, one is held for employment at the working and supervisory level and another interview for employment at the senior and high level positions. Obviously, the interview board structure and mechanism of questioning are bound to differ according to the job qualitative requirements which are drawn for above levels of jobs. As a result, you will be subjected to different types of interviews as stated in the next paragraphs and your preparation should match to a particular job in which you are interested.

Different Aspects of an Interview

The objective of an interview is to evaluate physical, psychological, mental and intellectual characteristics of your personality. Scientific methods and technological tools are used for data-based interview, situational interview, stress interview and tele-conferencing interview. Another significant aspect of an interview is the skill and abilities of an interviewer and his or her deep knowledge and experience for probing the human abilities and qualities. The interviewer should also be a patient listener. Duration of interview may last for 30-45 minutes for general jobs and extend beyond this period to 4 to 5 days for selection of defence officers by the Service Selection Boards and senior level executives.

Matching your Personality with Specific Service Requirements

It is advisable to know about the job scenario and the competitive environment which is full of challenges of the present century. You can't afford to be selective and complacent at the initial stage. In fact, whenever the opportunity comes to your way, you should never hesitate to grab it. Even though you fail to succeed, it offers you tremendous and valuable experience and exposure of going through the selection process. Of course, you should not act recklessly but should know essential requirements of any service career. In this respect, you are advised to take the following steps to ensure that your personality matches to a particular job requirement :-

(a) **Know the Career/Job Market** – Keep an eye on what jobs are available and which organisations are the best to work with for offering career prospects.

(b) **Achievements of Proper Qualifications and Professional Training** – Achieve proper and higher educational qualifications and avail training facilities for different types of jobs. Try to gain some practical experience on a job work and exposure of industrial practices and culture.

(c) **Write a Good Self-Explanatory Application Form** – This is a very important document written by you about your Self, indicating your intention and what best abilities you can offer. You should highlight and emphasize those aspects of your Self which the employers are generally looking for such as experience, communication skill, quality consciousness, creative skill, commercial and economic awareness, integrity, time management and physical fitness and endurance. In other words, enclose your comprehensive **resume called Bio-data.**

(d) **Prepare to Project your Personality Effectively** – This pertains to your ability to express and communicate to your employer about your positive aspects and convey the impression that you would be an asset to his organisation. This depends upon how effectively and emphatically you project the positive aspects

of your personality and performance.
- (e) **Keep Learning and Improving your Knowledge.** This helps you to widen the scope of different jobs, assignments and mission works. Besides, it helps to extend your employability.
- (f) **Remain Aware about the Employer's Needs and Requirements.** It helps you to prepare for the interview and expect the questions accordingly. For this purpose, you should carefully examine the advertisement and its job requirements and also about the company's reputation and standing in the market.

Criteria For Selection

Most of the employers state their selection criteria in their job advertisements. It basically pertains to the requirement of minimum educational qualifications and professional training about a particular job. You should always aim at qualifying yourself in this respect. You should also ensure to gain sufficient experience and exposure to a particular job environment so that you can easily adopt and adjust yourself. Employers do not generally wish to spend much time on your training and they want to directly put you on the job.

Now, you should ensure that

- (a) You must have the aptitude to do a particular job.
- (b) Your response and urge to do and perform should be natural.
- (c) You should examine your aptitude and find out what type of jobs suit you best and where you use your abilities in an optimum manner. If you do this exercise, you will be able to avoid mismatch and remain mentally prepared to face and project yourself accordingly.
- (d) You must pay special attention to your family background and its financial position especially when you wish to appear for the competitive examinations at the state and national levels. Here, it takes a minimum of two to three years period in order to complete the process. Obviously, you should have adequate financial support. Besides, engineering and medical education has a very high fee structure and long course duration. Unless you get a scholarship, you won't be able to manage if your parent's support is inadequate.
- (e) Finally, the most important factor is your health and physical fitness. If you wish to join Defense, Para-military services, your physical fitness matter a lot and you have to take a close look at your health condition. In fact, physical fitness is required for maintaining sound mind and concentration on the job. It ensures your stamina, endurance and capacity to work hard and continuously.

Casting your Personality According to Employer's Expectations

While preparing for the interview, you should be conscious about the demands and expectations of your prospective employer who offers you employment and accepts your financial liabilities. He will invest in your training and prepare you for the job. Naturally, he is looking for certain qualities in your personality and wants to ascertain whether you will be able to deliver the goods in a reliable and dependable manner. If you are aware about this requirement of any employer, you can have an edge over your competitors in the selection process. Now, what are those aspects that you should know from employer' point of view during your preparatory stage? These are given below.

(a) Clear objective and vision about your future as a driving and steering force to your career.
(b) Positive and healthy personality with minimum body movements, amiable behaviour, dignified conduct, cheerfulness, positive outlook and mindset, physical stamina for hard work.
(c) Proper professional skill with adequate training and experience.
(d) Application skill with an analytical approach for producing quality products.
(e) Learning desire for improving your working skills and adopting new technical developments for ongoing works.
(f) Focus on the job with no side attraction.
(g) Total loyalty and Integrity to the employer and his organisation.
(h) Dedication and commitment to the work and your immediate boss.
(i) Self-discipline for following rules, regulations and instructions without murmur.
(j) Cost and quality consciousness for ensuring economical use of resources for giving quality output.
(k) Work ethics and values for remaining away from vices, in-house petty politics and agitations which hamper your performance and lower your output potential.

Once you know these expectations, you should do self-assessment and self-appraisal in order to ascertain that you will be able to match with the expectations of your prospective employer and accordingly prepare yourself to face the interview.

Projection of Outer Personality

There are two parts of any interview. One pertains to the projection of your outer personality before the board members as you enter and position yourself. Another point pertains to what the members of the interview board expect from you on behalf of employers' specific demands. Let us see the first part as to how you should project your outer personality. Remember that your role in this part creates first impression about your outward personality related to appearance, conduct, manners, posture, expression, body movement and most of the members are likely to be either impressed or unimpressed by your outer personality.

So, here are some of the tips for projecting your outer personality :--

(a) Be properly dressed and styled for the occasion.
(b) Seek permission before entering the room. Walk gracefully toward your chair without making any unnecessary noise.
(c) Pay compliments to all members in a humble manner by saying 'Good Morning or 'Good Afternoon Sir'.
(d) Look confidently at the Chairperson first and then at the other members of the

interview panel while expressing the greetings.

(e) Occupy the seat only when told or seek permission before sitting.

(f) Sit straight and look confidently at the members in front.

(g) Listen to questions carefully and answer them meticulously in audible and clear tone. Avoid fumbling for words. Add proper salutations like ' Sir ' 'Madam' to your answers in response to questions. .

(h) Express yourself confidently. Say frankly NO if you don't know the answer instead of waffling.

(i) Don't make any unnecessary body movements and be careful about your body language.

(j) Be humble, courteous and pleasant in your answers. Do not lose your temper or get irritated even if the question happens to be trivial, stupid and ridiculous or humiliating as it may be meant to assess your mental make-up, mindset and sensitivity to awkward situations.

(k) Say Thank Sir and depart gracefully when the interview is over.

Assessment of Inner Personality

The second part of the interview is directed to actually assess your personal and performance characteristics. In this respect, members are interested to find out your nature, character, attitude, behaviour, abilities, mindset and outlook. While the members can physically observe your personality, they have no means to see your other aspects except your resume. So, their questions are primarily directed at you in order to discover the following *trait profile of your personality* apart from observing its physical features.:-

(a) Aptitude

(b) Nature and Character

(c) Drive and Motivation

(d) Professional Knowledge level

(e) Attitude

(f) Ambition and objective

(g) Communication skills

(h) Self-Confidence level

(i) Effective intelligence

(j) Responsiveness and grasping levels

(k) Social behaviour and relations

(l) Leadership tendencies

(m) Administrative and organising skills

These are related to your mental, emotional, intellectual and behavioural traits. While you should have mentioned most of them in your resume, members are interested to ascertain them and observe your reactive and proactive mood and response. The I.Q.

factor is already assessed from your academic performance and written text if held. So, the focus is maintained on the above stated factors.

Group Testing

You are often required to work together with other workers, supervisors and senior officials. You are also member of a team or group working on an independent project. For this purpose, you are given a task and you form a member of the team. Now, you are observed for your following personal traits :-

    (a) Adaptability and accommodation.
    (b) Team-spirit and togetherness.
    (c) Cooperation and coordination.
    (d) Helpfulness and support.
    (e) Promptness and common sense.
    (f) Initiative and awareness.
    (g) Boldness and courage.
    (h) Mutual respect and regard.
    (i) Interpersonal skill.

Questioning Standards for Senior-level Jobs

The scope of questioning which covers the above stated aspects of your outer and inner personalities is generally adopted for candidates for initial employment at working and supervisory levels. Now, when you are interviewed for senior or high level jobs, the scope of questioning and modality for conducting interview is totally different. The composition of the interviewing board members is different and the criteria of selection are also different. Here, emphasis is given to assess the management skills and leadership abilities of the candidates who have generally put in 5 to 10 years of service and they have sufficient professional experience. So, the focus of interview shifts to test their soft skills in order to assess their suitability for performing managerial jobs with leadership qualities for leading as heads at various levels. Your personality is thus subjected for assessing its functional and qualitative domains in the field of soft skills such as:-

    (a) Self-image and Self-esteem factor
    (b) Self-confidence and Self-reliance factor for decision making
    (c) Performance effectiveness and excellence
    (d) Response and grasping level
    (e) Drive, motivation and determination
    (f) Loyalty, integrity and dependability
    (g) Planning, administrative and organizing abilities
    (h) Delegation of power, monitoring and accountability
    (i) Communication skill for verbal and nonverbal expression, presentation and

　　　　public speaking
(j) Innovative and creative skill for reforms, improvement and updating for leading in the competitive market
(k) Negotiating skill, tactfulness and diplomacy
(l) Temperamental state under extreme stress, strain and challenging conditions
(m) Human liaison skill for public relation, contact and promotion
(n) Mission and objective orientation, focus, firmness and consistency
(o) Physical fitness, stamina and tenacity

　　It is evident from the above that wide in-depth aspects of your inner personality are thoroughly examined and critically assessed for finally deciding your suitability for discharging senior and high level jobs which carry high level responsibilities, independence, accountability and leadership commitments. Obviously, the members of the board have high caliber, vast experience, knowledge and high status and they are selected from higher levels within and outside organisations. In this type of interview, remember that your personality is totally assessed from different angles and perspective and the focus of the interview is to discover your soft skills as stated above which are definitely required for executing senior and high level jobs of high responsibilities.

Awkward Questioning

You are cautioned to expect some awkward, frivolous and sometime ridiculous questions from some members of the board. These questions do not apparently have any relation or relevance to your job but they are directed at you in a casual manner in order to assess your response, reaction and temperament. You should maintain your posture cool and composed, think over and answer them in a positive manner. You should be serious and polite in taking them on and answer them in a logical and rational manner. You should never treat the question stupid nor show your negative reaction. In case, you don't know the answer say frankly **SORRY, I DON'T KNOW.** In case, the question happens to be controversial, you should refrain from expressing your opinion but just say that **SORRY, I DO NOT WISH TO COMMENT.** Here, you are advised not to waffle and boast. Some board members may divert your attention to current political scenario and test your general knowledge and find out your mental alertness for reaction to different scenarios. You should remember that *these awkward questions are thrown at you like a spit-fire with the purpose of ascertaining your psychic frame of mind and mental reaction.* You should naturally be prepared for such eventualities.

Points to Remember

In this interview, an employer want to select a candidate who could become part of his organisation, deliver the goods in honest and truthful manner, would be reliable and dependable and behave in a gentle, polite and amiable manner. He is not giving much importance to your professional skill as you can be trained to do any job. Bu your mental, emotional, psychological and physical conditions are very important for becoming a good worker, good subordinate and staff / team member. Personally, I have given higher weightage to these factors than their professional skill and experience. The reason is that once you become a member of the team, the employer has to depend on you in all respects. Hence, *personal traits like your loyalty, integrity, honesty, dependability assume prime importance. So, accordingly, efforts are made to discover these qualities in candidates while examining their bio-data and also during the interview.* .

Key Factor Self-Confidence

As you go through the process of preparation on the basis of your Introspection and Self-Assessment, you will definitely gain self-confidence. In this process, you become aware about your inner power, strength, potential, abilities and skills. You also come to know certain negative and weak areas of your personality which you should   correct and control for overcoming their ill effects on selection prospects in the interview. Thus, this entire process if it is properly, sincerely and meticulously executed   enables you to gain substantial confidence in yourself. Consequently, you can face the interview with full confidence, boldness and courage. Your facial expression and body language will be improved in revealing your confidence. Your psychological fear about facing an interview will be automatically over

Finally, you should remember that it is your personal responsibility for getting selected in the interview. All relevant useful information and guidance are given in this chapter for enabling you to boldly face and become successful in any public interview. Since the scope of any interview is vast and unpredictable, self-confidence, boldness, thorough preparation and general awareness will positively help you in coming out successful. Now, you have got total perspective of the entire process. And even if you are not successful in a particular interview, you don't get disheartened because your preparation will always help you for the next interview which you will perhaps face with redoubled energy, strength, experience and confidence,

Reasons for Rejection/Failure in an Interview

Despite your best and honest efforts if you are rejected in the first interview, you should not get disappointed, dejected and disheartened. It is the right opportunity for you to take a close look at your personality and retrospect as to what have gone wrong and how you could not properly project your personality. Instead of blaming outside agencies, you are advised to look into the following aspects of your preparation and projection :-

      (a) Lack of adequate professional knowledge and its proper projection

      (b) Lack of proper communication skill and expression

      (c) Unawareness of employer's job requirements

      (d) Slow response and reaction to questions

      (e) Casual and indifferent approach

      (f) Lack of ambition, vision and focus for future career prospects

      (g) Poor show of manners, etiquettes and conduct

      (h) Lack of team spirit, cooperation and support

(i) Lack of current affairs and general knowledge amounting to unawareness of outside environment
(j) Lack of drive, confidence and initiative
(k) Lack of marketing skill for projecting strong points of your personality
(l) Poor physical appearance, fitness and improper body movements

Remember that you should not take your first failure seriously. You should rather consider it an opportunity to learn and relook into various aspects of your personality and overcome the drawbacks as stated above. You should seek proper advice and guidance from the competent persons. With the strong will, determination, and positive attitude, you will definitely succeed in the second attempt.

Concluding Remarks

Selection and placement in any job is possible only through the interview against published or otherwise known vacancies and job requirements. The interviewing method has certain drawbacks and candidates should be aware while preparing for it. Outer and inner personality of the candidate is deeply probed and profile of certain performance related attributes are ascertained for finding his suitability. There are different types of questions specifically designed for verifying these aspects and there is an unpredictable mechanic of questing by the members of the board.

Your personality plays a dominant role since it is a visible factor that causes impression and influence on the members at the first glance. You should take cognizance of various personality related factors while preparing for the interview. You should adopt the process of Introspection and Self-Assessment for gaining Self-confidence. You should always approach interview with full confidence and proper preparation. Even if you don't make it, do not get upset and discouraged. The experience, knowledge and wisdom gained in this interview and by overcoming your drawbacks as observed by you will definitely be useful and helpful to you in your subsequent interviews.

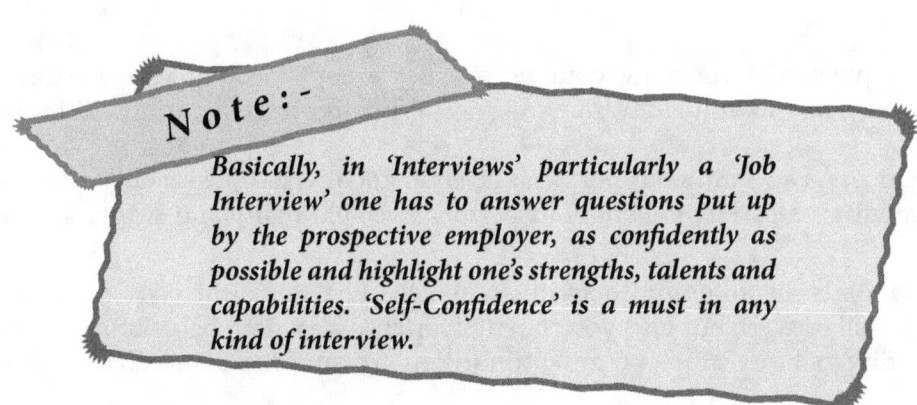

Note:-
Basically, in 'Interviews' particularly a 'Job Interview' one has to answer questions put up by the prospective employer, as confidently as possible and highlight one's strengths, talents and capabilities. 'Self-Confidence' is a must in any kind of interview.

CHAPTER - 17

PROJECTION OF PERSONALITY IN YOUR PERFORMANCE & SUCCESS

Abstract

Performance on the job is the most important demonstrative activity of your personality for proving its suitability. In fact, your performance opens the gateway for achieving your career advancement and better career prospects. As a result, your personality

performance by adopting the technique of self-interrogation and ascertain whether

of the fact that both your positive and negative attributes play the effective role in causing good or bad performance and that determines your suitability for performing different roles of higher responsibilities with higher ranks and status. It is only your performance on the job that determines your career prospects and advancement.

Expectation about your Performance

You are employed on different types of jobs and it is naturally expected that you should effectively performance well for giving substantial output with quality and value. So, .your performance is recognized for its importance, quality, relevance and positive contribution to your organisation. Irrespective of what you are capable of, your performance is the demonstrative visible activity in which you are seen, observed, assessed and tested for the capabilities of your personality. Your performance is the only visible factor which

assessing your

. There is no other way of physically verifying your personality except through your performance on the jobs, assigned to you from time to time. While performing, you will indirectly

on performance. As a result, your performance will get affected positively or negatively and consequently, assessment about your performance in quality and substance is done accordingly.

Performance is an all round activity in which it is not only your physical and professional skill on a job but also your talent, response, reaction, behaviour, awareness and adaptability to the existing operating conditions are carefully observed and assessed.

roles as and when assigned to you. Let us see different types of roles you need to perform while working in any organisation.

Different Functional Roles

Besides the importance and relevance of your basic performance, you are required to perform different roles with different functions, duties and responsibilities. They need different skills, training, knowledge, technique and experience. You have to show your proficiency, competence and suitability in these roles. So, you have to really prepare and train yourself under someone's guidance. Besides, you should know the demands of each role and its characteristics. Let us take a look at those roles as under :

- (a) Basic worker on a job
- (b) Supervisor/Superintendent.
- (c) Head of the Section/Department/Group.
- (d) Executive/Administrator/Controller
- (e) Organizer/Policy maker/Co-coordinator .
- (f) Event Manager.
- (g) Teammate/Subordinate/Team Leader.
- (h) Group/Mission/Project Leader.
- (i) Speaker/Lecturer/Teacher.
- (j) Advisor/Counselor.
- (k) Student/Candidate while attending training courses, workshops etc.
- (l) Negotiator.

It should be noted that while performing in different roles, you need to demonstrate your different personal attributes for making your role effective and result oriented. Your performance and its success depend upon personal qualities of your personality like leadership, positive attitude, motivation, vision, professional knowledge, behaviour and conduct.

Development of Skills

There are two types of skills, one is called *Hard Skill(Cognitive)* and another is called *Soft Skill (Non-Cognitive).* Hard skills are also referred to as " *On the Job Skills* " pertain to your professional knowledge which you gain by going through various professional training courses for specific fields in proper training institutes. It enables you to perform your specific job for which you are specifically employed. It is basically at the working level. So, you have to learn a new job whenever you are shifted to another one or when you join another organisation which deals with different works or products or projects. Here, the skill of an individual worker is not transferable and he has to learn again for handling a new job. Thus, *you have to demonstrate your ability to learn new job skill and adapt yourself to a new operating environment.*

Non-cognitive skills refer to your abilities and potential for planning, organizing, controlling, managing, administrating and conducting various functions and activities. These are basically personal attributes and functionally related to your personal skills. These are described in **Management Parlance** as under :-

(a) Behaviour, Conduct and Values
(b) Personal Characteristics
(c) Intellectual Abilities
(d) Performance and Stability
(e) Work Motivation
(f) Interpersonal Skill
(g) Administrative Skill

So, they are called *Soft Skills.* These are achieved over a period while serving in different roles in different organisations under different working conditions. Here, *your personal, especially positive attributes play a special role in enabling you to respond, absorb, assimilate and communicate them properly and effectively. These skills are eventually transferable.* So, when you join a new organisation, you carry these skills with you in the form of *your expertise, experience, wisdom and knowledge as your personal baggage* and you find them useful there in a similar manner as before. There is a requirement of marginal change in approach and style which depends upon different environmental, geographical and demographic conditions. Of course, these skills are required for appointments at senior and higher levels and your valuation in a new organisation is done on the basis of the depth of your professional knowledge, experience, exposure and achievements for handling different types of managerial jobs.

Hence, it is essential that you should be aware about these types of skills and their demands. You should therefore *focus your attention and efforts in developing these skills confidently and competently at the earliest so that you shortly become an effective performer and achiever under different operational, organisational and administrative controls and conditions.*

Self-Interrogation for Assessing Your Performance

Before somebody assesses your performance, it is always advisable if you can yourself assess your performance. When you observe your performance from your viewpoint, you come to know whether you are delivering good or average or poor performance In fact, before someone comments on your performance, you know the quality, style and standard of your performance. Then, you can withstand criticism or remarks from others. Besides, you can take appropriate actions for correcting certain drawbacks or control your reaction, anger and temperament as and when interrupted. So, you are advised to interrogate yourself about your performance in the following way :-

(a) Have I got proper qualifications and experience for the job I am selected for?
(b) Do I remain focused and committed to my job?

(c) Do I follow strictly and faithfully rules, regulations, orders, discipline and instructions?

(d) Do I perform my job sincerely, honestly and truthfully?

(e) Do I keep myself updated with the latest development and technology in my field by attending seminars, workshops, tutorials as and when held and also through my personal efforts?

(f) Am I really playing the key role so as to be called *'dependable'* from the view point of my boss while discharging my responsibilities of diverse nature?

(g) Do I try to shoulder additional responsibilities without being told thereby showing my initiative, readiness and willingness?

(h) Do I support my boss wholly and willingly without questioning his authority?

(i) Do I plan for continuous learning in order to increase my knowledge and wisdom?

(j) Do I seek advice from the competent persons without any hesitation whenever I get stuck?

(k) Do I observe proper and effective time management system? Do I always complete my job or assignment within the given time schedule and need no reminders?

(l) Do I voluntarily participate in the group discussion, panel discussion, brain storming sessions and periodic meetings?

(m) Do I maintain social contacts, relations and develop interaction with persons of different classes, professions and levels?

(n) Am I a patient, good interactive listener and try to get feedback on my performance?

(o) Am I humble, cordial and amiable in my behaviour, conduct and relations?

(p) Do I often get angry or irritated or lose my temper whenever any unpleasant thing happens?

(q) Have I ego or do I boast about my performance and do I talk much about my achievements?

(r) Do I try to evade my responsibility and pass the buck to somebody else?

(s) Do I follow certain values and moral standards in my professional and personal life?

Incidentally, this is also the indirect way of writing your own **Personal Performance Report** on your performance. In fact, you get an opportunity for critically examining your actual performance and ascertain if it is up to the mark as expected by the standard norms. Such type of personal assessment if done honestly and sincerely will certainly help you and clarify most of your doubts, complaints and grudges about your superior officers if you happen to miss the bus for promotion.

Performance Oriented Verification of Your Personality

These are some important performance related questions which cover the official, social, ethical and behavioural aspects of your life. Here, you are interrogating yourself on your performance and seeking honest, truthful answers for your own information and assessment. Once you get answers to these questions, some affirmative and some negative, your positive and certain negative attributes are also revealed and *they really determine the benchmark for your self-development, performance improvement and career advancement.* The list of self addressed performance related interrogative questions for verifying your personality is given below.

- (a) Have I willingness and positive attitude to perform?
- (b) Am I competent and suitable for jobs of higher grades?
- (c) Have I enough drive and motivation for pushing myself forward?
- (d) Have I foresight and vision for my career prospects?.
- (e) Have I sense of self responsibility and self esteem?
- (f) Am I totally dependable, dedicated and committed to work?
- (g) Do I always concentrate on my duties and responsibilities?.
- (h) Am I time conscious for completion of my work schedule?
- (i) Am I calm, composed and have quiet nature?
- (j) Do I work with team spirit, cooperation and togetherness.?
- (k) Have I got tolerance, endurance and mental toughness?
- (l) Do I behave with politeness, gentleness and amiability?
- (m) Am I thoughtful and patient for listening to others without interruption?
- (n) Am I inquisitive and curious for gaining knowledge and wisdom?
- (o) Have I non-vindictive, non-reactive and non-provocative attitude even while facing criticism or adverse remarks?
- (p) Am I egoistic, boastful and arrogant and liking self eulogy?
- (q) Am I bold and courageous in taking risks and facing challenges?
- (r) Have I self-confidence and self-reliance?
- (s) Am I temperamental and hyper-sensitive?
- (t) Have I emotional, irritating, restless and casual attitude?
- (u) Am I selfish, greedy and indifferent?
- (v) Am I arrogant, critical and adamant in my expression?
- (w) Do I possess a mindset for thinking positively?
- (x) Am I flexible in my viewpoints, thoughts and approach?

Well, you are now in a position to truly assess your performance in light of the treasure of your positive and negative attributes which have obvious bearing and influence on the quality and standard of your performance. Here, you become the first judge and you come to know about your performance. At the same time, you come to know the strong and weak points of your self and you can certainly think of their positive or negative impact on your performance. Before it gets adversely affected, you can prudently and judiciously take remedial and corrective actions so as to avoid ill effects of your negative attributes on your performance and consequent damage to your career. At the same time, you become aware of your strong attributes which offer you moral and natural strength and enhance your power and potential. Obviously, it results in boosting your performance and consequently improving your career prospects.

Prominent Attributes of your Personality for Giving Effective Performance

When you begin your service career, you come across different working stages at different times and levels of command and control functions. Besides, you come across different supervisory and officiating persons of different temperaments at working and management levels as immediate and superior bosses as well as subordinates and colleagues. As a result, there is a continuous demand on your personal qualities in order to demonstrate your abilities, potential, behaviour and relations for giving an effective performance. On the other hand, your employer expects you to deliver a result oriented performance and become soon an effective team member and asset to his organisation. How should you match the situation so that both parties are finally benefited? For this purpose, there is a need for you to possess the following positive attributes :

(a) **Integrity, self-discipline and loyalty**
(b) **Adaptability to get along with others under given condition**
(c) **Industriousness i.e. hard-work, diligence and perseverance**
(d) **Honesty, sincerity and truthfulness**
(e) **Politeness, amiability and gentleness**
(f) **Determination, firmness, steadiness, consistency and mission orientation**
(g) **Dedication, devotion, involvement, responsibility and accountability**
(h) **Dependability and commitment**
(i) **Time-consciousness, promptness and initiative**
(j) **Drive and motivation**
(k) **Communication skill in expression for group activities, discussion and reporting**
(l) **Professional competence and creativity**
(m) **Credibility and respectfulness for management**
(n) **Ethics, etiquette and work culture**

You should note that your immediate and superior bosses expect you to possess the above stated qualities and they try to assess your performance in view of these qualities. Whenever you perform as per their expectations, they are happy and try to grade you for higher progressive promotions and appointments. Accordingly, you receive good annual confidential reports and recommendations for higher promotions.

What is important to note in this exercise is that your performance is the key factor directly responsible for career progression and indirectly your personal attributes also which ultimately speak for the quality, relevance and contribution of your performance. Thus, your personality is involved and indirectly reflected in your performance. Hence, your personality and performance are closely interrelated for giving success in your mission.

Maintain a Positive Attitude in Performance

Since your personality is indirectly reflected in your performance, the primary factor that keeps you active in performance and maintains its shine is the positive attitude of your personality. It is associated with your positive mindset and positive thinking. As a result, you take success as well as failure in the positive stride and spirit. You don't get flabbergasted at the time of crises. You maintain calm, composed, cool and balanced posture without showing any sign of stress on your face. You also avoid your immediate emotive and volatile reaction and initiate positive thought process for tackling the unpleasant situation. So, the following features of your personality give you positive attitude :

(a) A positive self image.

(b) Confidence and trust in your abilities and potential.

(c) Avoiding criticism, foul language and negative remarks thereby creating a positive environment.

(d) Planning your approach and activities properly, thoroughly and meticulously with anticipation for possible pitfall.

(e) Banishing the thoughts on past events and refer them only to learn from mistakes and errors committed for taking their positive cognizance.

(f) Believing consciously in what you are doing with due consideration to its relevance and organisation's interest.

(g) Seeking the advice of your superiors whenever in doubt.

(h) Maintain always your high morale, ethics, values and conviction in your positive thought process and action.

(i) Reading books on various topics and subjects for improving your knowledge, outlook, vision and thought process.

(j) Programming your subconscious mood, attitude, behaviour and habits in positive manner.

(k) Keep motivating and empowering yourself for achieving excellence in executing and managing your jobs

(l) Avoid having ego about your achievements and be humble to give credit to your sub-ordinates or team members and senior officials including mainly your boss.

(m) Never say NO to shoulder additional responsibilities and accept with smile and confidence.

Let us now see now how your personality plays an effective role in achieving **success**.

Concept of Success

Success or successful act is one when you get or achieve what you desired on the basis of your planning, efforts and using resources. As per general life expectations, success is finally associated with achievement of desired wealth, fortune, power or fame or their combination. Every individual has his concept of success which could be short term or long term. Short term success is limited to achieve an immediate objective such as passing final examination with merit or getting admission in a professional college or passing a UPSC or state level competitive examination. It varies from person to person according to his needs, family background, ambition, available guidance, support and resources. Another definition of success lies in a particular way of thinking. This is a bit philosophical and pertains to your way of thinking about relationships, goals, material and spiritual benefits.

Linkage with Personality

How success is related to personality and why it should be considered as a part of your personality. You are already aware that your nature, character, behaviour, conduct, relations and performance depend upon your personal attributes of positive and negative types. Now, your personal attributes are integral part of your personality. When the positive attributes are dominating in your personality, your success is certain or you will certainly succeed. When the negative attributes are dominating, you failure is certain or you are certainly to fail or you certainly fail to achieve your goal. So, it is finally your personality which is reflected in your success and most of the success gaining factors and environment revolve round your personality. Thus, *success gets an individualistic perspective and projection for measurement and assessment.*

Approach

When you want success in your mission small or big, you should approach with firmness, determination and strong will power from your mind. Your mental make-up and attitude play significant role in driving you to succeed. You should therefore focus on strong positive aspects of your personality. You are intuitively and instinctively driven to plan, organize and manage effectively various aspects of the mission or project. Hence, your approach right from the beginning has to be positive with the firmness of your mind for achieving success. Of course, *you are warned not to be over-zealous, reckless, impatient, rigid and over-confident in your approach and overlook the constraints of the operating conditions and environment.* You should remain patient, cool, composed, open-minded and flexible while working on your objective.

Key Aspects of Your Personality for Achieving Success

What are the key factors of your personality that play the significant role in achieving success? These factors are stated as under :

(a) *Setting final objective and milestones* for step by step achievement
(b) *Vision and clarity* of your objective
(c) *Positive mental attitude and positive thinking*
(d) *Focus and concentration on objective with dedication*
(e) Assume total *responsibility and commitment*
(f) *Strong will-power and determination for achievement*
(g) Keep the boss informed and seek his/her advice as well as from others
(h) *Interact frankly and tactfully* with your team members and seize upon their suggestion
(i) Remain *time conscious and keep the target of completion* in view
(j) *Plan and organize your activities for utilising your resources* in an economic manner
(k) Maintain *total belief and confidence in yourself*
(l) *Behave politely and gently* and conduct yourself in a dignified manner
(m) Never criticize and bother about initial failure. Sort out with *cool and composed head without losing mental balance.*
(n) Take *care of your health* and relieve stress and fatigue from time to time
(o) Keep the interest and reputation of your organisation at your heart. Remain *supportive and cooperative* to your boss for his responsibilities
(p) Keep yourself away from loose talk and in-house politics
(q) *Never get in an egoistic mood after* achieving short-term success
(r) Keep *driving and motivating yourself* for achieving excellence in your job

These factors are the general steps or measures which become forerunner for achievement of success in any field. It requires intelligent application of these steps and steering yourself successfully with your dedicated efforts and commitment. What is given above constitutes an excellent roadmap for achieving success in any mission by harnessing certain positive attributes of your personality. Make a mental note this roadmap of key factors that you should practice and adopt under any environment. You eventually become competent to face risks and challenges that may arise on your way. You are empowered with sufficient courage, strength and boldness to face them in a systematic manner. As a matter of fact, when you follow them in letter and spirit, *your personality is enriched to the extent that you are placed on the path of success with your own efforts planning and vision.*

Concluding Remarks

It is certain that your personality plays the dominant role in your professional and lifetime performance and activities. Different attributes of your personality are demanded for different types of jobs and activities in different functional and executive roles, having different levels of responsibility and executive power. It is an essential act to do *self-assessment* and *self-appraisal* for ensuring that you are doing your job properly and correctly because your performance is being observed and assessed for determining your suitability for promotions and career advancements. You should act yourself as the first judge and take appropriate remedial actions if there are certain deficiencies found in your performance. You should not wait for somebody else to tell you about your deficiencies and shortcomings and you should certainly not take it as an insult of your personality. The aim of this chapter is to appraise you about your basic responsibilities and how you should invoke your personality for the purpose of delivering successful performance with excellence. You should also be aware that your personality plays a positive role in achievement of success in any mission whenever you undertake it, jointly or independently.

> **Note:-**
>
> *A Positive Attitude, Honesty, Hard Work, Commentment and Confidence are essential for giving Effective Performance and fore achieving Success in life.*

CHAPTER - 18

HAZARDS FOR DETERIORATING YOUR PERSONALITY

Abstract

Personality is your personal property which you should protect and keep safe from

and soundness of your personality. Your personality has to go through the rigour and hardship of the modern highly competitive environment. So, it is perpetually subject

should remain conscious and vigilant about them. You should organize your working schedule, maintain habits and take proper corrective steps in such a way that their adverse effects are kept to the least possible level. In this chapter, various hazardous factors that you normally come across in your professional career are adequately discussed along with their potential ill-effects that are caused on the health of your personality. It should be noted that some cause direct effect and some indirect. You have to overcome them by undertaking self-preventing struggle and adopting self-healing measures.

Present Career Scenario

Most of our young generation is passing through a rich, high voltage living style and culture with the fast, mobile, automatic and luxurious availability of facilities, means and transport. Manual work, contact with the earth, pollution free atmosphere, healthy diet and stress free working schedule are progressively diminishing from the normal working environment. With the fast life style, facilitated by the progressive technological developments and advancements and all types of facilities being available at your door step, you are getting exceedingly engrossed to keep pace for staying on the job and be ahead in the race of your career advancement.

While this process is on, you unconsciously neglect your health because of the spirit of your youthfulness. *But over the period, you don't come to know when you have lost your physical, mental and spiritual vitality, health and luster of your personality. You*

modern working conditions and facilities, competitive environment and strenuous work schedule.

Under the present working scenario, it is essential that you should remain aware about the hazardous factors that *keep working on you in the background and keep sapping your energy, vitality and spirit of your personality.* You should therefore know how your personality is subject to slow deterioration as you keep pacing with your career prospects and achieving materialistic allurements.

Hence, the purpose of this chapter is to appraise you about the damaging effects of various factors and working conditions which you have to face and pass through. Obviously, *it becomes your duty to protect your personality from the ill-effects of the hazardous factors and still remain healthy by maintaining wellness of your body and happiness of your mind and spirit.*

Time for Realisation

In this respect, the pertinent question is – When should you realise the impact of the modern working environment? At the time you enter service or start the business, you are young, strong, energetic, keen and enthusiastic. You work hard, boldly face tough working conditions and still focus on your work and stay on it. While you are in the age group of thirties or forties, you don't feel the impact on your health and you keep the momentum of the work. As you reach middle age or pass forties, you start feeling the impact of the past work schedule and habits on your health and personality. It becomes noticeable in the form of mental fatigue, backache, loss of sleep, pain in joints, tiresome, angina pain and so on. This is *the right time when you should take cognizance of your hazardous working condition and personal habits and simultaneously take necessary remedial steps and precautions for keeping wellness of your health and protect your personality.*

Basic Questions

Now, the pertinent questions that arise are: –

(a) Is your personality safe?

(b) Does it ever remain healthy?

(c) Are there known and unknown undesired factors that indirectly cause its slow deterioration?

(d) Are you conscious about this eventuality?

(e) Do you think that this health aspect of your personality is relevant and needs your personal attention?

(f) Are you aware that the responsiveness and effectiveness of your personality keep continuously varying under influence of the environmental factors?

These are the host of pertinent questions that are today found relevant for maintaining health and effectiveness of your personality under the present operating and competitive environment of the 21st century. You generally focus your efforts and attention on development of your personality under constant advice and counseling without bothering about the factors that cause its slow deterioration. Under the present highly competitive and employment shrinking market condition, your life momentum is fast and your attention is naturally focused on your career advancement for staying ahead in the competition or at least sustaining yourself in the position. Obviously, you remain unaware about the slow poisonous workload, work style, working hours, competition, personal ambition and hierarchical pressure that slowly keep adversely working on your personality. And one day, you don't know when your personality has lost its spirit and lustre thereby making you unenergetic, inefficient and prematurely feel old.

Hazardous Factors

What are those factors that have harmful effects on your personality and eventually become its enemy.?. Are they visible or invisible and arising from the psychometric forces or become dominating because of your mental and physical weakness? Let us examine these factors one by one and assess their damaging potential on the health of your personality.

1. Disease and Ailments : These factors cause disorders in the overall health of a person. They affect your cheerfulness and reduce your strength, stamina and power. Due to medication and constant visit to doctors, you become demoralized and your spirit keeps sinking, depending upon the diagnosis of ailment. Thus, disease and ailment affect your outer personality and moral strength. However, when you keep certain traits of your inner personality strong such as willpower, endurance, tolerance, determination, positive attitude, outlook and focus on end objective, your outer personality will not get much affected and you are able to ward off the ill-effects of disease and ailments on your personality.

2. Parental Care-Treatment and Harsh Upbringing : During the child growth, if a child receives abusive and biased treatment from father or mother or both, it causes harmful disturbance on the mind of a child. Due to mental disorder caused in the early stage of upbringing, children become exceptionally emotional, sensitive, suspicious, anxious and fearful. This disturbed childhood later leads to impaired social bearing and mal-adaptive unsocial habits thereby causing certain chronic distortions in their personalities. It takes time for the children to overcome such a backlash of their childhood even with proper personal caring relation.

3. Environment and Surroundings : When children are born and brought up in an unhealthy, extremely backward and ragtag environment with no civic facilities and existing anti-social atmosphere around, they experience the worst part of the human life and their mind, attitude, thinking and habits are set accordingly. As they grow up, they have to struggle much to come up. However, certain impressions of their harsh and adverse childhood are left on their mind causing some aberrations on their normal growth. That leaves certain distortions in their outer personality in the form of undue body movements, slang in language, roughness in behaviour and hesitation in communication and social activities.

4. Mental Health : Certain persons develop tendencies about nervousness, anxiety, unstable temperament, unbalanced outlook, impulsivity that seriously affect their personality and its longevity. Mental health depends upon mental stability and mental attitude. Too much negative thinking and getting involved in wayward thinking sap your mental energy and diverts it to wasteful and unproductive work. As a result, you are not able to concentrate on your work. You habitually remain engrossed in wayward thoughts and your performance gets disturbed. As regards nervousness, some children are endowed with certain psychological abnormality on account of genetic factor or some may develop during childhood due to unhealthy upbringing or receiving mal-treatment and injustice. Some may be the victim of suppression, tyranny, abusive action or shock caused by sudden death of their parents leading to cause nervous breakdown and consequently disorder in their personality.

5. Stressful Work Schedule and Work Style : When you follow a very busy and tight work schedule with event after event without proper rest and neglect lunch timing, your physical and mental power to cope up needs to work fast. In the process, you ignore many health precautions. Since your mind is not relaxed from severe work schedule, you are bound to feel mental fatigue and exhausted at the end of the day with no desire to do any physical activity. Similarly, if your work style like sitting, walking, viewing, conduct and body movements is not done in a proper manner, aging of your certain body elements will be fast thereby slowly deteriorating your outer personality. You should therefore work out the schedule of your office activities in such a way that your body and mind timely receive proper rest and peace.

6. Workaholic Habits : If you work continuously without taking breaks in between and remain occupied on a job or keep sitting in the office chair without doing any productive work, your body will ache and become stiff. While doing so, you don't observe proper schedule of lunch or afternoon rest timing but sit late in the evening, your digestion system suffers thereby causing liver disorder. Besides, you are depriving your body to take fresh air and do some physical exercise. In the process, you become restless, irritating, temperamental and hyper sensitive. Your staff as well as your family members also get irritated and start disliking you and your personality thereby creating isolation and loneliness for you.

7. Unhealthy Habits and Vices : Habits like smoking, heavy drinking, chewing tobacco are highly harmful to your health and become biggest risk factors while adopting healing measures from diseases of liver cirrhosis, heart breakdown and lung cancer. Similarly, vices like gambling, bouts of drug, indulgence in unhealthy sex, heavily sap your energy and gradually make your personality sick, sullen, cheerless, ugly and prematurely old.

8. Sexual Disbalance and Mismatch : It relates to your personal life in which if both wife and husband are not matched in nature and habits, it creates mismatch in your sexual relation. As a result, it leads to your mental dissatisfaction, frustration and depression. You remain cheerless, dissatisfied and mentally-off-balance. Besides, disturbed married life causes irritation and restlessness and leads you to become either workaholic or alcoholic or develop suicidal tendency. Remember that sexual satisfaction from the conjugal life makes you feel satisfied, cheerful and your personality looks bright.

9. Lack of Love and Affection : If the children don't get proper love and affection during the childhood from their parents or close relatives, they develop hard mental attitude with isolation, indifference and inferiority complex. They become detached from the community resulting in them the sense of anger, hate, jealousy, vindictiveness towards the society and develop bad habits in early stage. Thus, distortion takes in their personality and leads to formation of their negative mindset and attitude.

10. Ambitious Nature and Dominant Attitude : If you are a highly ambitious person and you strongly desire to dominate, you become a single track driven person with straps on your eyes thereby disabling you to look around. You become inflexible, adamant and self-centric person thereby leaving no scope to improve and modify your attitude. Hence, you remain a deprived person, preoccupied with self-interest and self-indulgence. As a result, you remain isolated from your colleagues and friends.

11. Self-Ego and Self-Praise : These factors are developed in you at a later part of your career on the basis of your achievements and position in your organisational hierarchy. The day you start showing ego and praising yourself, you rough shod in behaviour and indirectly hurt your colleagues. The bloated air and sense of your personality cause jealousy and envy, thereby leading to cause harm in your higher promotions because positive traits of your personality are responsible for your achievements geting overshadowed by your ego and self-praise.

12. Give up Attitude : If you adopt a give up attitude, you close all tracks of inputs and feedbacks and stop the way for your self-improvement and development. That brings your personality to the dead end with no hopes to recover from the past. This pessimistic attitude makes your personality regressive and depressive with no hope to try for any alternative for coming back on the track.

13. Self-Consciousness and Inferiority Complex : When you are too much conscious about your weaknesses, shortcomings and lack of self-confidence, you remain mentally disturbed and apprehend possible failures or losses or committing mistakes in your on-going performance. These apprehensive feelings keep you engrossed and preoccupied and consequently cause deteriorating effects on your personality.

14. Competitive Race for Promotions : When you find many contenders vying for promotions along with you and going ahead of you, you become nervous and feel complex for not being sufficiently prepared or upgraded in your performance. This fear and apprehensions keep worrying you and eventually, your personality suffers from showing its real potential.

15. Working Environment, Relations and Workload : These aspects have a lot of bearing on the mental state of the executives. Some of them are not found to cope up with the demands of their boss, his peculiar working style, priorities, likes and dislikes in addition to the depleted office staff, uncooperative working staff and pressures from the higher management. Since you remain in the worried and tired state, your personality become cheerless and lustreless and you start prematurely looking old due to constant strain, stress and worries.

16. Failures and Misfortunes : Whenever they occur unexpectedly, you become nervous, discouraged and disheartened. You become demoralised and lose the sense of correct direction. These negative traits are basically weak aspects of your personality and get manifested at the time of failures and misfortunes. On the other hand, when your career proceeds smoothly and suddenly, such events occur in your life, and your personality becomes the first victim for showing its adverse effects of agony, sorrows and frustrations. You need to overcome these with *courage, boldness* and *wisdom*.

I have just mentioned here these important negative factors which are invisible and remain unperceived for causing slow harmful influence on your personality without giving any clue and notice. These factors are mostly mental, psychological, work incidental and every one of us has to pass through them. *Demands of the present 21st century related to the workload, global competition and human aspirations have incredibly gone up. The above stated features and their ill effects project the other side dark picture of the resulting prosperity, career diversities, global reach-out and wide scope for individual advancement and achievement.* Consequently, expectations of the employment agencies go up from your abilities, performance, work engagement and quality output. As a result, your personality is caught in a situation where you have to stretch out yourself and face the onslaught from both sides. Now, it becomes entirely *your show and absolute responsibility to cope up and manoeuvre your personality so that it can remain fit, safe and intact while achieving your objectives.*

Self-Struggle

This exercise has pointed out that the health of your personality is subject to the hazards of diversified nature. Your personality has to face them at various stages of your career activities. It you want to ward off their harmful effects on your personality, you have to firstly undertake personal struggle to understand and realise their adverse consequences and then adopt precautionary approach for avoiding them as much as possible. Your wisdom and self-interest should be focused on remaining aware and conscious of such an eventuality and keep yourself fit and healthy by adopting healthy schedule of work, proper diet, controlled habits, adequate exercise, social interaction and proper entertainment. In the process, you have to control your mental state and keep it strong and robust by divorcing it from wayward negative thoughts and concentrating on your jobs and responsibilities.

Whatever may be the distractions or temptations, you should primarily remain occupied on your job with devotion, dedication and sole purpose focused on the interest of your organisation and self-health. With such a noble objective, you are able to give definite direction to your personality by maintaining strong will power, positive attitude and objective outlook. Remember that whatever may be the early setbacks or failures or sufferings, it is your strong mental power, will power, ambition and determination that will pull you out of the morasses of hazardous and adverse situations and conditions.

As you maintain the health of your personality throughout, you win half the battle in your life because you are able to enjoy the fruits of your achievements. Remember the paradox that you have tons of fortune, wealth, reputation but if you have a bad health and sick personality, will you be able to enjoy the materialistic fruits of your achievements? Certainly not. Hence, there is a close relationship between health of your personality and achievements in view of the personal derived benefits, comforts and enjoyment are concerned. It is always advisable to keep this aspect in view while running after one's career and its ambition. You should try to strike a proper balance for achieving ultimate objective of real mental peace, happiness and contentment in life.

Self-Healing Process for Your Personality

It is obvious that you have to adopt self struggle and controlled schedule of activities with self-imposed discipline. Consequently, it becomes a self-healing process in which your personality is engaged in observing a healthy behaviour, emotional balance and integrated social relationship while working in different segments of your service career. With increasing medical treatment cost, causing your absence from the job on becoming ill or diseased or suffering from accidents or bad habits of excessive working or drinking, self-healing consciousness and self-awareness enable you to maintain your personality healthy by controlling psychological disturbances like chronic anger, anxiety, stress or depression. Self-control, commitment, and bold positive attitude for facing challenges cause less worry, fear, anxiety and emotional stress.

These are incidentally the guidelines for you to observe as your **Self-Actualization Programme for keeping yourself fit and your personality healthy. Here, the focus is on your personal efforts, struggle, awareness and realisation. If you ignore or overlook, you and your personality face the consequences.**

Suicidal Tendency

Before concluding this chapter, I would like to mention about this type of the emerging tendency among the youth which primarily occurs due to unbalanced, inconsistent and unstable mental attitude with the fear psychosis and inferiority complex, becoming the major part for causing *extreme depression* and *frustrations*. **It mainly arises from the weak and sick personality, having predominance of the negative trait characteristics.** The persons, having such a weak or sick personality are highly intellectual, talented, hardworking, self-conscious and obedient but they are highly temperamental, hyper sensitive and introverted with the unstable mental attitude as stated above. Such persons easily fall prey to the pressure of their parents or to their own ambition whenever the failure occurs in higher examinations or miss the promotion or face the severe work pressure from the boss. With their mind being overpowered by negative thoughts and having extremely sensitive and temperamental nature, they remain aloof and keep deeply brooding over their failures with fear, wayward thinking and wild imagination for feeling for them the end of the road and life. Such a mental state leads to extreme depression, desperation, frustration and consequently suicidal tendency. Thus, it becomes a case of extremely sick personality with no self-healing efforts and self-control on their mental, emotional and psychic characteristics of negative types.

Concluding Remarks

In the present highly competitive world, you need to understand and realise the health hazards and their continuing adverse impact on your personality in an unseen and indirect manner. Thus, health and personality have become interrelated issue in a number of ways. Eventual illness and health disorders occur from psychological disturbances like chronic anger, anxiety, depression or stress. Similarly, mental disturbances occur quite often from an unhealthy personality as the body affects the mind. *Work stress, strain* and *work pressure* cause a fast aging of your personality.

It is generally observed that persons who are hostile, competitive, ambitious and aggressive are more likely to suffer from heart diseases than the easy-going persons. Remember that hard-work activities or a challenging job will not cause hazards to your personality. It is your highly ambitious nature, self-centric attitude, aggressive work style and psychological behaviour that will lead you to depression and ill-health.

The positive aspect of functioning with calm, relaxed approach and a positive attitude become the self-healing factors along with playful and contended posture of your personality. It is now entirely your responsibility and exercise for steering your personality through the hazardous path of your life events and activities.

> **Note:-**
> *Typical hazards, physical or non physical which are described in this chapter have the slow poisoning effect on your personality. You must consciously take cognizance of them and adopt corrective measures for reducing their adverse effect on your personality. In fact, you need not wait fore someone to warn you about them. It remains your personal exclusive responsibility to protect your personality from such hazardous factors.*

CHAPTER - 19

GENDER DIFFERENCE IN PERSONALITIES

Abstract

Males and females follow the conventional and traditional course of working and functioning based on their individual personality. Both are required to go through the same rigor of interviews and perform on the job for meeting the expectations of their employers. Apart from having visible difference in their outer personalities, physiological and biological factors have caused difference in their inner personalities thereby each having different attitude, mindset, thinking and outlook. Now, it is entirely up to you how to exploit the strong and weak aspects of the gender difference in their personalities. In this chapter, their personal characteristics are critically examined and some differences highlighted for you to take cognizance while making best use of them on the assigned jobs. In fact, the females do possess some of the good traits but they can't use them due to environmental conditions and family traditions. Whenever they get encouragement, they show equally good results at par with their male counterparts and sometimes better too.

General Aspect

to application of these aspects to both male and female. The aspects so far discussed are classical, conventional and normal for discovering and understanding their general personalities. It implies that when you consider male or female as a separate gender, these aspects are universally applicable to each of them.

career advancement. Both male and female equally get the gift of personality at the time of their birth from the genetic and cosmic sources. Both of them have to go through the upbringing and nurturing through the prevalent situation and face peculiar circumstantial forces of favorable and unfavorable nature. They receive similar education and get similar opportunities in life for training, employment and career advancement. Here, a question normally arises whether a male or female proves to do better in performance and whom you would prefer for giving better performance in a particular job.

Scope

The scope of this discussion under this chapter regarding gender difference is **limited to their performance and working on the jobs and outdoor career activities. As such, it is relevant to observe if there is any significant difference in their nature, character, behaviour, talent, style and modalities while performing in offices, institutes, industries, banking and any other organisation.**

Preference

In view of this scope, you come to the basic issue of your preference of a male or female for doing a general purpose and special type of jobs. Although, this appears to be an invalid question in view of the fact that females are successfully making their grade and progress in all fields of govt., semi-govt., and private sectors, *it always remains your psychological and physiological viewpoint and doubt that cause influence on your attitude and thinking for looking at the personality of male and female from an individualist angle. Hence, it is necessary to consider broad perspective about personalities of both male and female in an unbiased and rational manner with emphasis on their natural and innate individual strong and weak areas for effective and optimum utilization as more of assets and less of liabilities from human resource (HR) point of view in any organisation.*

Physiological and Biological Factors

On the basis of these basic factors, a male is obviously distinguished from a female. It reflects on outside physical body features of their personalities. Since these are natural, well known and obvious aspects of their outer personalities, it need not be discussed and elaborated here. Since masculine and feminine classification are physically seen in these aspects, each has obvious certain inner forces which are generally reflected in male and female as under :-

(a) **Male** – *Strength, power, ego, aggressiveness, assertiveness, dominance, adventure, result-orientation, objectivity, sexuality, liberty, promiscuity, freedom of movements, etc.*

(b) **Female** – *Emotionality, sensitivity, sensuality, submissiveness, communicative, passivity, subjectivity, caring, supportive, patience, fearing, delicacy, dependent, protective, productive, etc.*

These are general personal characteristics which are born out from their masculinity and feministic factors. Due to liberality and lifting of many restrictions on females, availability of facilities for higher education and opening of employment opportunities, these trait characteristic differences are undoubtedly diminishing or overlapping. So, it becomes the question of what type of upbringing, facilities, opportunities, liberality and unbiased attitude are available in a community and society and females are certainly making best use of them and showing their splendid and remarkable performance and perhaps excelling in their managerial and leadership skills in political and nonpolitical fields. However, the percentage of such type of females is few compared to males because of the above stated trait differences. As a result, in general class of male and female, a noticeable distinction will remain because of the inborn physiological and biological factors, resulting in some strong and weak points in either male or female.

Traits and Characteristics of Males and Females

Let us try to examine these unique traits or characteristics of males and females in the succeeding paragraphs :-

1. **Self-Image** : Males are more conscious of their self-image and try to project it in the form of ego, pride, self-esteem and specific body language. Females don't exhibit self-image despite their outstanding performance.

2. **Ambition, Power Dominance** : Males have ambition and nurture aspiration to gain power and dominance at any level initially over a small group or section and progressively desire to rise for senior and high levels. Females have short term objectives and do not think for bigger size picture for themselves. They remain happy to handle immediate issues and develop desire whenever they get support from their family members.

3. **On-job Performance and Dedication** : A male learns a job but does not wish to stick to it for a long time. He looks for change and diversifying. A female likes doing repetitive job and remains focused and dedicated on it without looking for an immediate change in her career prospect.

4. **Emotionality and Sensitivity** : Females are more emotional and sensitive than males. Their reactions to unpleasant events are instant and fearsome. It takes time for them to harden their feelings and reactions but they remain within them in the silent form and may erupt later.

5. **Dependability, Loyalty and Integrity** : Males remain loyal and dependent so long their personal interests are safeguarded and taken care of. The possibility of their loyalty for diversion is fairly high on getting tempting offers and allurements. Hence, special care has to be taken to retain their loyalty. Females are loyal and dependable without much expectation and they are difficult to get tempted unless they have personal grudge. They continue to be loyal unless they get in trouble and someone wants to exploit them.

6. **Possessiveness and Sense of Belonging** : Females are generally possessive towards their children, husbands and personal belongings. They often express words like **My** and **Mine** in their normal talking. Males are liberal, casual and delegate power to others. Sometimes, female's extreme sense of possessiveness become irritating and repulsive in parental care of children and their personal life.

7. **Patience, Tolerance and Endurance** : Females have a great deal of patience, tolerance and capacity to endure unpleasantness and monotony. Their extreme patience and tolerance is seen in cooking and neat up-keep of households. They bear with patience and endurance shortages, drawbacks and inconvenience in office and family functions without complaint or demur. In fact, their patience for doing repetitive jobs and religious rituals like worshiping is remarkable and males become restless and depressed while performing monotonous jobs over a long period. Of course, females remain sulking within them and it erupts only when flashpoint is reached.

8. **Caring and Helpful :** Females are more caring, helpful and supportive than males. They get involved in this process by virtue of their tender nature and attitude. Males are generally casual and get involved only on seeing their personal interest.

9. **Self-Confidence and Self-Reliance :** Males undertake given jobs with self-confidence They hardly seeks any advice or look back once they are professionally trained. Females are hesitant and shaky initially but once they do it, they perform confidently and independently. Females are more careful and cautious and so they take little time to develop self-confidence and self-reliance than males but they concentrate fairly well and proceed for completion with confidence.

10. **Communication Skills :** Communication skills of females are better than males. They are focused on the subject with specific points of logic, clarity, continuity and emotional appeal. They are good at nonverbal communication. They are also sensitive to non-verbal cues and expressive with impressions on face. Males' focus is on conveying his objective and purpose with analytical approach, aids and examples. Of course, there is more throw, force, emphasis and articulation in male communication, while, female communication carries emotional appeal, softness and repetition of certain issues in a monotonous manner.

11. **Listening Skills :** Females show patience in listening without interruption. They are initially hesitant in talking. But once they start, they are less prone to listening. Males often need to be advised about the importance of listening first and then react.

12. **Leadership :** Males take initiative and responsibility in leading small groups from the front. They remain committed to the cause of the mission along with their teammates. Females have to prove themselves and need to be given the chance to lead. They are also hesitant whenever they are called upon to do so. Females have to make beginning from small groups and look for detailed briefing while males jump to perform big roles of leadership

13. **Intellect, Memory and Intelligence :** Females are endowed with intellect and memory a shade better than males. Memory of females is sharp. So, they are proficient in reproduction of what they have learnt. With their intellect, they are sharp to pick up and learn fast. But their intelligence gathering skill being limited from outside sources, their investigating, analyzing and projecting expertise is not the same as males.

14. **Administrative, Organising and Managing Skills :** Females are equally competent to administer and organize but they need to have rank, status and executive powers. But, males have an edge because of openness, wide contact and aggressive approach and they do become bold, harsh and impolite while dealing with unwilling and uncooperative members of the team. As regards managing, females are proficient and skillful in managing office, households and outdoor activities but their reach out over the outdoor management is limited.

15. **Influenciability :** Females are susceptible to influence and easily persuaded to change their views and beliefs. It takes time and patience for the males to get influenced and sometimes, they remain adamant and dogmatic on their preformed views.

16. **Confidentiality** : It is said that ladies can't generally keep any secret long and divulge it anytime in an unconscious and unusual manner. Hence, females can't maintain confidentiality of important issues for a long period and may divulge it at the slight provocation and self-eulogized mode. While males maintain it hidden at heart and never divulge even they are threatened or provoked. Keeping this aspect, females are generally kept away from discussion of highly secret matters. However, this is a debatable point for specific ladies who have reached top positions in their organisational hierarchy.

17. **Mindset :** Females are seen to focus on small and immediate objectives without taking cognizance of its long term consequences. The males observe and analyze the issues in a broad manner and they show their broad and seamless mindset and outlook. Besides, females have generally positive outlook and are optimistic about the outcome from their personal sincere efforts. Males need to be advised to have positive mindset and it takes time to pull out them from their negative mindset.

18. **Sociability :** Within a family, females are seen more sociable as they try to reach out their relatives and get them together. They take initiative in maintaining relations and togetherness in their families. Of course outside, they are selective in social factor. Males are also selective and take time to form friendship. While males mix with their friend too often, females select the occasion for attending the function of social togetherness.

19. **Learning Skill** : Females learn and absorb the professional skill fast. They intently concentrate on learning new jobs and reproduce in a proficient manner. They are keen to learn and enhance their capabilities by gaining knowledge. They wish to compete in their professional knowledge with their male colleagues. Male are found slow and unwilling to learn new things. They do so when compelled or foresee their career prospects.

20. **Compliance to Rules and Regulations :** Females always work within laid down rules and regulations. They don't show defiance and rarely jump the rule. They don't show interest in framing or modifying existing rules. Male do work within rules and regulations but they become uncomfortable over a long period and work for suggesting changes. They tend to jump over the rules on certain occasions for serving personal interest.

21. **Envy, Zealousness and Vindictiveness :** Females easily become envious and zealous in their personal matters while males become envious in their administrative and official affairs like promotions, assignments. Females sometimes become vindictive in their personal affairs when purposefully wronged. Females don't get upset even if they are left behind in promotional and administrative rising unlike males who generally sulk while serving under female dominance.

22. **Adaptability and Accommodativeness** : Females are easily adaptive and accommodative to any environment and do not complaint. or object and they try to adjust and make its best use. Males are selective and look for environment of their comfort. They have grudge and voice their discomfort if the environment does not suit them.

23. **Introvert/Extrovert :** Females are generally introvert, while males are both introvert and extrovert. Females would not like to open out unnecessarily. They form small groups of their own and don't like to reach out unless specifically invited

24. **Quality Consciousness and Excellence :** Males lay down the rules for quality and excellence and females faithfully follow them. Females have good observation while checking quality and remain watchful for ensuring it. Males aim at achieving quality and excellence but like to supervise.

25. **Decision-Making and Negotiating Skills :** Males are fast in taking decision and sometimes become autocratic. Females are analytical, logical and careful while taking decision and so they take time. But once decided, they stick to it and are very reluctant to change unless persuaded. Their negotiating expertise is logical, rational, focused and persuasive. Males tend to be vague, unfocussed and temperamental with certain body movements. Females show patience in listening to the views of others and answer with much deliberation. Generally, it is pleasant and meaningful to negotiate with ladies as they come fully prepared with proper homework.

26. **Advice and Counselling :** Females are hesitant in seeking advice and counseling. When they face problems, they take time to open out and be specific for their particular problem. Males are quick to seek advice but they take advice from the competent persons.

27. **Knowledge Upgrade and Advancements :** Females are generally happy with whatever knowledge they have gained as required for a particular job and look for using it at the earliest. They go for its enhancement when forced or urged to do so. Of course, they have certain limitations and compulsions to do so freely and willingly. But, when opportunity comes, they are determined to avail it. Males have to compulsorily go through this phase if they wish to avail promotions and higher responsibilities.

28. **Networking :** Females are capable to do networking, but they hesitate to do lest it is misunderstood. Hence, they have to depend on their own proven talent, abilities and splendid performance for availing promotional prospects. Males are slow in developing contacts and do so when their personal interests are involved.

29. **Risks and Challenges :** Males show courage, boldness and fearlessness in facing and tackling challenges. They try to find out a way from the difficult situation even by timely seeking advice. They maintain cool and remain unperturbed. Females become shaky, perturbed and even nervous. They look for someone's support and assistance for pulling them out.

30. **Reward, Award and Recognition :** Males are anxious to get quick reward in the form of promotion or pay rise or allowance. They look for their work getting recognized. Females are patient and continue the job without being anxious for rewards. They are patient to wait for their term and they don't bother even if they miss it

Assessment

I would like to repeat that *these are specific observations on general class of males and females.* They are always overlapping when females possess abilities, talent, potential and whenever they get opportunities to show off their traits. Unlike males, whatever weak areas of females are seen, they are not natural product by virtue of birth but forced on them by the physiological factors along with their protective upbringing and traditional restrictions. With the openings and lifting of restrictions and making equal opportunities available, females excel in academics and professional fields. They pass competitive examinations and prove their talent and abilities at par or more than the males in open competition.

Then, *whatever has been described and discussed so far is invalid?* Here, comprehensive efforts have been made to bring out and project natural differences of small or large magnitudes in the inner personalities of male and female in an objective and pragmatic manner. It is well known that these are created by their physiological and biological factors and mental structure and attitude. There is no doubt that there are certain strong areas in females and certain weak areas in males. These specific trait areas become part of their natural personality. While it makes no difference in employing either a male or female on a particular job, both satisfying the same job criteria, you will minutely observe subtle difference in their soft skills which influence their performance and its work output.

With emphasis on equality of gender, it is unfair to make distinction in their work and performance. Both are observed and judged on the same scale of promotional criteria. However, it is a judicious job of assigning work to a male and female for making the best use of their personal abilities. Then, the question arises *what for there should be a debate of gender difference in their personality.*

It is pointed out that there are general obsession and misunderstanding about their personalities while evaluating suitability of male or female for doing a particular job of responsibility. The preconceived notion of male dominance or female inferiority prejudices the mind of authorities.

Hence, a clear picture needs to emerge out in a realistic manner about the ingrains of their personalities and trait specifics which remain in the hidden form especially in females and no efforts are made to discover them. Given equal opportunities and removing restrictions on the females, they make the best use of their abilities and trait specifics for general performance and much more on particular jobs in specific roles. In fact, their natural feminine body structure and gestures put certain restrictions on their individual free movements and cause personal safety problem for protection from antisocial and evil-willed elements. But once, they are in a group, they become bold and overcome their natural fear from any possible threat.

When you see ladies occupying top positions in politics, banking, judiciary and executive branches of both Government. and Private sectors, these ladies are found strong-willed, highly ambitious, determined, mission-oriented, dominating, aggressive leaders, having tremendous organising and communicative skills, administrative power and remarkable oratorical skills that sweep the audience. They have overcome male resistance and hurdles to their leadership by skill fully using their soft skills and management techniques. They have excelled in managing resources and delegating powers and responsibilities. Unfortunately, proportion of such dominating and ruling class of females is much less and their cases cannot be taken for study for the general class of females. However, *at the onset, you can't rule out the latent potential of a female personality for rising like a phoenix from the most adverse and unfavourable conditions.*

Now, *what have you specifically observed and gained from this gender study of their personalities?*

There is always an up-man-ship in the male personality for feeling a superiority complex over females. Strong areas of female personality are overlooked and capabilities of all females are underestimated because of their obvious feminine features and their constraints. The general projection of human personality is applicable to both males and females in their individual category. When you start comparing a male personality with female and keep gender inequality in your mind, you are likely to go wrong and will not get the proper result. Hence, you need to know the basic natural differences in their traits or characteristics which are born out from the physiological and biological reasons. These differences are reflected in the form of strong and weak areas of both male and female personalities. In fact, *you should be concerned and your expertise and wisdom focussed on making the best use of their naturalised strengths and weaknesses and blend them in a harmonised manner for deriving maxismum benefits from their services to your organisation.*

Concluding Remarks

Finally, it is pointed out that the gender differences in the personalities of male and female, although they appear to be innate are generally changeable as they are strenuously influenced by a combination of biological *tendencies, motives, abilities, social obligations, expectations and situational forces.* By properly understanding various forces that influence a male or female and condition his/her personality, efforts are made in this chapter to project their gender differences in a realistic manner, while performing any job in an organisation or industry. Disregarding the masculinity or feminist aspect of an individual, *equal opportunities should be offered to both in a secure, open and competitive environment.* As a result, each gets an opportunity to make the best use of his/her personality so that they are able to climb up the steps of promotional ladder on the basis of their merits as high as possible in their respective positions in organisations.

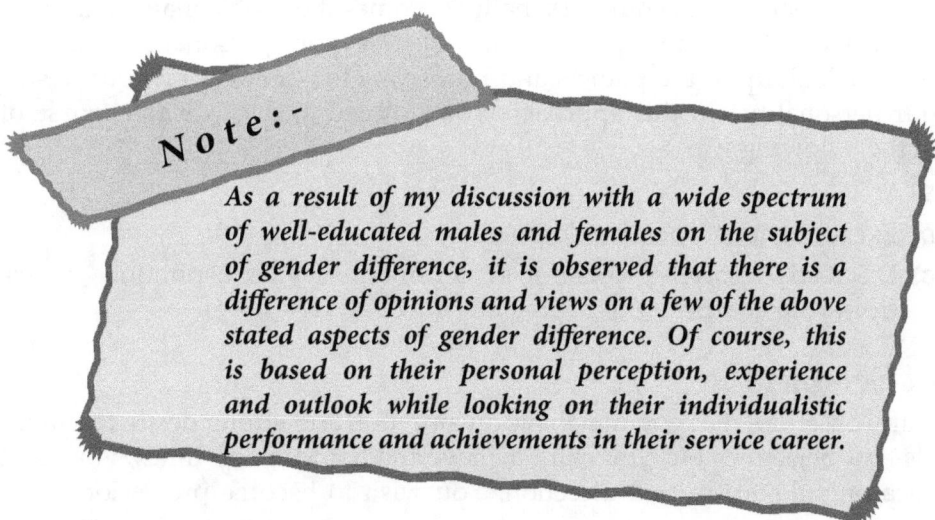

Note:-

As a result of my discussion with a wide spectrum of well-educated males and females on the subject of gender difference, it is observed that there is a difference of opinions and views on a few of the above stated aspects of gender difference. Of course, this is based on their personal perception, experience and outlook while looking on their individualistic performance and achievements in their service career.

CHAPTER - 20

DESTINY HIDDEN IN YOUR PERSONALITY

Abstract

your destiny. Hence, it is essential to know your personality for executing its proper development. In fact, your personality remains the most neglected part when you

and negative types play very important role in advancing or retarding your career prospects. In other words, your dominant negative traits cause failure and dominant positive traits result in success. Success or failure in your career is simply interpreted as the effective dispensation of your destiny.

Relationship

As you approach towards the concluding part of this book, you are reminded about its title pertaining to discover destiny in your personality. It means that the unknown, mystic and occult aspect of your human life called destiny is indirectly related with your personality. It implies that your personality is instrumental for materializing the events of your destiny. In other words, your personality becomes the visible manifestation of your destiny and you can consequently read your destiny in your personality. Unfortunately, the Astrologers look up to the planets and horoscope for discovering your destiny and not in your personality. In this approach, you proceed to discover the course of your destiny in the following way :-

    (a)

    (b) Executing its proper development

    (c) Discreetly applying steps for achievement of your aspirations as expected from your destiny

Present Scenario

It is generally observed that you may have an ambition and strong desire to pursue your lofty goals and objectives but you can't achieve them and many times, you can't even make a meaningful start in that direction. You wish to become professional in one of your interested fields but you unwittingly and unwillingly land up in another profession in which you have the least interest and you would have never dreamt of it. You may have many mishaps, failures and losses in your missions and business. You may meet an accident and surprisingly survive with or without a scratch. In all these cases and incidents, there is a strong tendency to blame your destiny. This is a simple, standard, routine excuse and easiest escapist route and explanation from the reality for your failure or non-achievement of your objectives in life. Whenever reasons, you analyze in such cases, you have invariably tendency to blame the outside forces and so, you feign helplessness by saying that it was out of my control. Thus, you remain oblivious of the main role of your personality and its effective contribution in such cases. *You evade to blame yourself and so you unwittingly bring the destiny in picture and overlook the reality. Thus, the basic issue of your personality really playing the effective role in your performance gets overlooked and sidetracked.*

Human Destiny

Human destiny is a mystic aspect of your life. It is imperceptible and invisible complex entity, having its roots in your beliefs, faiths, religion, philosophy, theology and spirituality. It is therefore deeply embedded in your mind, perceptions and feelings and comes forward to give us relief and solace from your failures and losses by giving impression that the event was destined to happen and you have no control on it.

Hence, human destiny appears to be abstract but comprehensible entity and implies occurrence of events and their associated success or failure according to a certain predetermined schedule which is a priori worked out and controlled by the divine forces and remains much beyond your free will and control. Hence, it is believed that it is endowed to you at the time of your birth and you carry its imprint throughout your life. So, whatever happens in your life, its control mechanism lies in this imprint. Thus, it is projected as the super-natural invisible power which is supervising, guiding and controlling your life events. So, it is eventually deemed to become responsible for the end result of success or failure in your life. Consequently, it becomes a singular unique source for explaining cause of a particular event in such convincing manner.

Since your destiny is endowed to you as a gift at the time of your birth by the heavenly forces in conjunction with the genetic factor contributed by your parents, it becomes a proper imprint of your nascent personality and its brain-mind combination for operationalizing the lifelong activities and events.

It is seen that persons have individually different nature, character, potential, talent, abilities and personality. They differently behave, conduct and perform and at no time, it is the same or identical. So, their personal qualities of both positive and negative types are substantially different and consequently affect their personality and performance in different manner. Since, success or failure of any event depends upon your nature, character, behaviour, talent, skills and performance and since they are integrally related to your personal attributes or qualities, it is evidently clear that your success or failure is basically correlated to personal attributes of your personality which has dominance of either positive attributes or negative attributes or perhaps, both may have a low presence. With this correlation, having practically seen from my observations and experience, it is definitely possible to establish a close link of your destiny and personal attributes of your personality. In other words, your personal attributes play important role in determining the end result and thus becomes the key factor for consideration between your destiny and success or failure in your service career. In this respect, you should remember that you are born with different nature, temperament, intelligence, aptitude, personality, potential and abilities and you carry them within your Self as the heavenly gift in the form of an imprint of your identity and individuality since the day of your birth. It is the combination of the positive and negative qualities with variations in their strengths and relative levels that make a person different from each other and consequently establishes his unique identity and existence. *Hence, human destiny obviously gets dispensation in the basic combination of the inborn personal qualities of his personality.*

To a common man, it is very difficult to understand and grasp the complex nature of this relationship between inborn personal qualities and his destiny. In fact, other side of the story reveals to us the events of failure or non-achievement of the life-long goals as the cases of lost opportunities. Numerous examples are found in cases of many persons for their losses or failures which appear to be out of their control. But after taking a close look and analyzing the reasons honestly, truthfully and dispassionately, it is observed that *the most of the cases of lost opportunities are ultimately attributable to personal qualities, especially of negative types such as indifference, casualness, selfishness, idleness, laziness, short-temperament, shortsightedness, narrow-mindedness, restlessness, short vision, etc. These negative qualities adversely affect their nature, behaviour, character, skills, abilities and consequently their actual performance and relations in service career.*

Since, the direct responsibility here rests on you, it is commonly observed that you would not like to blame yourself nor you like anybody pointing the accusing finger at you. On the other hand, you pass the blame on the outside forces or you invariably make your destiny the scapegoat and pass the entire blame of the failures on your destiny. Here, *the human intolerance, ego, ignorance and intransigence are responsible for him not to easily concede and voluntarily accept his mistakes and take remedial measures for correction.* Thus, a case study of the lost opportunities enables you to take a close look on the real perspective of the destiny and its intimate relationship with your personality of predominantly negative types as stated above.

Correlation

Let us put the destiny as an abstract entity on one side and a set of personal attributes of both positive and negative types of your personality on other side. Now, it is observed that the destiny and personal attributes, although they appear to be two independent entities to our mind, are basically correlated with each other in an intrinsic manner. As a result, these personal attributes of your personality are mostly found responsible for causing success or failure which is reflected in the form of gaining fortunes, prosperity, promotions, positions in your service career or failures and losses.

Thus it can be stated that
- *Success is an indicator for dominance of the positive attributes present in your personality*
- *Failure is an indicator for dominance of the negative attributes present in your personality*

This is a simple way of looking at your success or failure and ascertaining its cause which eventually becomes attributable to your Self. In this respect, it is pointed out that dominant negative attributes significantly contribute to cause a failure or loss while dominant positive attributes cause success or boost the chances of success like your promotions and finally career advancement in your service career.

It is well known that the human destiny depends upon the time, date, month, year and place of the birth of a person. Astrologers give much credence to this birth data for preparing horoscope and determining human destiny. It is obvious that the most of these personal attributes of positive and negative types are generated within a child in differential manner at the time of its birth. Now, it is difficult to explain why and how the positive attributes dominate over the negative attributes or vice-versa and in what manner their differential strengths and levels are set to occur.

At least, it can be logically and scientifically attributed to the genetic factor and presence of the cosmic forces, generated from the downward flow of cosmic energy from different planets while moving in their respective orbits along with the position of the sun and magnetic field of the earth, existing at the place of birth. It is also believed that the energy from the floating souls of dead human beings and animals adds to this cosmic force and then disappears from the space. The overall effect of this combined cosmic force finally determines the quality and standard of your outer and inner personality and consequently the course of your destiny.

Interconnectedness of Personal Attributes with Destiny

It is observed that human destiny and personal attributes of his personality are correlated. Now, *the question is how? What is the mechanism of interconnectedness? What is its profile? This intra-relationship is illustrated in the following manner.*

There are number of intermediate stages; *you have to go through for ultimately getting the desired and cherished fruits of your destiny in the form of wealth, fortune, prosperity, promotions, high status, recognition etc. which are known as the normal aspirations of the human beings. At every stage, there is an assessment and evaluation of your performance, behaviour, relationship and activities which you will demonstrate on the basis of your nature, character, abilities, talent, potential and conduct. These are integral part of your mindset, habits, manners, attitude, temperament and body movements. This is a continuous process which is elaborate and properly structured in any organisation. You receive promotions and awards only after you have gone through this entire process and receive due recommendations from your superior officers for quality, eligibility, acceptability and utility.* Thus, the fruits of your destiny do fall in your hands but only after you work hard, struggle intelligently and perform on the basis of your personal attributes in such a manner that it *should be recognized, approved and valued by your senior officials.*

This is a typical sequential process, depicting intermediate stages which progressively take place in any organisation. It is a normal procedure and the final result is seen only after the end of the complete process. A person who has reached high level of position has invariably achieved progressive promotions and has gone through these intermediate stages in his service tenure. A person who has reached the top position in any organisation is called a highly lucky person but before that he has gone through this rigorous and finally delivered the results and substantially contributed to his organisation. So *merely calling him lucky is to grossly underestimate and overlook his skills, talent, abilities and potential which he has actually demonstrated in his performance through his personal attributes especially positive types which have really played dominant role in his performance.*

Therefore, thus, outstanding performance becomes the true indicator of his dominant positive attributes which produce impact and effective influence at every stage. Besides, such persons are able to avail and utilise right opportunities at right times and adopt systematic approach without getting confused or misguided. They do not deviate from their mission path and go all out for achievement of their lifelong objectives. They have fixed their mission clear in their vision and proceed with a strong will power, tenacity, drive and motivation. They have firm determination and commitment to adhere to their short as well as long term objectives.

Positive Attributes for Winning Success

Now, what are those positive attributes of your personality? Let us take a look at those important personal positive attributes which substantially contribute in enabling you to achieve your career oriented objectives and take you to your destination. They basically belong to the hidden treasure of your latent positive qualities which are actualized in action and drive you to perform successfully. These are listed below

(a) **Adaptability** – To any situation, conditions, environment, staff, boss.

(b) **Commitment** – To your organisation and given or assigned tasks and objectives.

(c) **Confidence** -- Trust in yourself to execute the work successfully.

(d) **Dedication** -- To concentrate your attention and energies on the given task.

(e) **Dependability** – Of the boss and organisation on you for your honesty, credibility and truthfulness.

(f) **Integrity and Loyalty** – Pertains to your moral attachment, trust, belonging and faithfulness.

(g) **Knowledge** – Learning and training for acquiring new skills and updating your existing skills, pertaining to your profession, organisation and management required for high positions and senior appointments, and enables you to gain promotions. A totally voluntary act.

(h) **Dynamic Mountain Mover** – Means a person having tremendous zeal, drive, initiative, stamina, enthusiasm, keenness and motivation. He/She goes all out for achievements with *full force, energy and high spirit.*

(i) **Patience, Politeness and Humbleness** – It means to wait for proper opportunity and then strike. Related to your behaviour and conduct.

(j) **Communication Skill** – Pertains to your expression verbally and in writing for making contacts with others and express your views and opinions clearly, loudly and powerfully.

(k) **Responsiveness** – Pertains to your capacity and reactions for absorbing training and gaining knowledge. Indicates your vigilance, attentiveness and assimilation.

(l) **Talent** – Pertains to your intellect and I. Q. level.

(m) **Vision** – Capacity to look beyond the horizon and visualise your long-term objectives and mission.s

(n) **Will power and Determination** – Unless you have a strong will power and firm determination, you can't achieve your objectives or goals.

(o) **Willingness** – It is the readiness to undertake responsibilities and work of your own.

(p) **Urge** – A driving force of your inner 'Self' to achieve a particular objective or goal.

These are selected specific positive attributes which are key players and strong indicators of your favorable destiny. They exercise positive influence on your personality and performance and lead you to win success in your life.

Negative Attributes for Causing Failure

Now, what are those negative attributes of your personality that create setback to your destiny? These important negative qualities/attributes affect your attitude and mindset and result into your bad temper, relations, behaviour, conduct and adverse performance. They adversely influence your thought process and divert your thoughts in the wrong direction. As a result, your personality, performance and relations badly suffer. Consequently, bad and adverse impression and opinion are created about you in office and public. This proves to be quite damaging to your career and so to your destiny. Most of these negative attributes are inborn and some of them become evident at early stages of the teenagers and some erupt at later stages of their life as they grow. During this interim period, some of these attributes remain hidden deep in their mind and come out later at unforeseen and unpredictable times. These are listed below :

1. **Anger** – Related to loosing temper and getting into rage, sometimes violent and wild.
2. **Aggressiveness** – Readiness to attack or quarrel.
3. **Carelessness and Casualness** – Not being attentive and missing opportunities at right times .

4. **Craziness** – Irrational fondness and foolishness.
5. **Dominance** – Feeling a sense of superiority and riding high on them.
6. **Egotism** – Talking much or boasting about self and one's achievements only.
7. **Greediness and Selfishness** – Keeping self interest above all and tendency to grab.
8. **Impulsiveness** – Urge or sudden action without thinking.
9. **Indifference** – Showing no interest in jobs, relations and performance.
10. **Introvert** – Looking inwards to yourself, sticking to personal viewpoints and opinion.
11. **Possessiveness** - Excessive sense of possessing without respecting other's claim or claims.
12. **Rigidity** – Holding to personal views and not bending or yielding.
13. **Rudeness** – Showing bad manners and impolite behaviour.
14. **Stubbornness** – Unwilling to give way and difficult to manage.
15. **Temperamental** – Becoming excited and moody on slight impulse or stimulus.
16. **Sexiness** – Getting highly excited on sex matters.

These are prominent negative personal attributes which adversely affect your mindset and drive you to think in the wrong direction. *They become the adverse key players in causing your bad or unfavorable destiny because they will stand as obstacles and oppose the way to your destination. Obviously, it will cause failure in achievement of your mission and lifelong objectives.*

It is thus seen that *these positive and negative attributes of your personality become fairly prominent indicators of your destiny and whether it should result in good or bad destiny depends upon the dominance of concerned either positive or negative attributes.*

Concluding Remarks

It is seen from the above discussion that your personality with its positive and negative attributes plays very important role in finally achieving fruits of your destiny. It is the dominance of either positive or negative attribute in your personality that will eventually determine outcome of your favorable or unfavorable destiny. These attributes are integral part of your personality in an imperceptible form and indirectly influence your nature, character, mindset, attitude, talent behaviour and performance. The process of interconnectedness as described above amply demonstrates this indirect relationship of your personality with your destiny.

Hence, the secret of knowing your destiny and its direction lies in your personality and its personal characteristics. You need not go to the Astrologer for knowing about your future which is in fact hidden in your personality and you need to turn your *attention to yourself by adopting the technique of Introspection and Self-Assessment.* When the secret of your destiny lies within you, your efforts, going elsewhere for discovering are strange and escapist from the reality. Unfortunately, it is perhaps the *gross human failure for not acknowledging and appreciating his personality as the gift of the God given to him at the time of his birth and let his destiny remain hidden in it for him to discover and discreetly apply for personal benefits in his lifetime activities.*

While discussing the relationship of *destiny with human personality*, the scope was limited to occurrence of your career-oriented events and activities. In any way, your personality has no role in avoiding occurrence of natural external events or misfortunes except the *response, tolerance and reaction level of your personality,* while bearing its consequences.

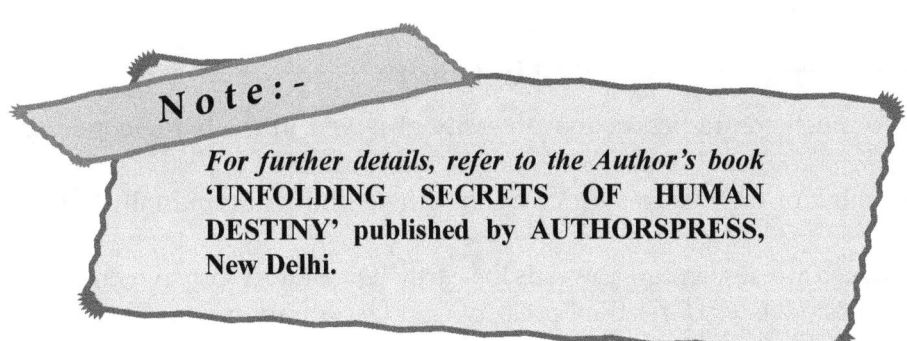

Note:-

For further details, refer to the Author's book **'UNFOLDING SECRETS OF HUMAN DESTINY' published by AUTHORSPRESS, New Delhi.**

CHAPTER - 21

INFLUENCE OF COSMIC LAWS ON HUMAN PERSONALITY

▪Abstract▪

There is so much contradiction and diversity observed in the living conditions and

rationally think of their causes for creation. When a human mind fails to think of a

its forces which are descending towards the earth. Its cosmic energy which is governed by various cosmic laws of rhythm, polarity, gender, vibration, etc. affects the nature

at a particular place, time and date of the birth of a child affects its appearance and brain structure. As a result, these genetic and cosmic factors give unique singularity and individuality to a child at the time of its birth. In this way, this chapter deals with the mystic aspect of human destiny which is eventually manifested through his/her unique personality.

Contradiction and Diversity in Human Personality and the Living State

It is observed that no two or more persons are the same or similar. They widely differ in their appearance as well as in their inner qualities. As a result, they have distinctly different personalities. They act, behave, conduct and perform differently because you observe wide variations in their personal characteristics and traits as seen before. Besides, there is a wide contrast in the living standards and performance of the people as under:-

(a) *Some earn and amass fortunes, wealth and prosperity and become rich,* while others remain poor.
(b) *Some become highly professional and skilled persons,* while others remain ordinary workers.
(c) *Some become managers, senior engineers and reach high positions,* while others stagnate at low grade levels
(d) *Some earn fame, reputation and recognition,* while others don't get it despite of their outstanding performance.

(e) *Some earn wealth and name with poor education and adverse upbringing,* while others remain mediocre despite of high education and good upbringing.

(f) *Some like to serve and render social services in rural areas,* while others in urban and metropolitan cities.

(g) *Some like to lead an ascetic and spiritual life,* while others want to lead materialistic life and are involved in family attachments and friends

(h) *Some are smiling cheerful,* while others remain gloomy, morose and sullen.

(i) *Some are calm, quiet and composed,* while others are impulsive, temperamental and emotional in behaviour.

(j) *Some are physically fit and healthy while,* others are sick and mentally depressed.

(k) *Some maintain forward and optimistic outlook,* while others maintain a gloomy, regressive and pessimistic attitude.

Occurrence of Unfortunate Events

Some grim, serious and painful picture of human life is brought to your notice as under :-

(a) A child is born with physical as well as mental defects, such as *mentally retarded, abnormal growth of certain body organs, crippled or handicapped.*

(b) Development of serious illnesses such as *paralysis, leprosy, cancer, liver or kidney failure.*

(c) *Sudden loss of fortunes and becoming pauper* from a wealthy state.

(d) *Early death of a son or daughter* at fairly young age.

(e) *Sudden death of close relative and friend* on spot in fatal accidents.

(f) *Certain sections and classes of people staying perpetually in misery* and extreme poverty.

(g) *Separation and divorce* in one's *disturbed married life.*

(h) *Natural calamities occurring in a certain part of the region* and losses and death therein.

(i) *Devastation from man-made disturbances,* etc. such as riots, torching, blasting in a particular area and damage there-from.

Incidents of Outstanding Talents

You come across certain children or persons who display unusual and ex-ordinary talent and genius in art, music, singing, dramatics and other faculties. This phenomenon is evident from the reality shows on TV such as :-

(a) A child shows outstanding talent and aptitude in singing, music and dancing.

(b) A person shows remarkable memory of photographic nature.

(c) A person possesses a forceful and remarkably strong flowing oratory causing mesmeric influence on the audience.

(d) A person shows remarkable talent for investigative and inventive activities.

(e) A person shows outstanding performance in drama, art and acting.

(f) A person shows divine power in curing certain acute ailments of long suffering patients.

(g) A person shows extremely high spiritual and religious power which is manifested from his radiant face, body language and expression like Swami Vivekanand, .

(h) A person has mass appeal from his remarkable leadership qualities.

You are accustomed to observe these events and incidents of diversified nature in normal course of your life. You always look at them with surprise, awe and unbelievable feelings. Now, pertinent questions and doubts arising thereof are as under ;-

(a) Why and how do they occur?

(b) Why do you see such a wide variation and contrast in human life?

(c) Why do you find such an unusual talent in certain children and grown-up persons?

(d) Why do some persons perform in an outstanding manner and receive progressive promotions in their service career?

(e) Why are some persons able to sway the audience by their oratorical skills and its delivery power?

(f) Why do some people face misfortunes and meet unfortunate events in their life?

(g) And finally, what are the causes for occurrences of these unusual events and incidences?

(h) If the present human being is so powerful with his brain and scientific investigative power, can he prevent or control or procreate them?

(i) Who is responsible to occur or cause such contrasting and uneven incidences?

(j) What is the time of occurrence for its cause?

These are really and highly baffling, intriguing and pertinent questions. Now, let us consider the birth of a child.

Birth of a Child

A child is born on a particular day of the year and month at a specific time given in the form of hour, minute and second. A genetic factor of the parents is responsible for its conception, growth and finally birth on a particular day and time. Hence, birth of a child carries two variable factors, one is genetic and another is time factor. Now, whatever contradiction and diversity are seen in human beings, it is attributable to these two factors. While the implications of the genetic factor are well known, the significance of the time factor has to be comprehended from the cosmos and influence of its cosmic forces and their governing laws.

Cosmos and Its Energy

It is observed that all cosmic phenomena and events are occurring in the universe and they are being controlled in a specific manner by the universal forces, also called **cosmic forces**. In our Zodiac, the sun is at its centre and planets including our earth are orbiting around it along their respective paths. The sun and planets have inter-gravitational forces while moving along their respective orbits and their force levels and directions vary according to their positions in their orbits with respect to the sun. Besides, the sun generates its forces through sunshine which has a large spectrum of different colour rays. Some of the light particles are attracted towards the poles of the earth and they substantially contribute to the earth's magnetic field.

Now, these celestial bodies generate cosmic forces by virtue of their interaction through the collision process of particles from them. These forces are spread all over the universe and descend towards planets including our earth due to its gravitation The cosmic forces which descend towards the earth set the atmosphere of the universe in motion and generate cosmic energy which is responsible for the nature and its human, animal and plant life to exist and survive.

The free flow of cosmic energy having rhythm and polarity is responsible for generating wind and water with the help of the solar energy and freely moves around and up. Due to the downward cosmic energy stream and rotation of the earth around, changes are occurring in the universe but these changes are smooth, gradual and unique. .All cosmic phenomena represent such gradual changes from one side to its corresponding opposite side such as season to season, day to night, light to darkness and so on. This smooth and gradual flow of the cosmic energy is universal and beneficial to the mankind for living, sustenance, growth and finally decay.

Cosmic Forces and Governing Cosmic Laws

Cosmic laws are characteristics of the universal mind which is in operation throughout the universe. These laws are basically called the Laws of the Nature. The nature which is more than flora and fauna is the physical expression of the material world and is manifested in the form of rains, wind, flame, flowers, rainbow, vibrant colours, etc. Now, everything in the universe is governed and controlled by the cosmic forces and their laws. They are always working on the nature and human life. Whether you are conscious of them or not, they do exist and affect your life. The more you know of them, the more you will understand about yourself and your life.

Cosmic laws are generally known by their effects. Now, the laws and causes of these effects are unseen, you are making efforts to learn and know the nature of the cosmic laws and abide by them. In the process, it enables you to overcome or avoid many unnecessary excessive hardships and soften your struggle in life. By knowing, understanding and applying cosmic laws in a positive, constructive and creative manner, you automatically promote your spiritual growth and evolution. You are also able to know the causes of your hardships and failures and take proper corrective actions and remedial measures.

Sufferings can be mitigated and pave the way for achieving peace, health and prosperity in life. It is also advocated that *the package of the cosmic laws is a heavenly gift to the mankind that enables you to align yourselves with the nature and if you do it sincerely, you will experience harmony, mental peace and pleasure in your life. If you oppose them you will find yourselves in a hell of your own making.*

Another important aspect of the cosmic forces is pointed out in the form of its influence caused on a child at the time of its birth. This force is present all over and its strength and direction vary as per the

(a) Place of birth and its location in a particular direction of the earth, i.e. north, south, east or west and its secondary directions

(b) Place with respect to ground conditions i.e. plane, hilly, jungle, seaside, mountainous

(c) Time at a particular place with respect to the position of the sun i.e. morning, noon, afternoon, evening, night, early morning

(d) Position of the Sun in the north or south hemisphere, etc.

Different Cosmic Laws

Now, these cosmic forces are governed by the cosmic laws and they exercise influence on the human beings according to their strengths and directions since the time of their birth. As these laws are complied, they offer unique identity to a person in the form of his personality. Let us look at these cosmic laws and their impact.

1. Law of Mentalism

This cosmic law embodies the truth that human reality is in essence mental and your thoughts are channeled by your brain. It points out that your thoughts are consciousness and your thoughts spontaneously influence your physical activities. You can change the circumstances of your life by the sheer will of your thoughts. Besides, every thought you have attracts the experience of its electromagnetic vibration. Your thoughts pass through the corridor of space and time. Your thoughts are magnetic and every thought you have is either creative or destructive and attractive or repelling for your desires. What you desire and think will manifest in your life and your individual thoughts will contribute to the fabric of collective human experience.

2. Law of Correspondence

It is also known as **law of interdependence or interconnectedness.** It states that there is absolute correspondence between the cosmic laws and phenomena of the various hierarchies of cosmology, consciousness and human life. It simply states that what is above is so below and what is below is so above, In simple words, if there is a mountain above, so there is a valley below and that is how the balance is achieved in life. Now, hierarchies are also true in human thinking. People will find the conditions of their life to match the hierarchical level of thinking. Remember that no matter who you think you are, there is always someone better or worse than you.

3. Law of Vibration

It states that everything is in motion, everything vibrates and nothing is at rest. This law explains that the difference between manifestations of matter, energy and mind result primarily from varying rates of vibration. Higher the vibration, the higher is the position in the scale of life. Everything is vibration including your thoughts which are scientifically classified as electromagnetic vibrations. Since thoughts are energy, it seeks its own vibration and attains its level. Here the message is that control vibrations of your thoughts, you will control your physical experience. He who understands the principle of vibration he grasps the baton of power.

4. Law of Polarity

It states that everything is dual, everything has poles and everything has its pair of opposites. Like and unlike are the same, opposites are identical but different in degree and their extremes i.e. top and bottom points meet like a *Yin-Yang* symbol of dualism. Examples are heat and cold, day and night, good and evil etc. When you change your polarity, you change your vibration. Here the point to remember is that two things are no doubt different in scales but they are the same in nature.

5. Law of Rhythm

This law is also known as *the law of change.* It states that everything flows out and in, everything has its tides, all things rise and fall. It is like a pendulum swing from left to right and right to left. It also means that what goes up must come down or what rises must sink. This law is manifest in the creation and destruction of worlds, in the rise and fall of nations, in the life of all beings and their relationships. So, everything has a cycle of change including your life. There is a message of consolation and caution in this law. It you are having a bad period or undergoing tragedy or pain, your state will swing back to the opposite direction by its own rhythm. The same is applicable to your mood/thoughts/emotions/fortunes and it will swing in the opposite direction.

6. Law of Cause and Effect

It states that there is a cause for every effect and an effect from every cause. Nothing merely happens and there is no such thing as chance of luck. In your personal case, the external circumstances of your life (behaviour-effect) are a mirror of your internal circumstances (thought –cause). You know that the effect of your thinking is on your effort to have everything or don't have. It means that the only way to have what you want in life is to cause thinking for it.

This is also called the *law of Karma and your achievements are the effect of your karma.* So, nothing moves or occur without a cause, Even for a death, it does not occur without a valid cause.

7. Law of Gender

It states that there is a gender manifested in everything. Everything has its masculine and feminine principles. The principle of Yin (feminine) and Yang (masculine) is the foundation of the entire universe and it implies everything in creation. This law is responsible for generation, regeneration and creation. Every person contains the two elements or principles of masculine and feminine. Remember that male and female are the creation of cosmos. One can't exist without other and both are required for procreation.

It is evident from the brief description given for each law that these seven laws are physically prevalent in your life and applicable at every stage of your lifetime activities. It is also amply seen that your personality is correspondingly influenced and conducted in an imperceptible form.

Main Characteristics of Cosmic Forces

It is seen that cosmos exercises its influence over the nature and mankind through its cosmic forces which have the following characteristics because of the above mentioned governing laws:-

(a) *It is dynamic, intelligent and conscious force associated with thinking activity.*

(b) *It has correspondence, interdependence and interconnectedness.*

(c) *It has gender and polarity.*

(d) *It has vibration and rhythm.*

(e) *It is karmic and follows the cause and effect.*

Cosmic Influence on Personality

This cosmic force which is associated with the above characteristics and governed by the cosmic laws is descending towards the earth and is present all over in its nature, environment and surrounding. Geo-magnetic force of the earth as specific to the location is mainly added to this cosmic force. It is also presumed that the energy associated with the hovering souls of dead human beings and animals is also added. Now, this combined force is present at the time of the birth of a child. It was also present right from the day of its conception and during its growth inside a mother's womb and caused its influence according to its position in space and time. Its influence becomes highly effective at the time when the birth takes place and a child finally comes out of the mother's womb with fully grown body features and specific alignment of brain structure.

The moment the child comes out, it is subjected to the combined cosmic force which immediately acts and causes changes body appearance and alignment of the cells in brain structure. While the effect on the body appearance is minimal, the effect on the alignment of the neurological cells in the brain is quite significant and the consequent shift in alignment depends upon its force level and its direction as present at that time of the day, month and year. Thus, there is a realignment of cells that significantly occurs in the brain of a child. This realigned structure of the brain of a child carries the seed of its characteristic mind and becomes unique imprint of its inner personality.

It should be noted that *the cosmic forces present along with the earth's magnetic field at the time of birth are well conditioned and programmed by its laws as they carry motional and vibrational energy with rhythm and polarity. As a result, its consequential influence is quite significant on the alignment of brain and body features of a child at the time of its birth. This is seen as the divine process and human body and its brain are treated as the heavenly gift which is gracefully endowed to you as your personality. It is obvious that whatever the God intended to offer you, your personality has become the Heavenly gift given to you as deserved at the time of your birth and then left to you to discover, understand, develop and utilize it the way you wish. Hence, the secret of your destiny is hidden in your personality which becomes your personal baggage and indirectly visible manifestation of your destiny.*

Concluding Remarks

It is very thoughtful and interesting to link the human life and its personality with the cosmos and its forces. There is continuous cosmic influence on your personality since the day of your birth and on your subsequent life activities. Since this action is invisible and imperceptible, its impact on your personality is not physically felt and realised but it gets manifested in many forms and occurrences of fortunate and unfortunate events in your life. The word, 'Destiny', of course, takes its place and effectively becomes responsible to give you solace, relief and satisfaction from the unusual incidents and misfortunes. Because of this cosmic study and its insight in human life and its personality, it is now evident that the cosmos and its celestial forces are actively behind the word Destiny and they are responsible to determine the direction of human destiny.

Hence, human personality and his destiny become inseparable and become the two sides of the same coin. It is also pointed out that your thought of linking your personality with the cosmos and its influential forces which are governed by the cosmic laws is a rational, pragmatic and logical step for explaining mysterious events. You are aware about the dictum that *nothing happens in the universe without the will of the God*. You now find a reasonable explanation in which you point out your finger at the cosmos and its forces. They silently act in the background and control the direction of happenings in your life.

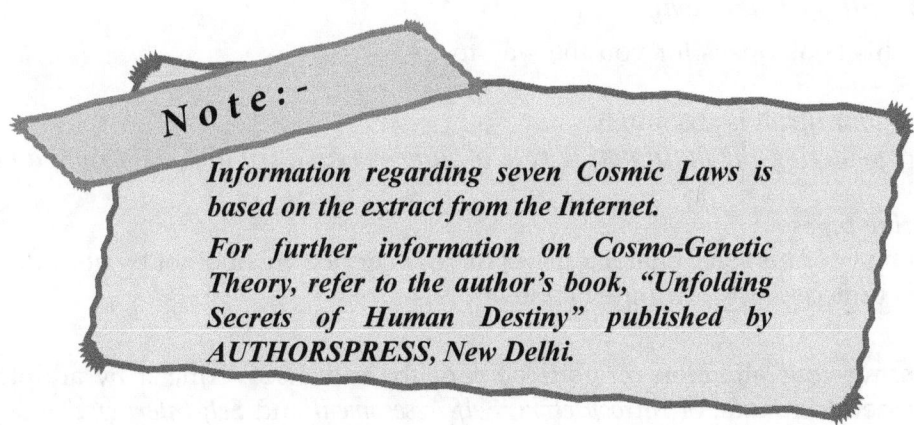

Note:-

Information regarding seven Cosmic Laws is based on the extract from the Internet.

For further information on Cosmo-Genetic Theory, refer to the author's book, "Unfolding Secrets of Human Destiny" published by AUTHORSPRESS, New Delhi.

EPILOGUE

CAN YOU CHANGE YOUR PERSONALITY?

While concluding the subject of this book, I would like to pose the question. Can you change your personality? After reading this book, I do admit that, this is an irrelevant and illogical question for the simple reason that you are now fully appraised about your personality and you have fully understood it. Obviously, you can now focus

improvement and development thereby causing necessary changes in them.

In fact, the purpose of this book is to discover the mental, psychic, intellectual, spiritual and physical aspects of your personality in a pragmatic and perceptible manner and pave the *way for proceeding to the next phase of its dynamic development*. Hence, you can treat
as the second phase.
undertaking its effective development in the second phase.

carry out the development program of your personality. With this approach, it is fully

In fact, this is the only logical, wise and noble way of understanding your basic and essential role in maturing the fruits of your destiny. In other words, *it projects the close relationship of your destiny with your personality or other way.*

Thus, this book opens for you the way to

failures in your life. It is absolutely
without considering the main active role of your personality and its strong and weak

and negative types
governed by your personal characteristics in your service life and not by your destiny to which you unnecessarily attribute blame or praise.

and focussing your attention on your personality and discovering it by adopting the self-addressed technique of *Introspection, Self-Assessment* and *Self-Interrogation* as stated in the chapter 15 of this book and then proceeding to commence a proper and systematic Personality Development program me with emphasis on your inner personality. As you proceed to the second phase of personality development, you should be aware about certain background information and associated assumptions about the basic developmental process having a normative sequence of the psychological growth and maturation. Therefore, it is advisable to bear in mind the following assumptions:-

1. Individual growth is a continuous process.
2. This process could be conveniently divided into specific life stages.
3. Each life stage is a developmental stage and is identified by certain characteristics which are common to all individuals and they have to pass through.
4. The society imposes certain responsibilities and demands on the individuals during these stages.
5. The demands of the society are uniform for all its members.
6. The demands differ from one stage to another as the individual progresses through each developmental stage.
7. Developmental crises occur when the individual fails to perceive the need to adjust to different situations.
8. The individual moves from one stage of maturity to the next after passing through a developmental crisis. There is no cross-over and he can't skip it.
9. The preparation for meeting a crisis or task occurs in the preceding developmental stage.
10. The development crises may rise during later phase of life too in different forms.
11. Meeting a crisis successfully leads to social approval and happiness.
12. Failure to meet the crisis results in disappointment and unhappiness.

With this approach, it becomes the systematic, sequential, thoughtful and visionary process in which you cater for all eventualities and contingencies with full awareness for probable occurrence of crises, failures and challenges. This information guides you to work out a solid, well designed plan for meeting crises in any developmental stage of your life. But before that, there is also a need for you to fulfill certain essential requirements as given below :

(a) Self-Awareness that I must improve my personality. Keeps this motto before me well displayed as reminder.
(b) Awaken to the fact that my personality has got certain strong and weak areas and I must try to exploit the strong points and correct and strengthen the weak areas of my personality.
(c) Ensure that I have set my personal mission, goal or objective in life and I remain ambitious to achieve my career accordingly.
(d) Remain determined, firm, strong and resolute for achievement of my career

objective/objectives.

(e) Keep my abilities focussed and concentrated on my personal efforts for developing and enriching my personality.

(f) Remain committed to maintain consistent, perseverant and vigilant approach in the entire program of my personality development.

(g) Search out for seeking proper and effective guidance and consultation from highly experienced, knowledgeable and competent sources.

(h) Realise, accept and own up mistakes or slips or omissions if done advertently or inadvertently in the past. Never keep brooding on them but be careful and cautious not to repeat them.

(i) Remain patient, calm, composed and optimistic about the result from my personality development program and I will remain focussed as before.

(j) Carry out periodic audit by monitoring results of my personality development program and promptly take corrective measures if so required.

This is the list of preliminary steps which you need to adopt if you wish that your personality development program should become successful, result-oriented and effective. It calls for your firm determination, total involvement and commitment and this is the main key for success of your program.

As a result, *you find an answer to the initial question for changing your personality. In the process, you are assured to achieve your desired objectives with full satisfaction, happiness and peace for having done your best possible efforts by harnessing all your abilities, strength, capacity and potentials.* With this advice, let me conclude this book with the hope for your success in your **personality development programme**.

Annexure 1 to Chapter 15

PERFORMA FOR WRITING REPORT ON YOUR OWN PERSONALITY

1. **Name**
2. **Date of Birth and Time**
3. **Place of Birth and its Location** (Plains, hill's, mountains, seaside, jungle, desert)
4. **Environment of Upbringing during Childhood** (Forward, backward, rural, urban) (Both items determine your handicap/opportunity level)
5. **Academic Performance** during last three annual examinations at School and college level as Excellent (above 91%), Very Good (81-90 %), Good (61-80 %), Average (41-60%), Poor (Below 40 %)
6. **Health Condition**
    (a) General Physique
    (b) Stamina and capacity for hard working
    (c) Physical Fitness
    (d) Endurance
7. **Appearance**
    (a) Shape and size of forehead
    (b) Height - tall, medium and short.
    (c) Shape and size of nose, eyes, ears, lips.
    (d) Habits and body movements (Determine the style and impressive level of your personality while conducting in public)
8. **Inner Traits – State**
    (a) Strong points of your nature and character and their strengths
    (b) Weak points of your nature and character and their intensity
    (c)

    (d) Interest areas like your hobbies such as music, singing, dramatics, painting, etc.
    (e) Likes and Dislikes, sense of time, etc.

9. **Intelligence Quotient (I.Q.)**
    - (a) Assess from your Academic performance as given above
10. **Attitude**
    - (a) Positive or Negative
    - (b) Forward looking or backward looking
    - (c) Progressive or regressive
    - (d) Reformative or Obscure
11. **Mindset – Mental Thinking, Approach and Viewpoint**
    - (a) Positive or Negative
    - (b) Optimistic or Pessimistic
    - (c) Encouraging or Discouraging
    - (d) Extrovert or Introvert
12. **Temperament (state level)**
    - (a) Anger – Loss of Temper
    - (b) Sensitive and Emotional
    - (c) Critical, Sarcastic or Abusive
    - (d) Adamant and Argumentative
    - (e) Egoistic and Self-praising
    - (f) Evasive and Shirking
    - (g) Serious or Casual
13. **Confidence Level**
    - (a) Very high
    - (b) High
    - (c) Cautious
    - (d) Needs preparation
    - (e) Average, Low
14. **Leadership**
    - (a) State your leadership qualities
    - (b) State leadership abilities like planning, organising, etc.
    - (c) Leadership areas like games, project work, task force, etc.
    - (d) Leadership temperament
    - (e) Type-of leadership like consultative, autocratic, independent, etc
15. **Decision-Making**
    - (a) Awareness about decision-making processes
    - (b) Capability to take the right decisions
    - (c) Do you take instant decisions or wait and watch?

(d) Do you consult others before taking decisions?

(e) Do you involve your colleagues or subordinates in decision-making?

16. Learning Skills
(a) Liking for learning and training
(b) Keenness for updating your knowledge and professional skills
(c) Belief in development and advancement
(d) Quest for improvements and growth of knowledge and wisdom
(e) Efforts for enrichment of your living and empowerment of your personality

17. Creative Power
(a) Awareness about your creative potential
(b) Creative thinking and approach
(c) Desire for creative generation
(d) Encouragement and support for creative efforts and production

18. Communication Skills
(a) Stage fear for public speaking
(b) Liking or flair for public speaking and self-confidence in facing the audience
(c) Level of preparation and use of presentation aids
(d) Power of expression, delivery and throw of your speech
(e) Display of emotions and facial expressions with hand movements
(f) Looking for public reactions and feedbacks for improving your style and conduct

19. Your Vision/Objective/Ambition Level
(a) Very high – reaching to the top level
(b) High – reaching to high levels
(c) Middle – reaching to senior levels
(d) Supervisory – reaching to sectional levels
(e) Working – remain as it is

20. Drive and Motivation
(a) Your motivation for basic needs
(b) Your motivation for elevation and enhancements
(c) Are you self-motivated?
(d) Level of your driving force and enthusiasm
(e) Source of your motivation like parents, teachers, ambitions, etc.

21. Strictly Personal
(a) Will power and determination
(b) Sense of responsibility and commitment

- (c) Loyalty and integrity
- (d) Responsiveness and grasping level
- (e) Initiative and awareness
- (f) Time consciousness and management
- (g) Control on self-ego, pride, temperament and habits
- (h) Dedication, dependability, reliability and resourcefulness
- (i) Quality consciousness and urge for excellence
- (j) Social response and behaviour
- (k) Optimistic vision even in failure or bad luck

22. **Character Traits**
    - (a) Moral strength to withstand pressure from top authorities for out of the way working
    - (b) Staying away from power and vices
    - (c) Credibility and trust level
    - (d) Compliance to observe commitments and promises
    - (e) Self pride and image level
    - (f) Compliance to values, ethics and etiquettes

23. **Achievements in**
    - (a) Personal and professional career
    - (b) Games and sports
    - (c) Research and development
    - (d) Public relations and social sector
    - (e) Wealth and fortunes

24. **Finally**
    - (a) Do you firmly believe that your personality effectively drives you to achieve your objectives?
    - (b) Do you now strongly feel that you can change your personality for achieving better career prospects?
    - (c) Do you realise that your destiny is concealed within your personality?

LIST OF REFERENCES

The references to various books have been quoted in the concerned chapters at appropriate places for advising you to seek further information on those portions of the Text. These books are however quoted below in the consolidated form for acknowledging reference.

1. Personality Classic Theories and Modern Research by HOWARD S FRIEDMAN and MIRIARN W SCHUSTACK.
2. Personality Development and Career Management by R.M. ONKAR, Published by S. Chand & Company New Delhi
3. Discovering your Personality for Managing Your Career by R.M. ONKAR, Published by S. Chand & Company New Delhi
4. Self Management by Introspection by R. M. ONKAR Published by AUTHORSPRESS New Delhi
5. Dynamics of Personality Development by R. M. Onkar Published by Datt Sons Nagpur.
6. Unfolding Secrets of Human Destiny by R. M. ONKAR Published by AUTHORSPRESS New Delhi

English Improvement/Self-Help

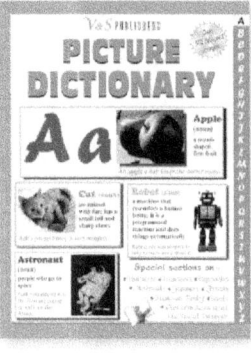

visit our online bookstore:
www.vspublishers.com

Career & Business Management

Visit our online bookstore: www.vspublishers.com

www.ingramcontent.com/pod-product-compliance
Lightning Source LLC
Chambersburg PA
CBHW080733300426
44114CB00019B/2577